AF874764

CREATE YOUR OWN COMIC BOOK

A Sketchbook & Drawing Guide for Kids

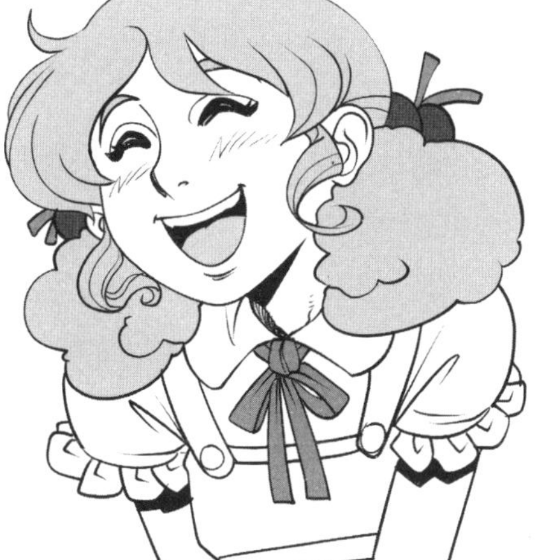

TUTTLE Publishing

Tokyo | Rutland, Vermont | Singapore

HOW TO USE THIS BOOK

The panels and templates are already laid out for you . . . so are you ready to create your own comics, make your own manga?

A quick comic or a longer story playing out over many pages or volumes? We've got you covered! Fill in the blanks to tell your story as only you can!

Start with the basics and build your world from there: character creation, poses and panels—and don't forget the speech balloons.

Remember there are no rules. No training or classes are required. Artists of all levels can create memorable characters and dynamic, page-turning stories. All you need is a free hand and a free imagination.

Fill in the frames as your story emerges before your eyes. Let your characters and your creativity soar!

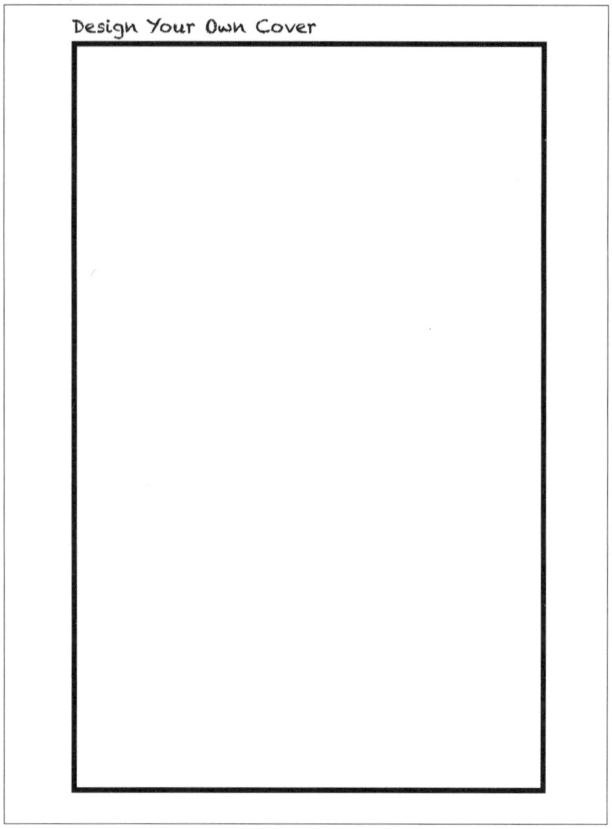

Cover Templates

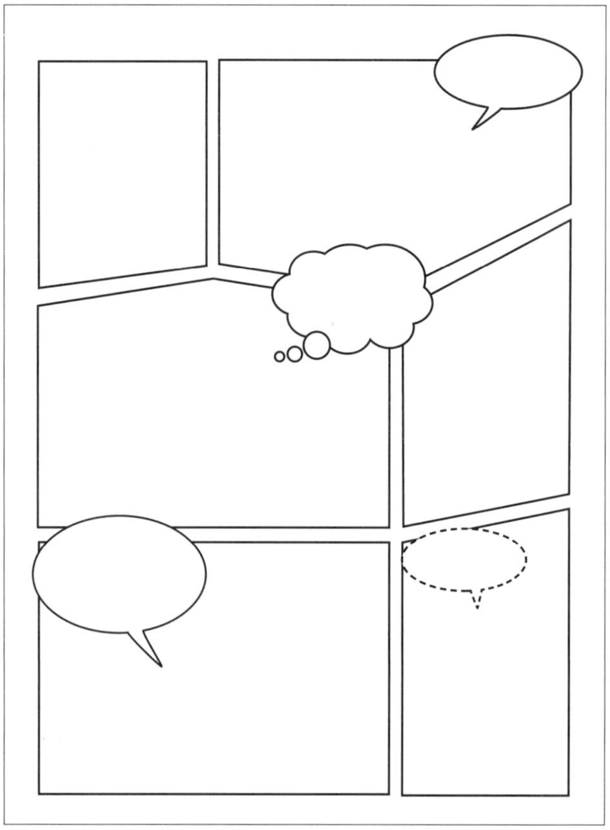

Page Templates

DRAWING A MANGA FACE

Let's start with one of your character's most important parts: the face! Follow these four steps to give your creation some unique features and an appropriate expression.

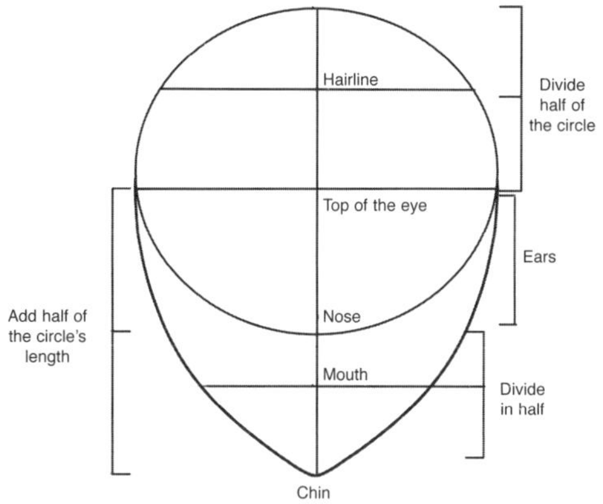

STEP 1

Outline the skull and jaw. The crisscrossing lines in the center help you place the nose and eyes.

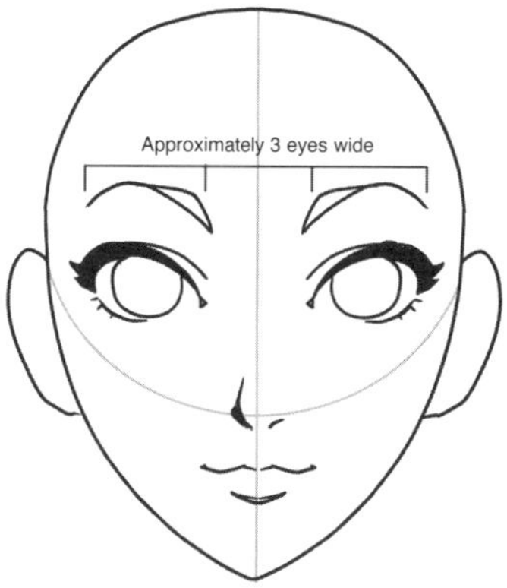

STEP 2

The mouth is added to the bottom of the circle. The bottom of the eyelid touches the eye line.

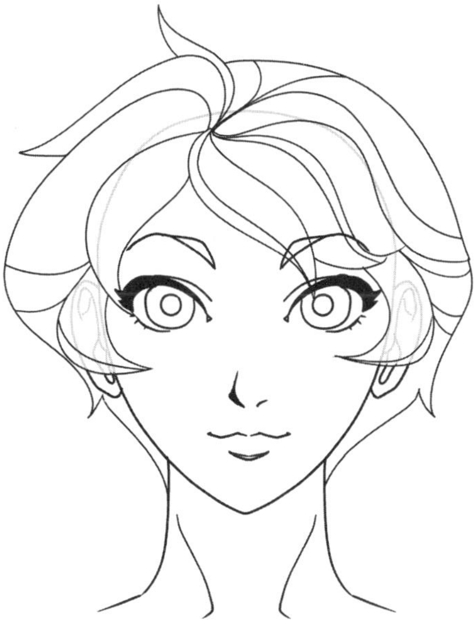

STEP 3

A simple line can indicate the nose. The hair adds size and volume to the head.

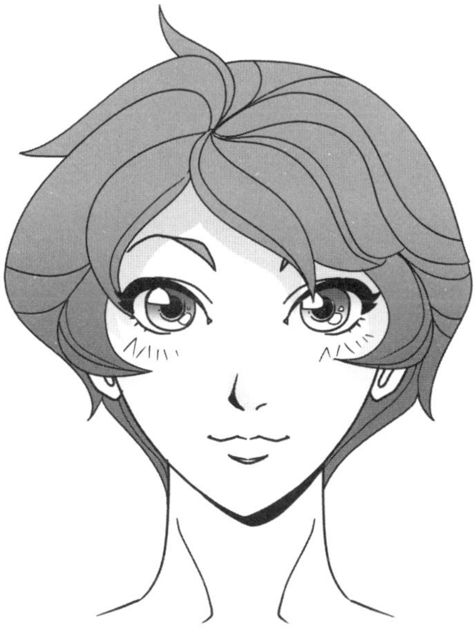

STEP 4

Now add details and finishing touches: shadows, highlights and strands of hair.

PRO TIPS

The nose is about halfway between the bottom of the chin and the eye line. The distance between the eyes is about the width of a single eye.

WHAT'S YOUR STYLE?

There's no one way to tell—or draw!—your story. But which style suits you best? Cutesy Kawaii, charming chibi or the fantasy fun of furry world? Realistic or fantasy-based, find the form that fits your vision and voice.

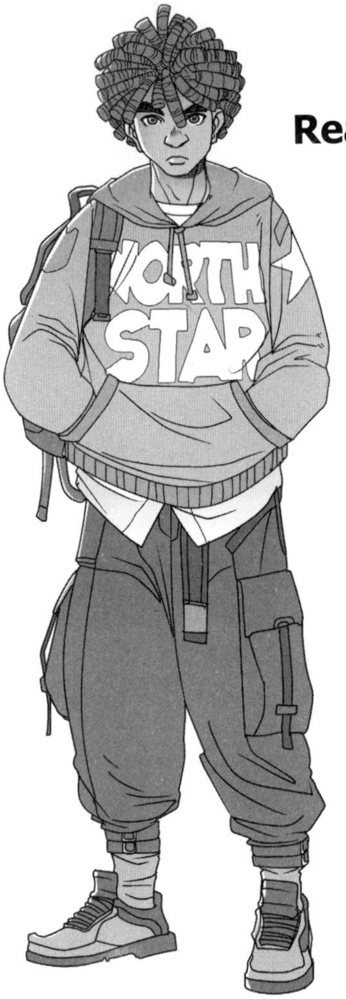

Realistic

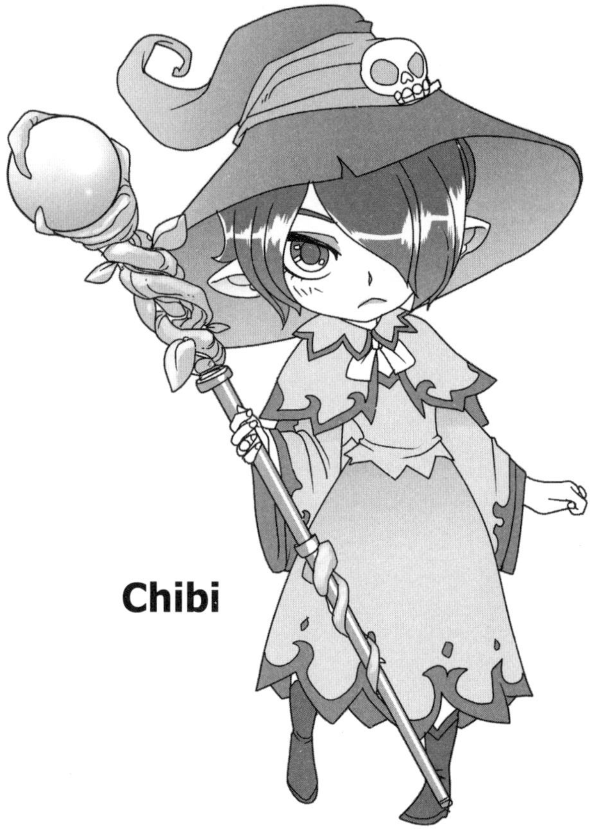

Chibi

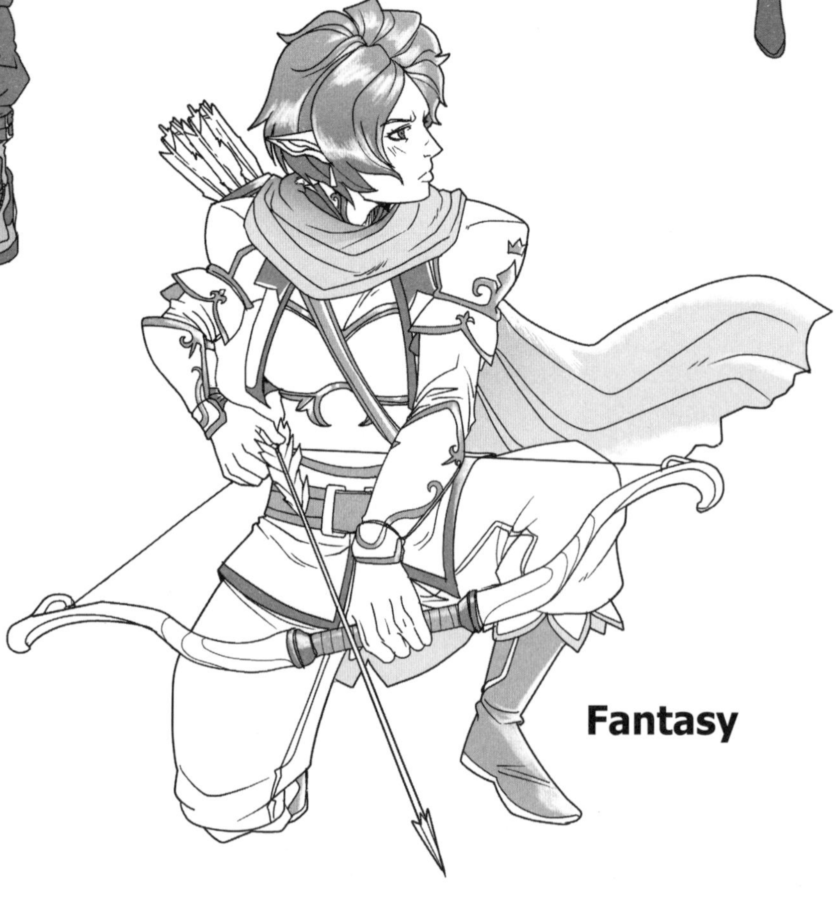

Fantasy

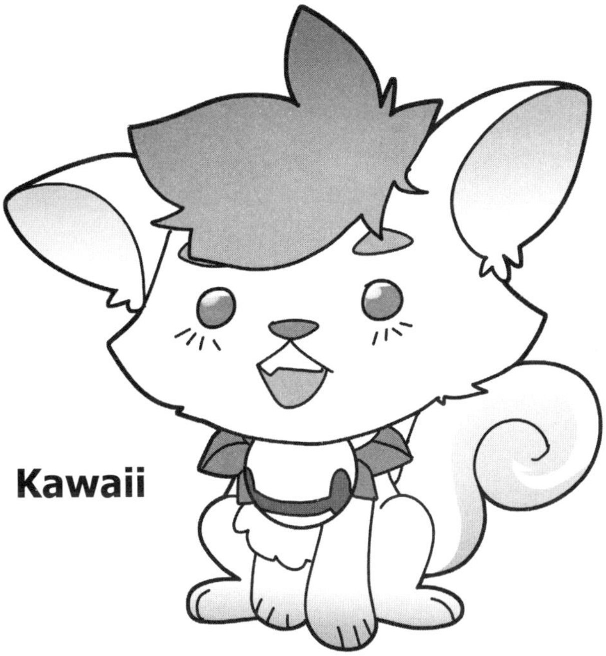

Kawaii

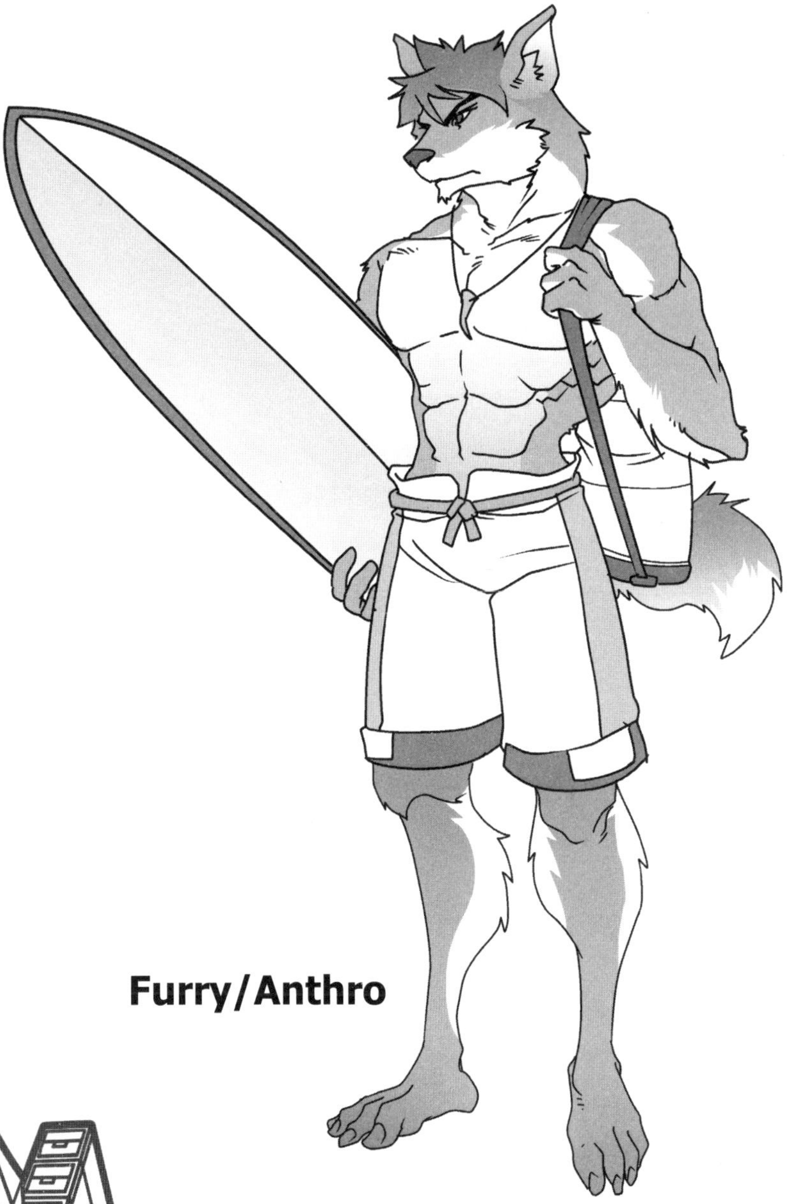

Furry/Anthro

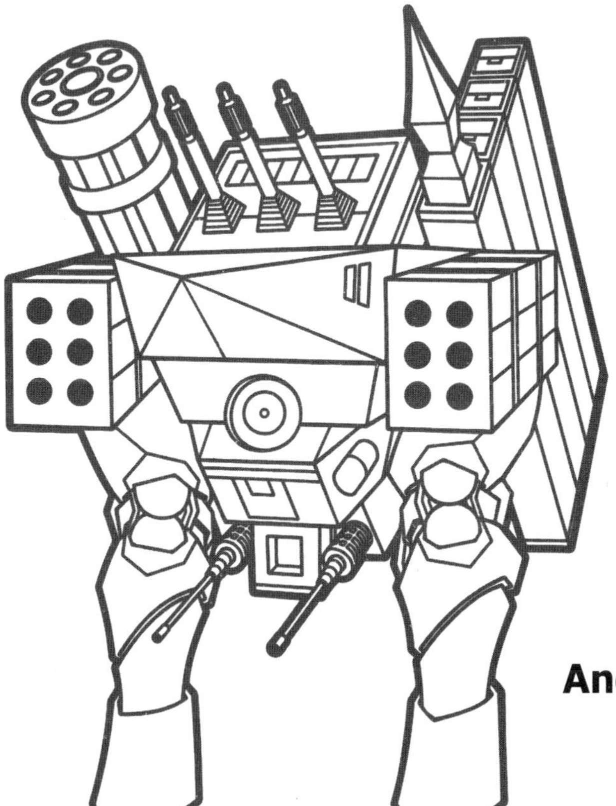

Android

CREATING CHARACTERS

Follow these four characters to build your characters from a basic body blueprint to a fully fleshed presence. A simple sketch soon turns into a memorable manga character!

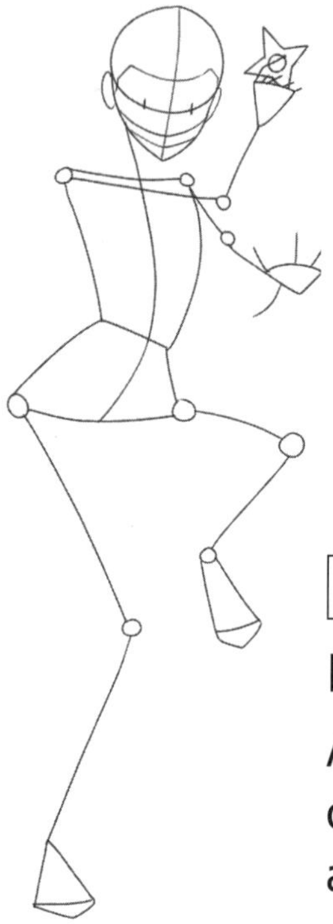

STEP 1

Basic Outline

A few simple lines sketch out the general shape and basic outline.

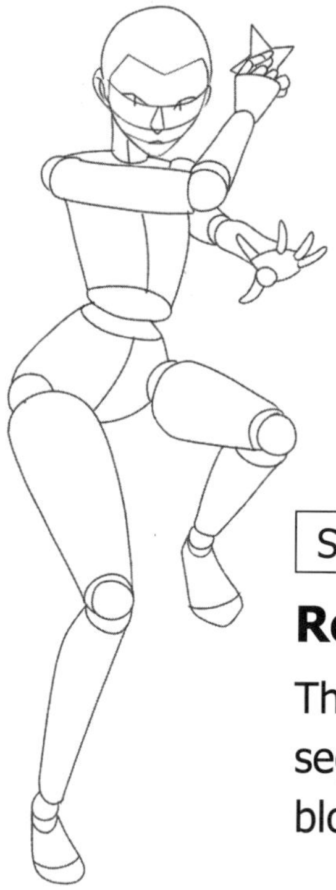

STEP 2

Rough Draft

The body is divided into segments using basic, blocky shapes.

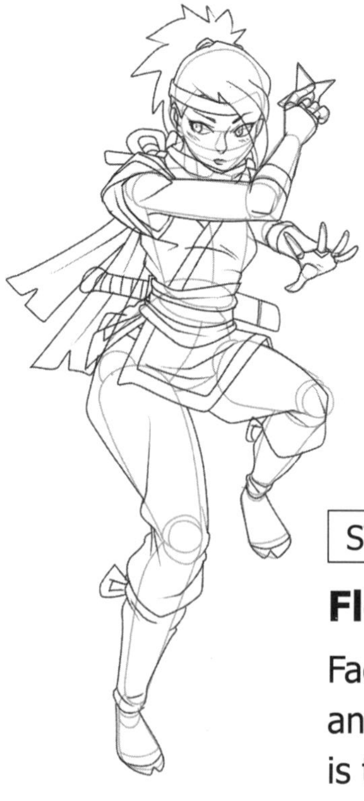

STEP 3

Fleshing Out

Face and features, muscle and hair: your full character is taking shape!

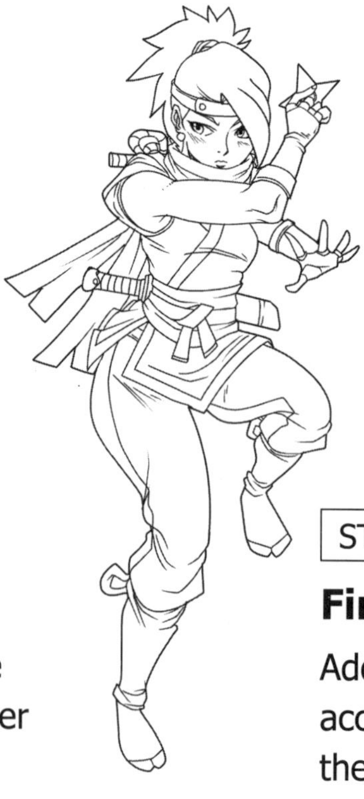

STEP 4

Finishing Touches

Add the final details: clothing, accessories and don't forget the shoes!

DRAW A FURRY

What's your favorite animal? Blend it with some human traits to create a funny and fabulous furry. The same four steps apply.

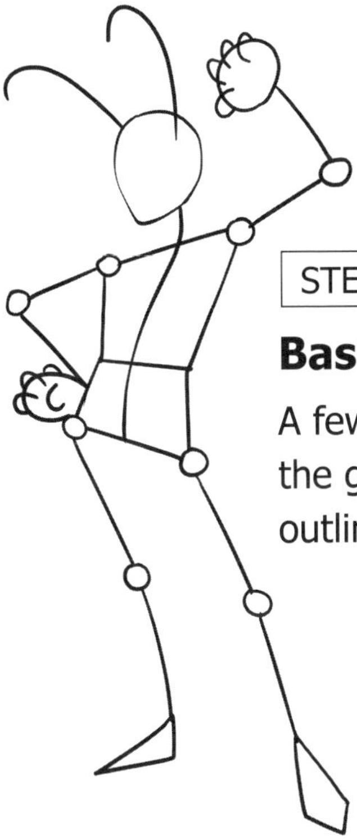

STEP 1

Basic Outline

A few lines suggest the general shape and outline of your character.

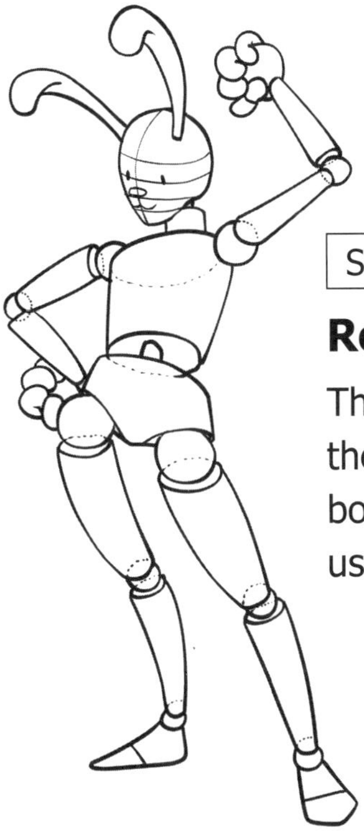

STEP 2

Rough Draft

This is sometimes called the "blocking-in" stage. The body's divided into segments using basic shapes.

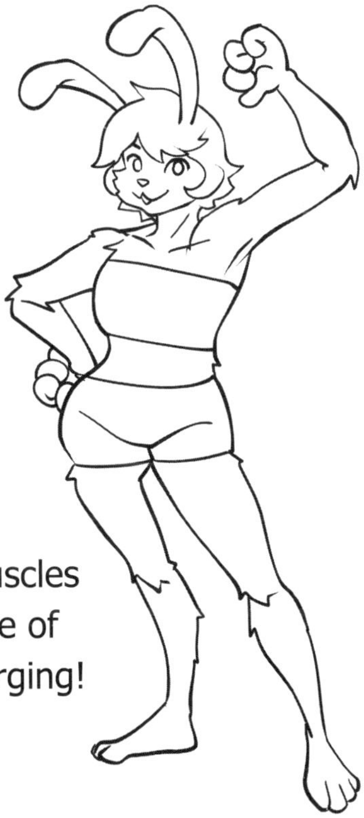

STEP 3

Fleshing Out

Face and features, muscles and hair: the full figure of your character is emerging!

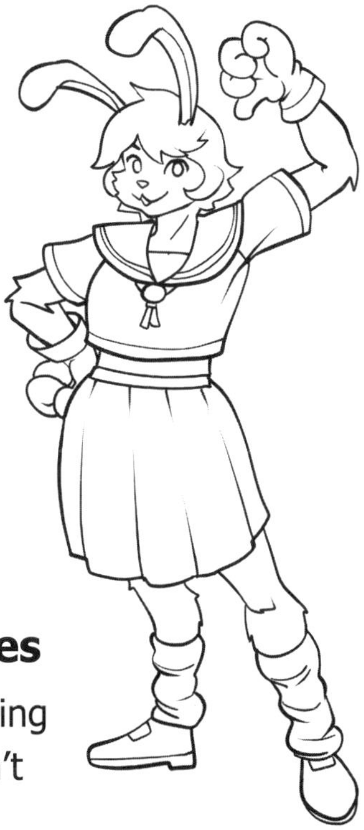

STEP 4

Finishing Touches

Wrap it up with clothing and accessories. Don't forget the shoes!

NOW YOU TRY IT: THE PRACTICE PAD

Now it's time to draw your way through the four stages. Sketch the basic shape, then add curve and contour. Before you know it, a muscled monster appears in a powerful pose.

Basic Outline

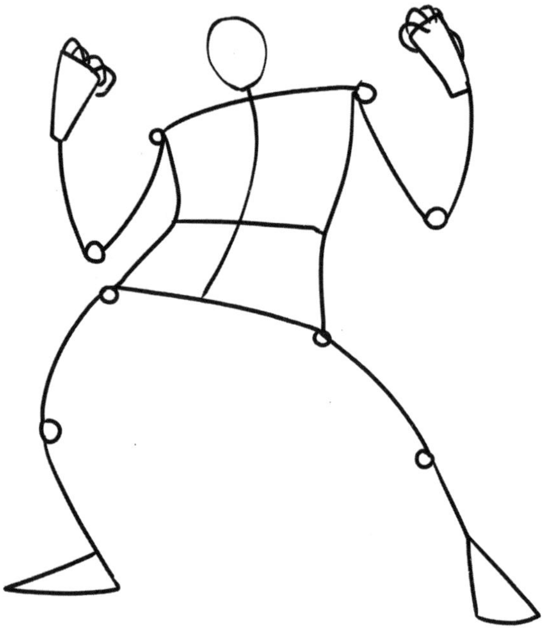

Rough Draft

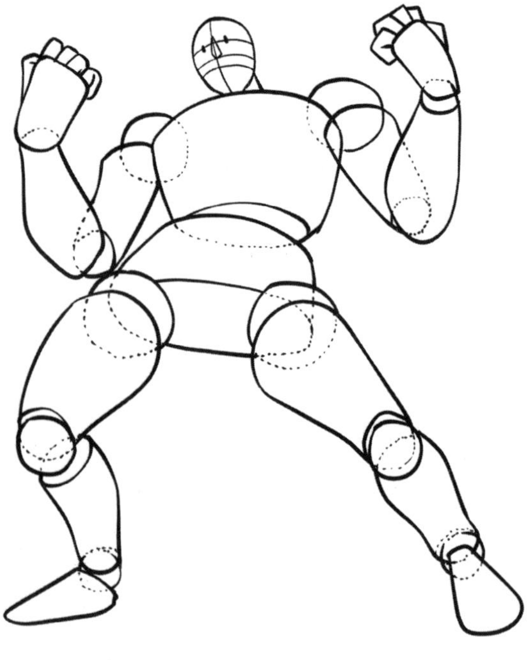

Fleshing Out

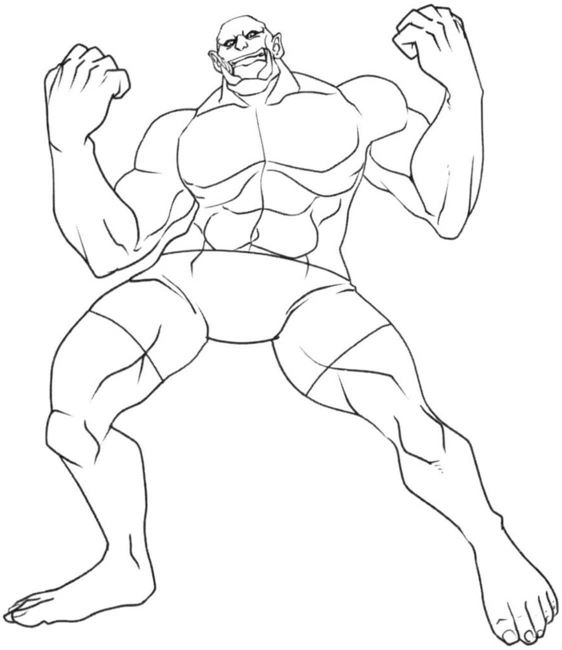

Finishing Touches

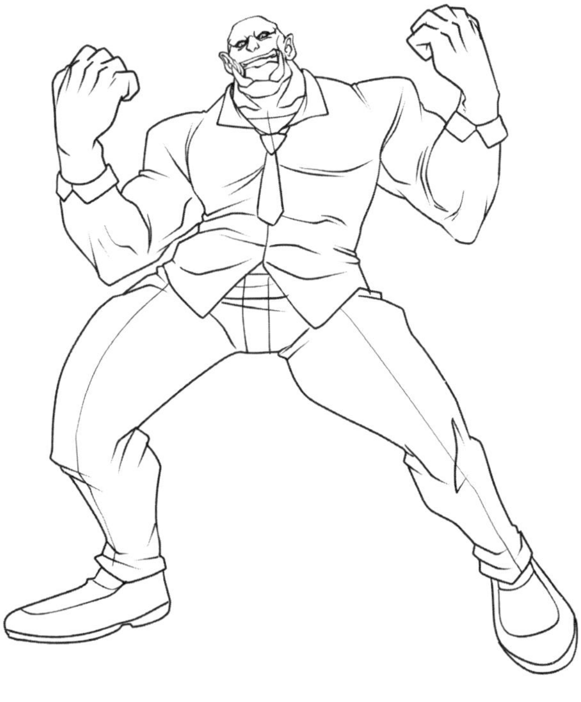

EXPRESS YOURSELF

Expressions tell your readers exactly how your characters are feeling. A clear and easy-to-understand expression helps convey emotion and advance your story as well.

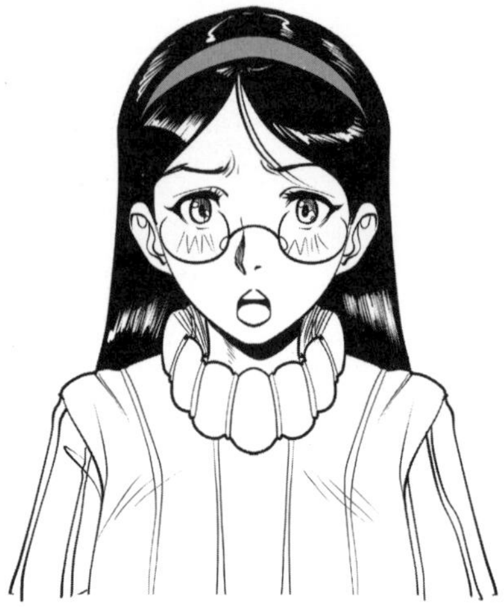

Concerned

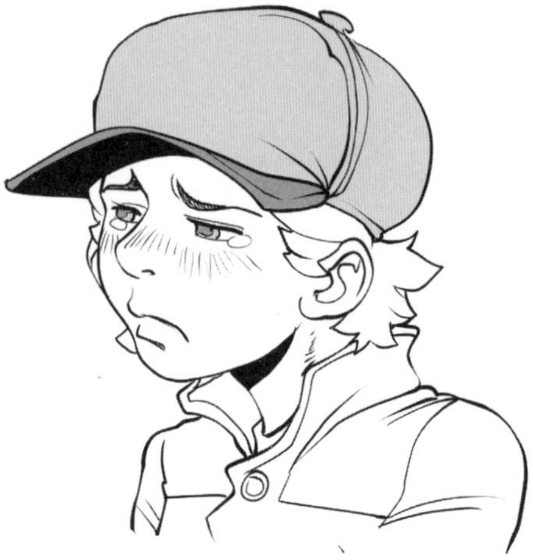

Sad

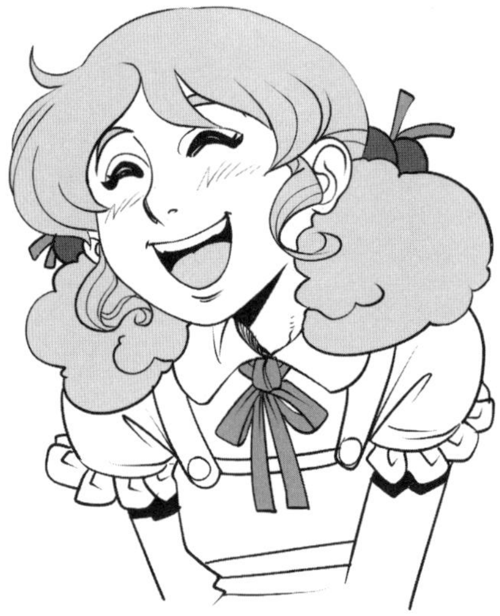

Cheerful

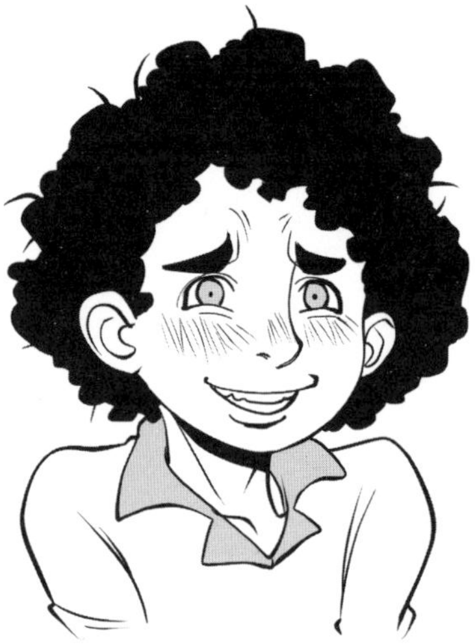

Embarrassed

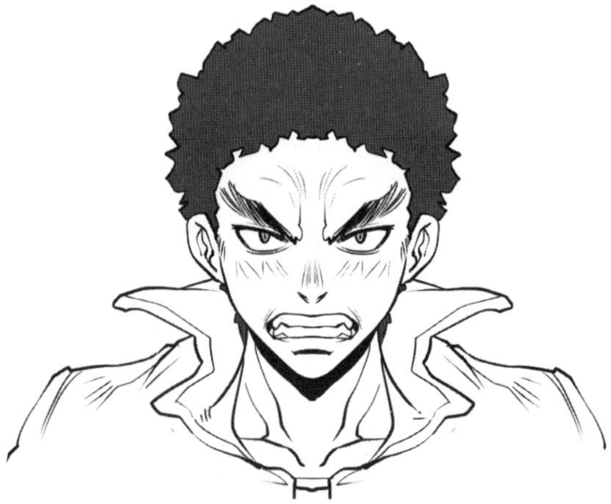

Angry

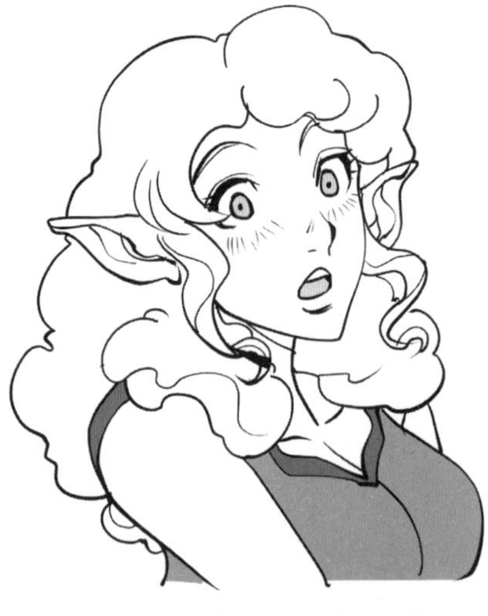

Surprised

SOUND EFFECTS

Make some noise! Sound effects are another great storytelling tool, just as effective as dialogue or description. Use the shape and look of the lettering to help suggest the sound.

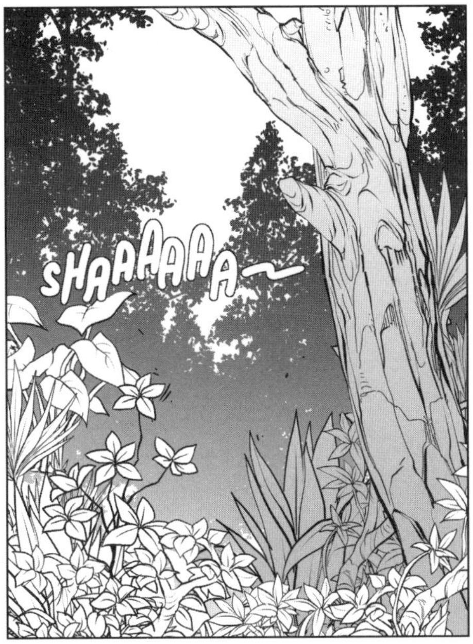

Silent Forest sound effects

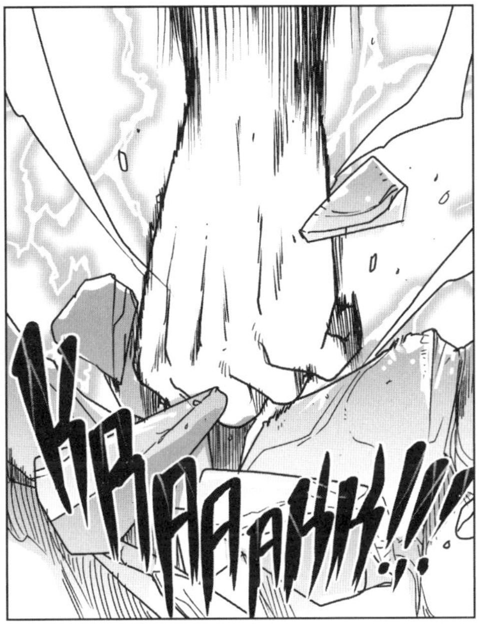

Cracking sound effects

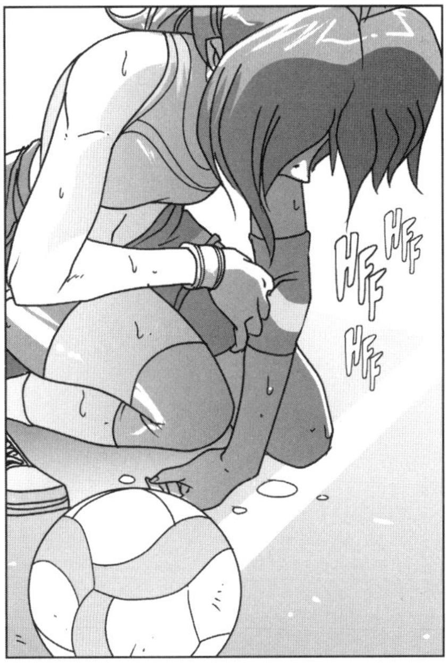

Gasping sound effects

TELLING THE STORY

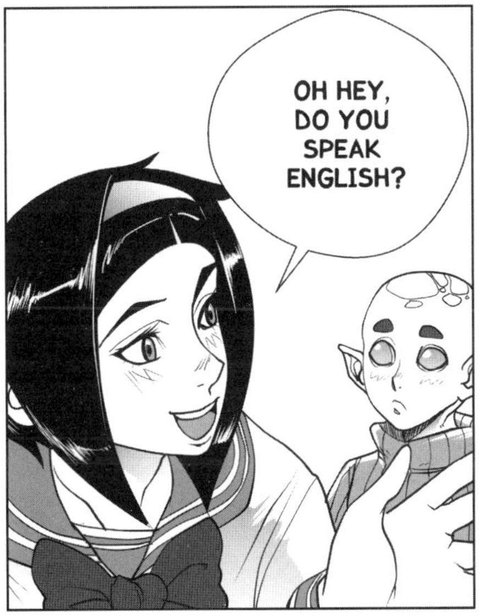

Question
This sets up the scene.

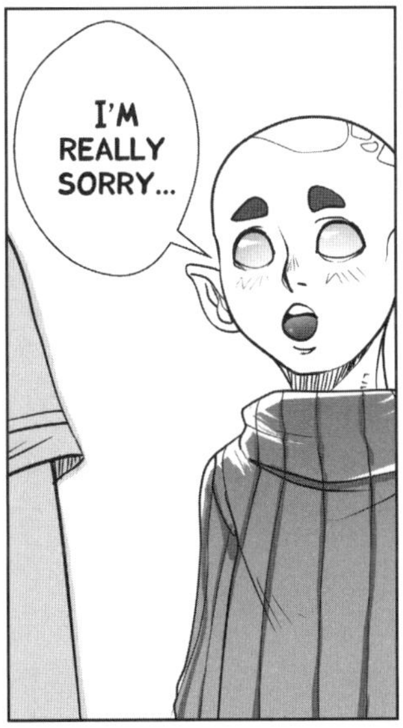

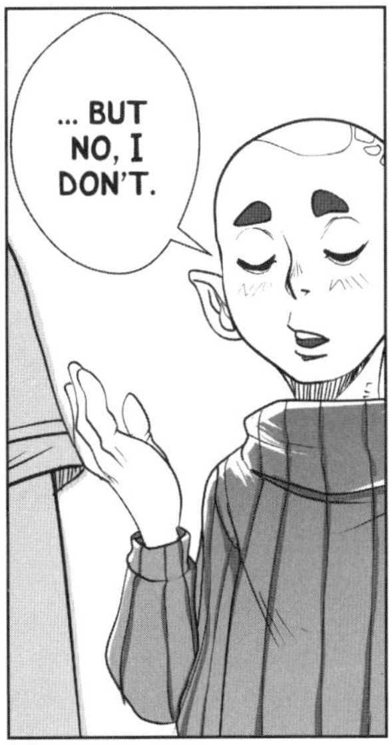

Answer
The response is revealed.

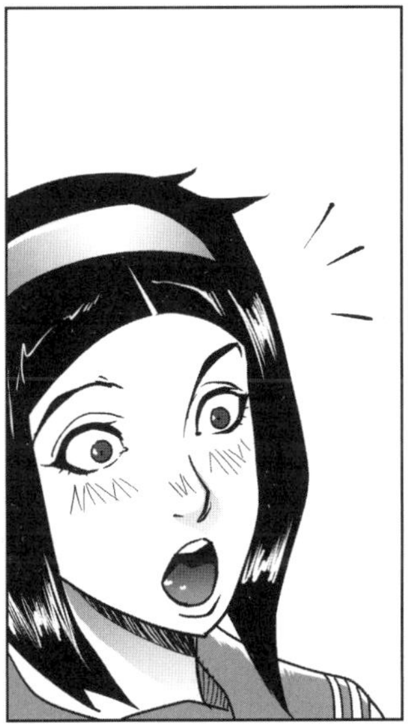

Reaction Shot
Say what? Now no words are used, and her expression tells the story.

AWESOME ACTION & POWERFUL POSES

Set your characters in motion. The proper pose captures your reader's attention and adds visual variety to your story.

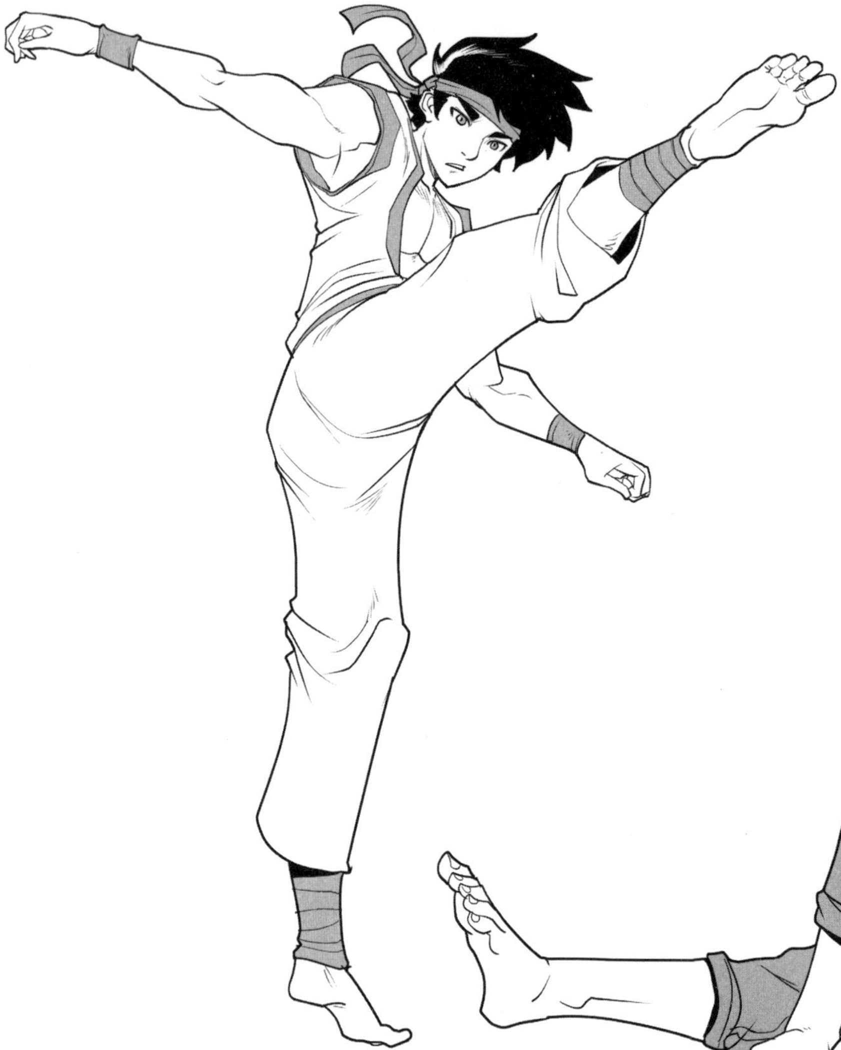

PRO TIPS

Powerfully posed characters also add depth, dimension and perspective to your scene.

Pay extra attention to the placement of the arms and legs.

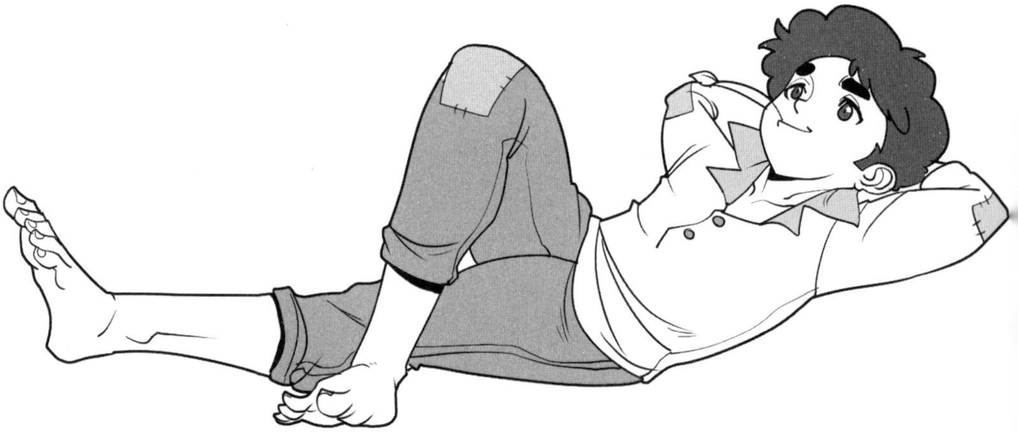

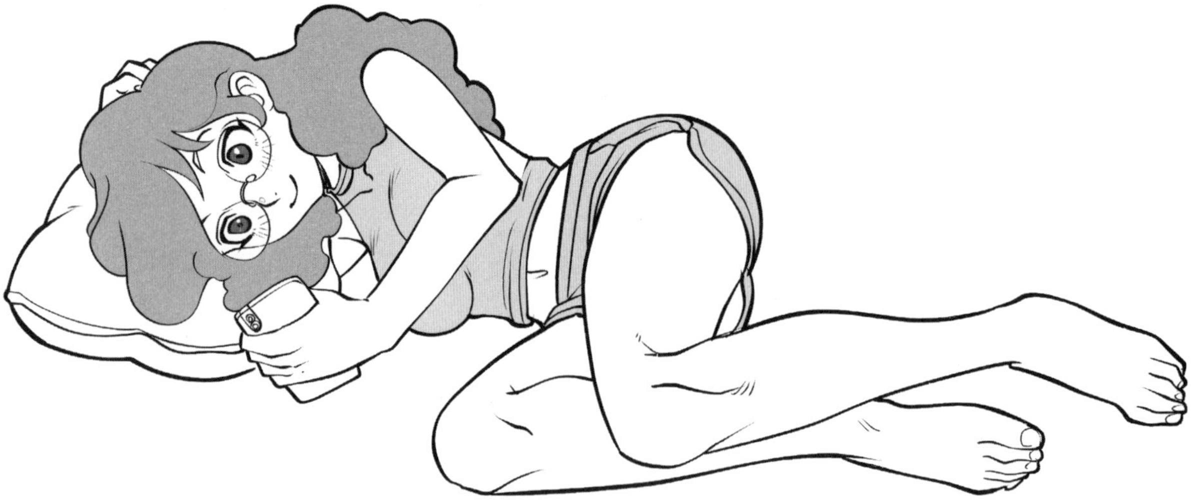

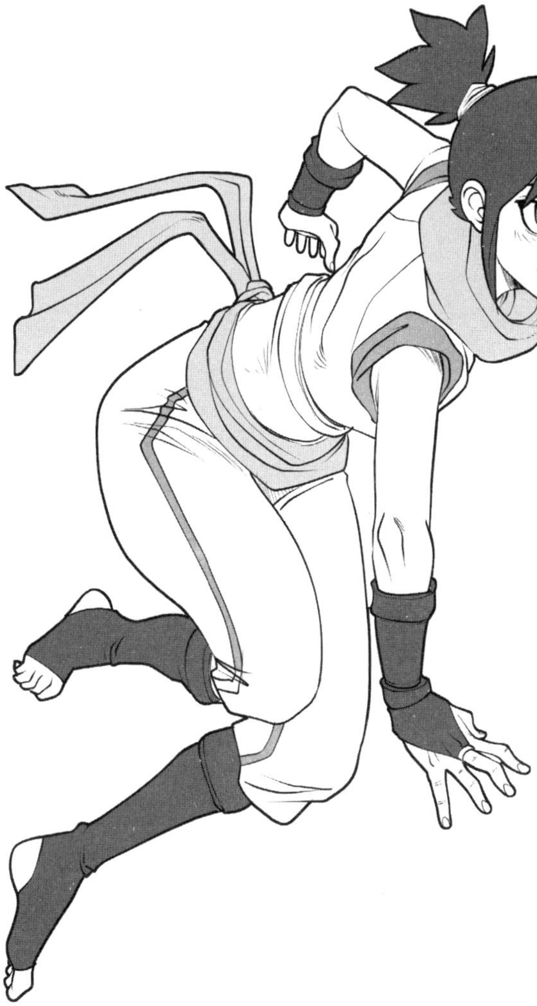

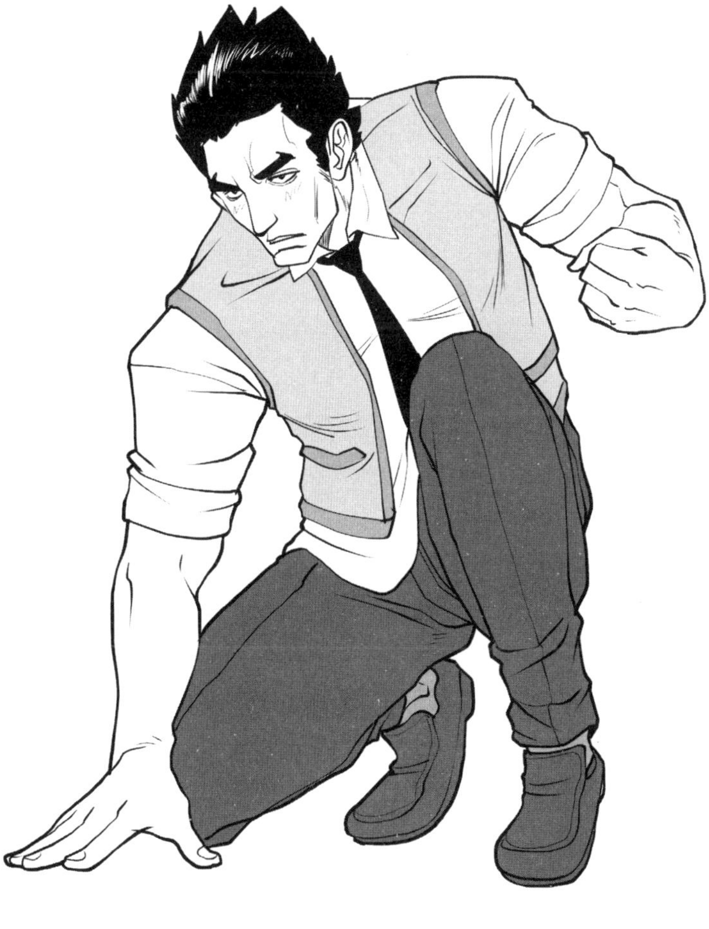

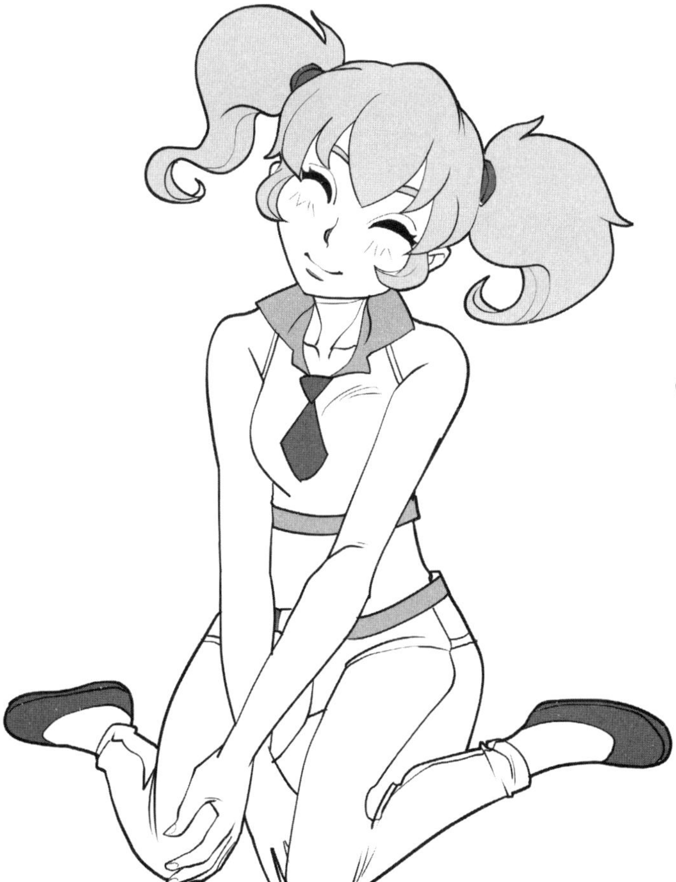

FLEXIBLE SPEECH AND THOUGHT BALLOONS

Here are some common balloons and text boxes. Cut them out, then place and trace them. Use the balloons already in place or design and add your own. Create the shape that's needed to fit your characters' words. Just make sure they read left to right, top to bottom.

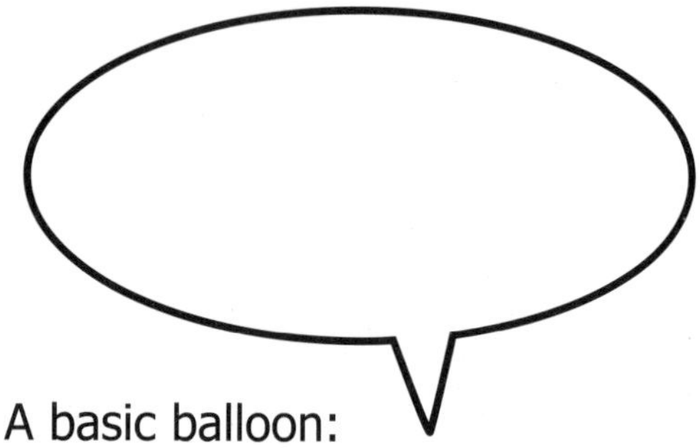

A basic balloon:
when your character
has something to say

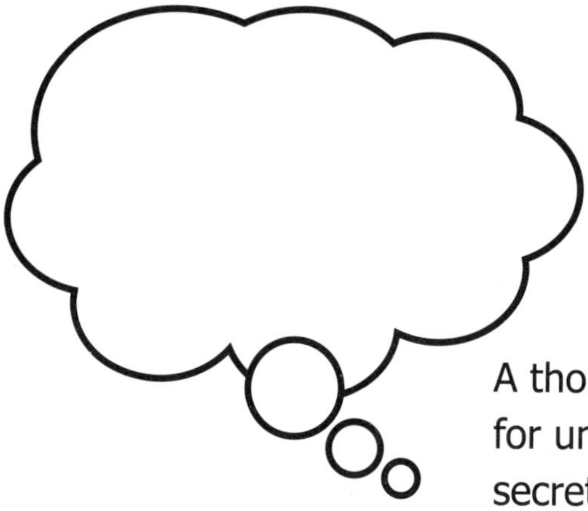

A thought balloon:
for unspoken words,
secrets & daydreams

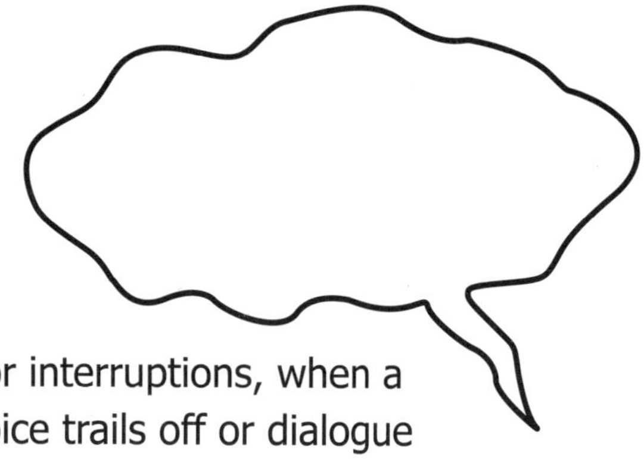

For interruptions, when a
voice trails off or dialogue
is left unfinished

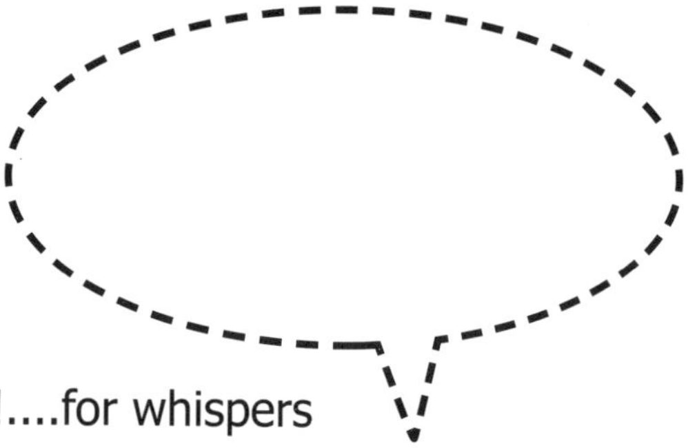

Shh!....for whispers
or words not to be
heard by everyone

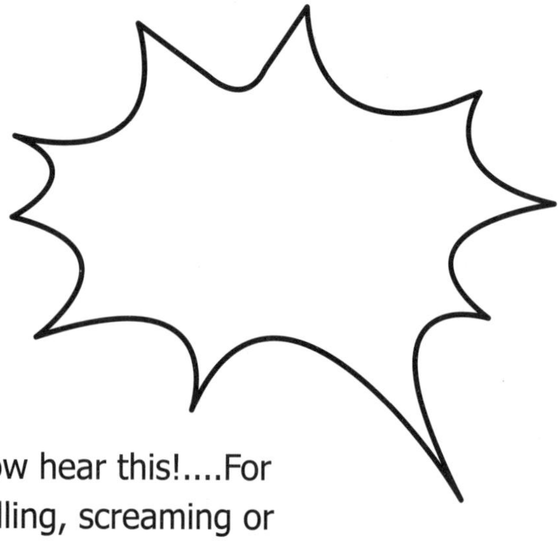

Now hear this!....For
yelling, screaming or
making an announcement

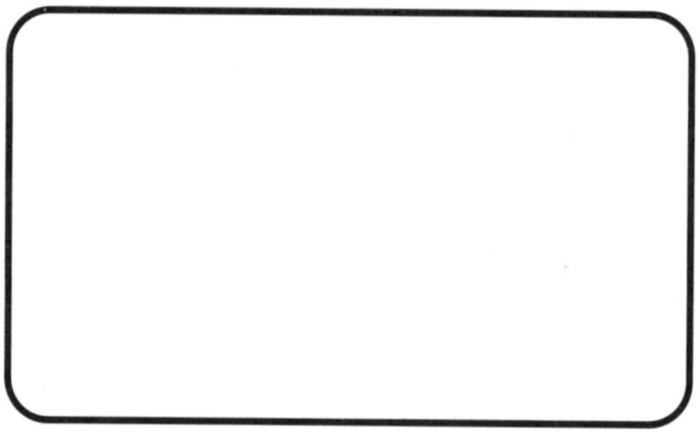

A basic text box for captions,
narration or general information

ANGLES & PERSPECTIVE

One way to tell your story is to start with a wide-angle view, an establishing shot. Then move in closer to the action, panel by panel, ending with the intensity of a close-up.

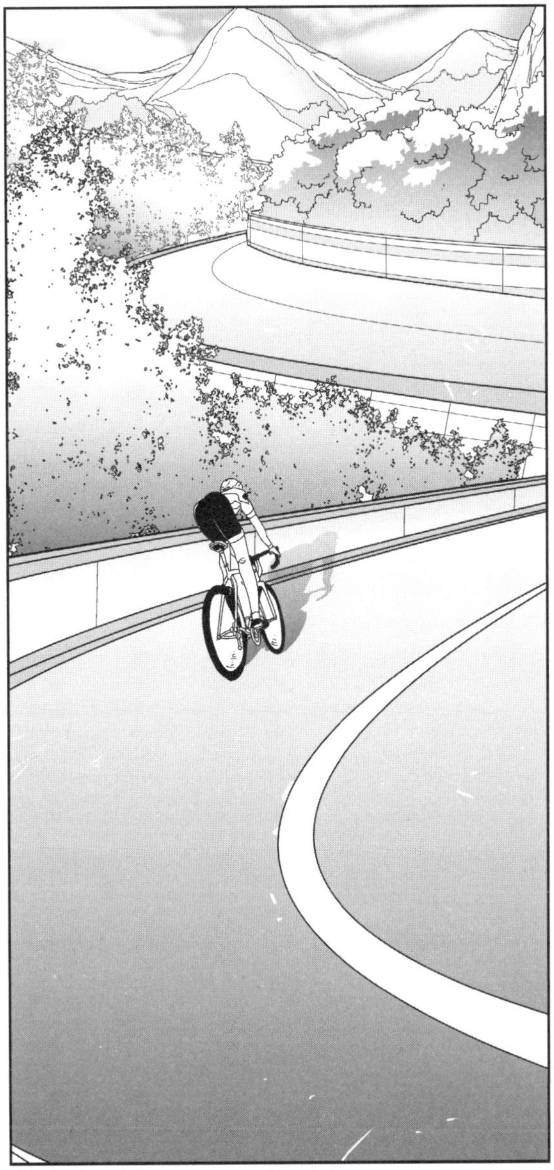

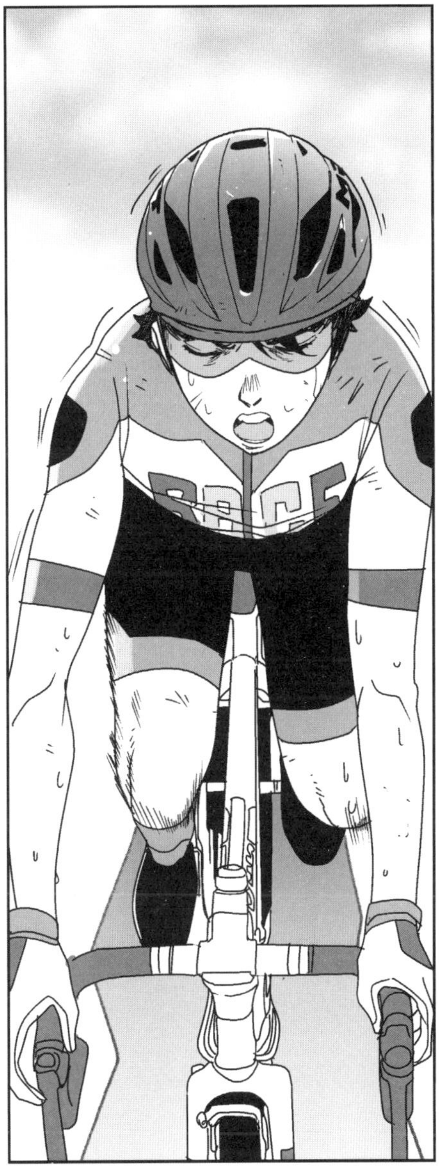

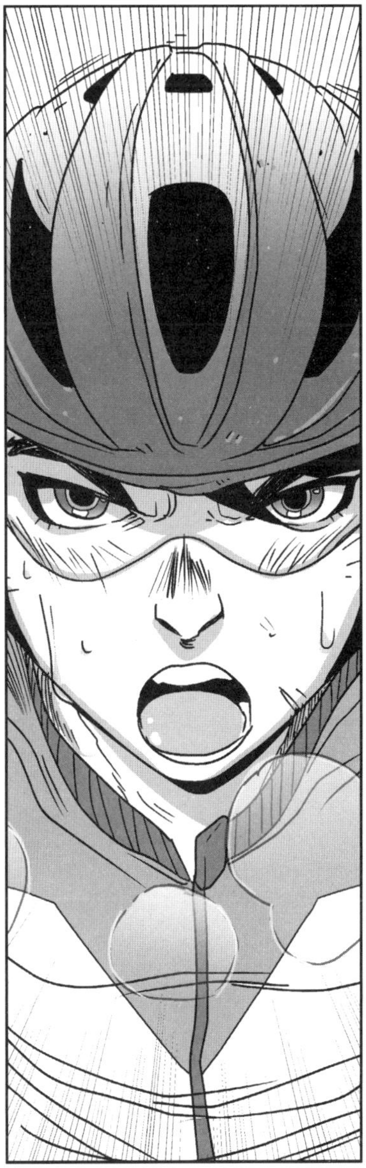

ESTABLISHING THE SCENE

A wide-angle view helps set the scene. Where are we and what's going on? This angle helps make that clear.

ZOOM IN

This is sometimes called a medium shot: closer to the action but not too close.

CLOSE-UP

In your face! Great for intense or emotional scenes. Or when you want to draw your reader directly into the action.

PANEL BY PANEL

Panels are created the same way characters are constructed. The same four steps apply. Start simple, adding details and complexity as you go. Your story's taking shape before your eyes!

STEP 1

Sketch in the basic outlines.

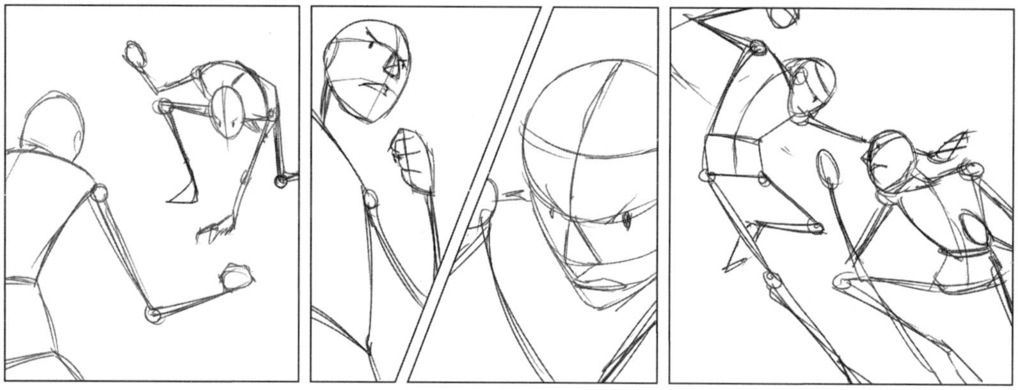

STEP 2

Flesh out and block in the forms.

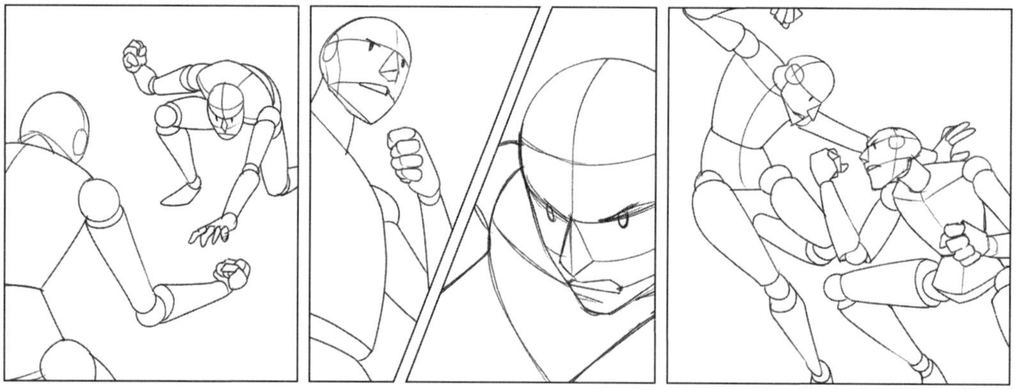

STEP 3

Add features and details.

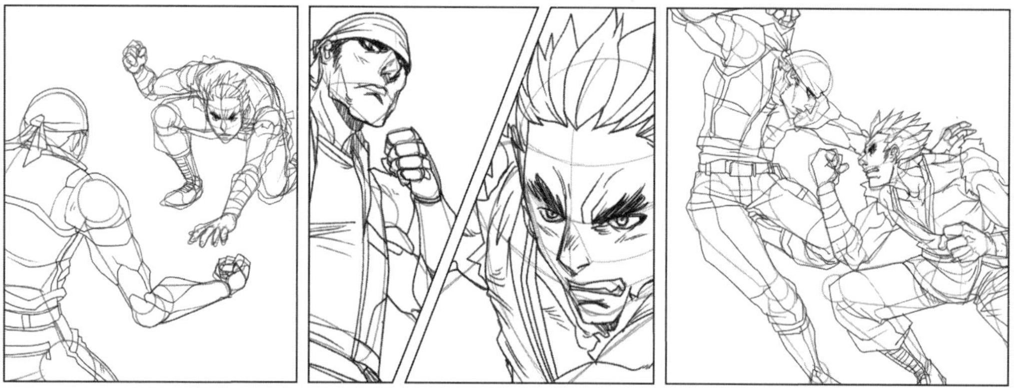

STEP 4

Finishing touches: ink or color it.

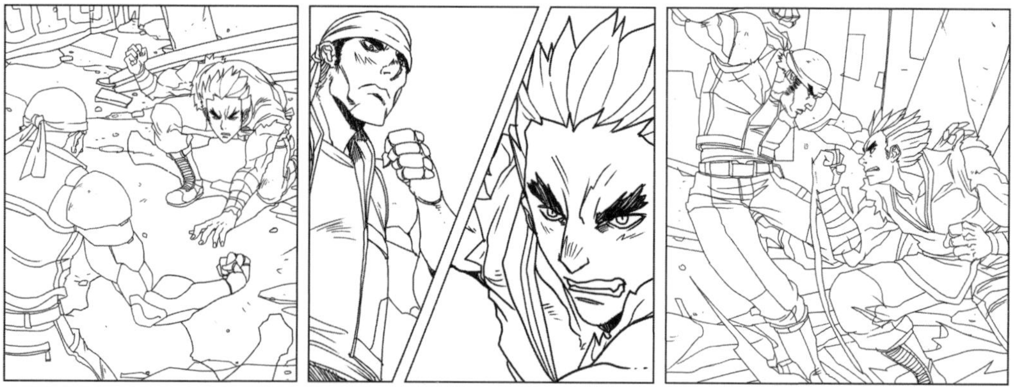

Design Your Own Cover

Design Your Own Cover

Design Your Own Cover

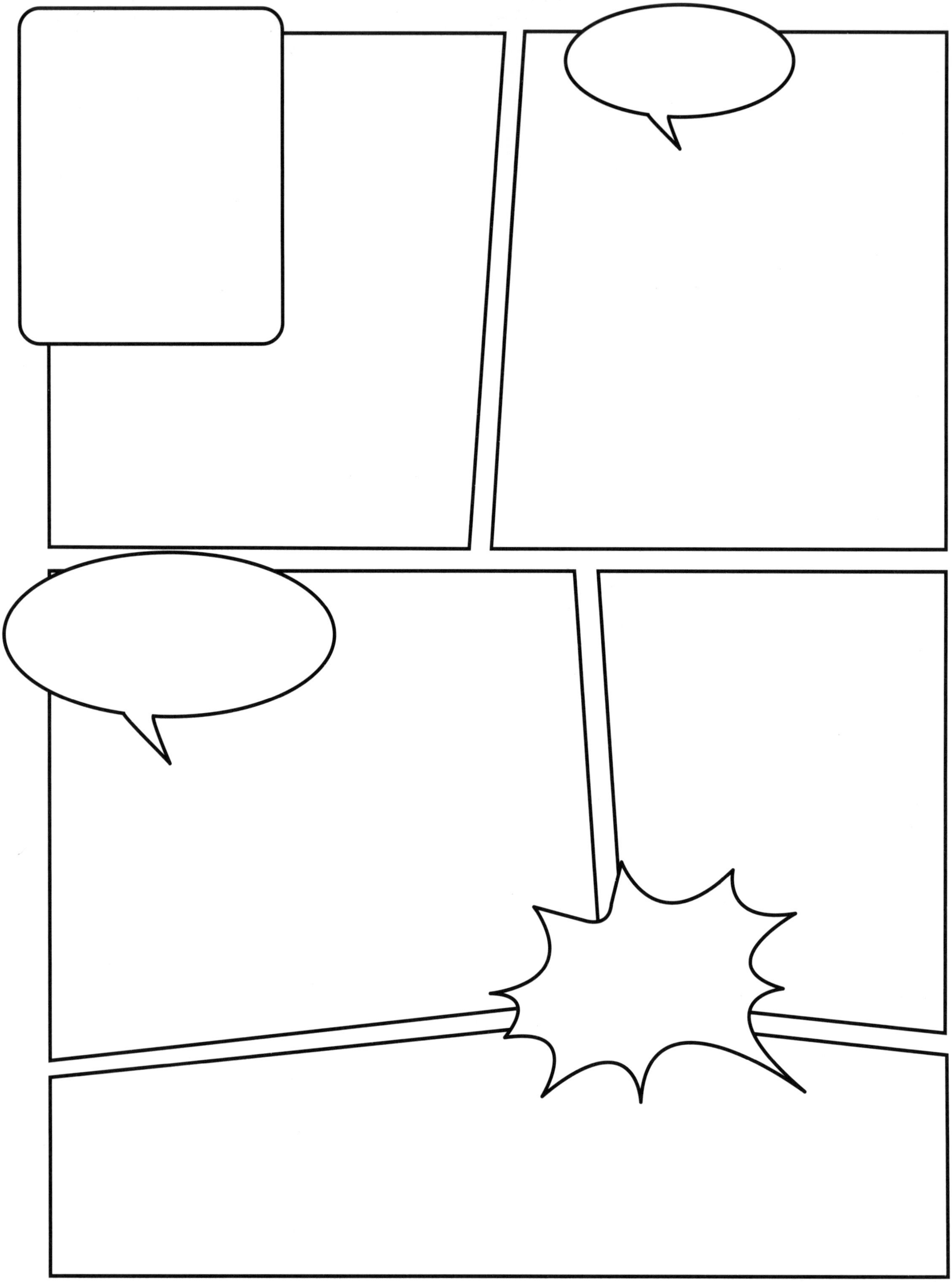

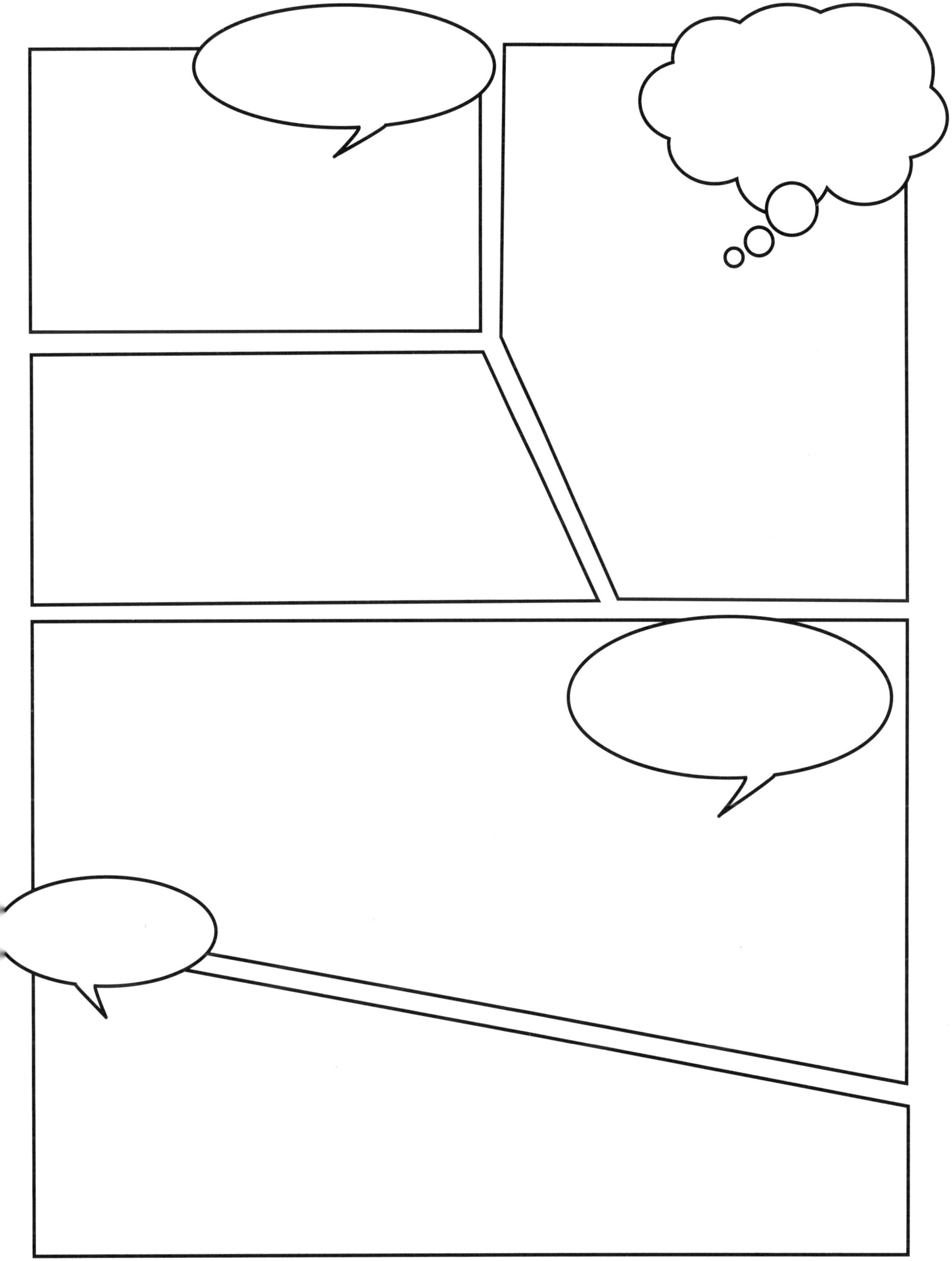

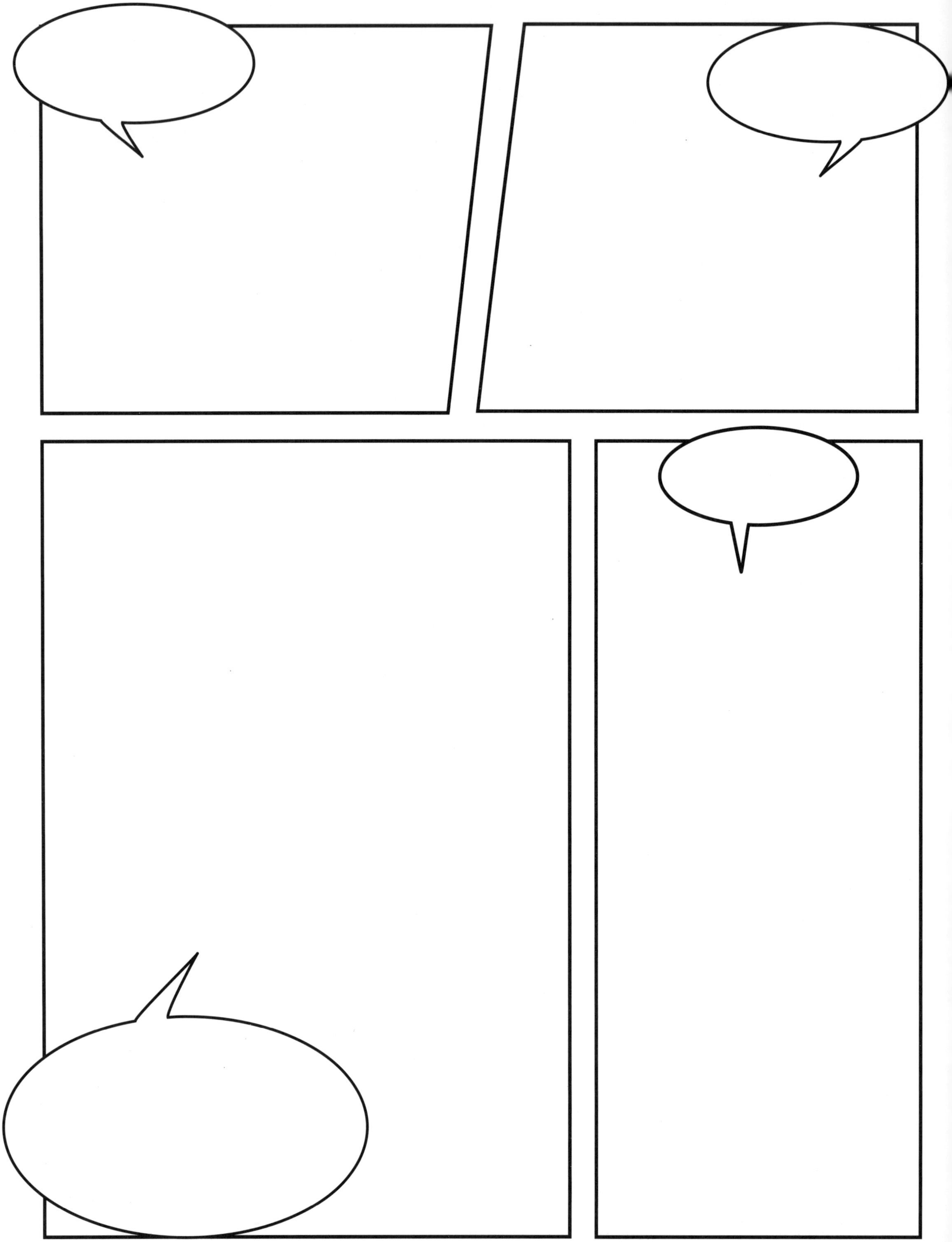

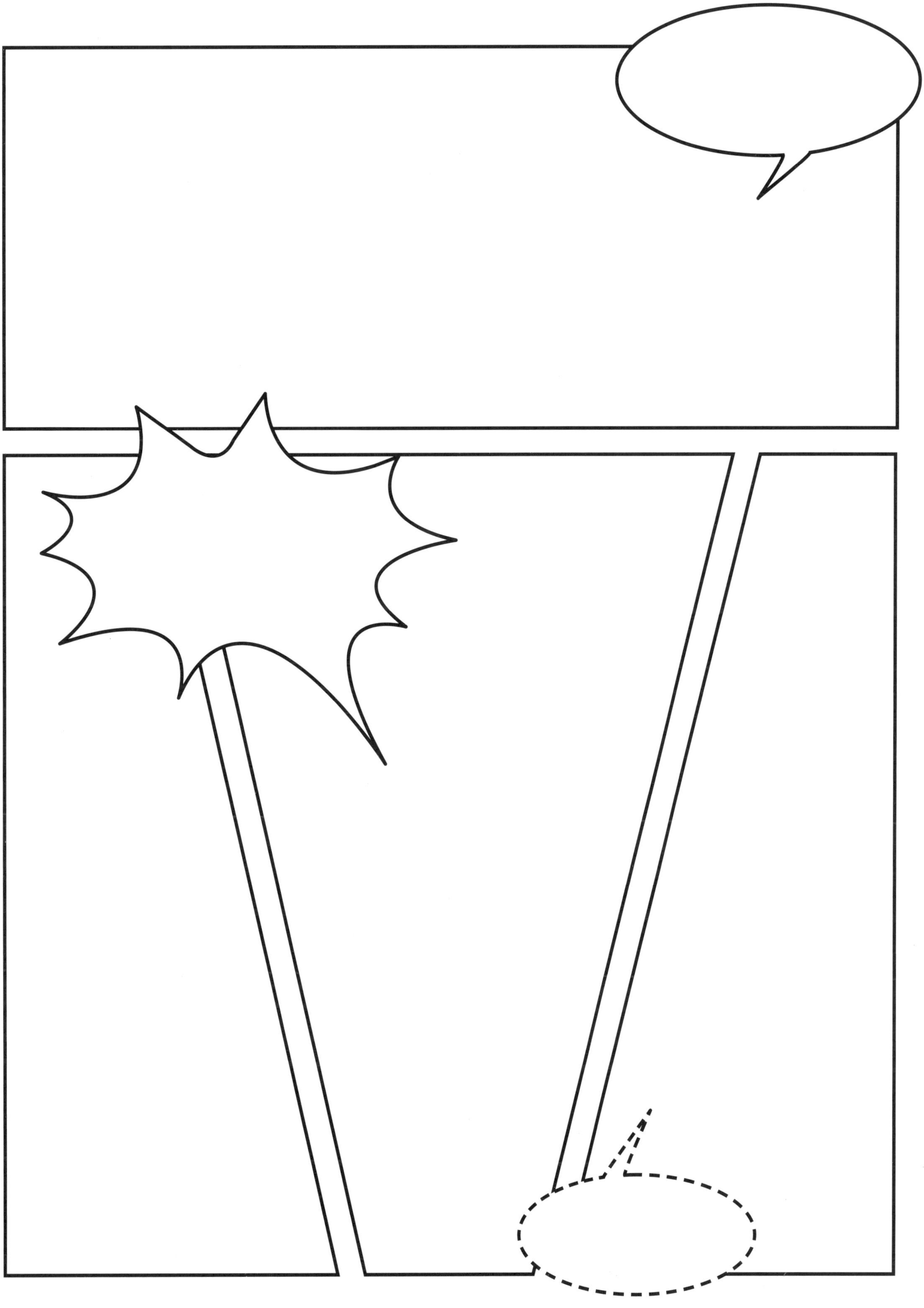

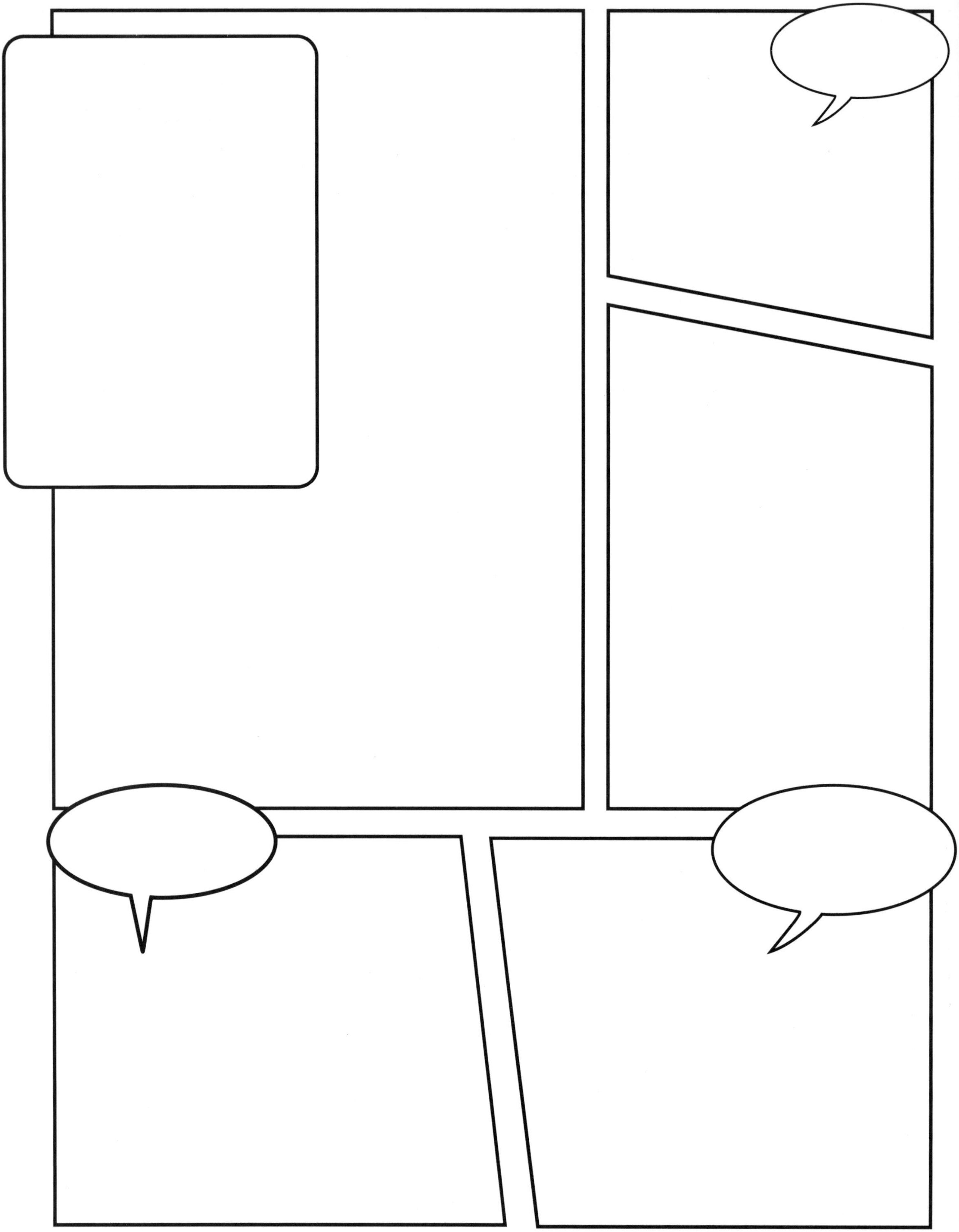

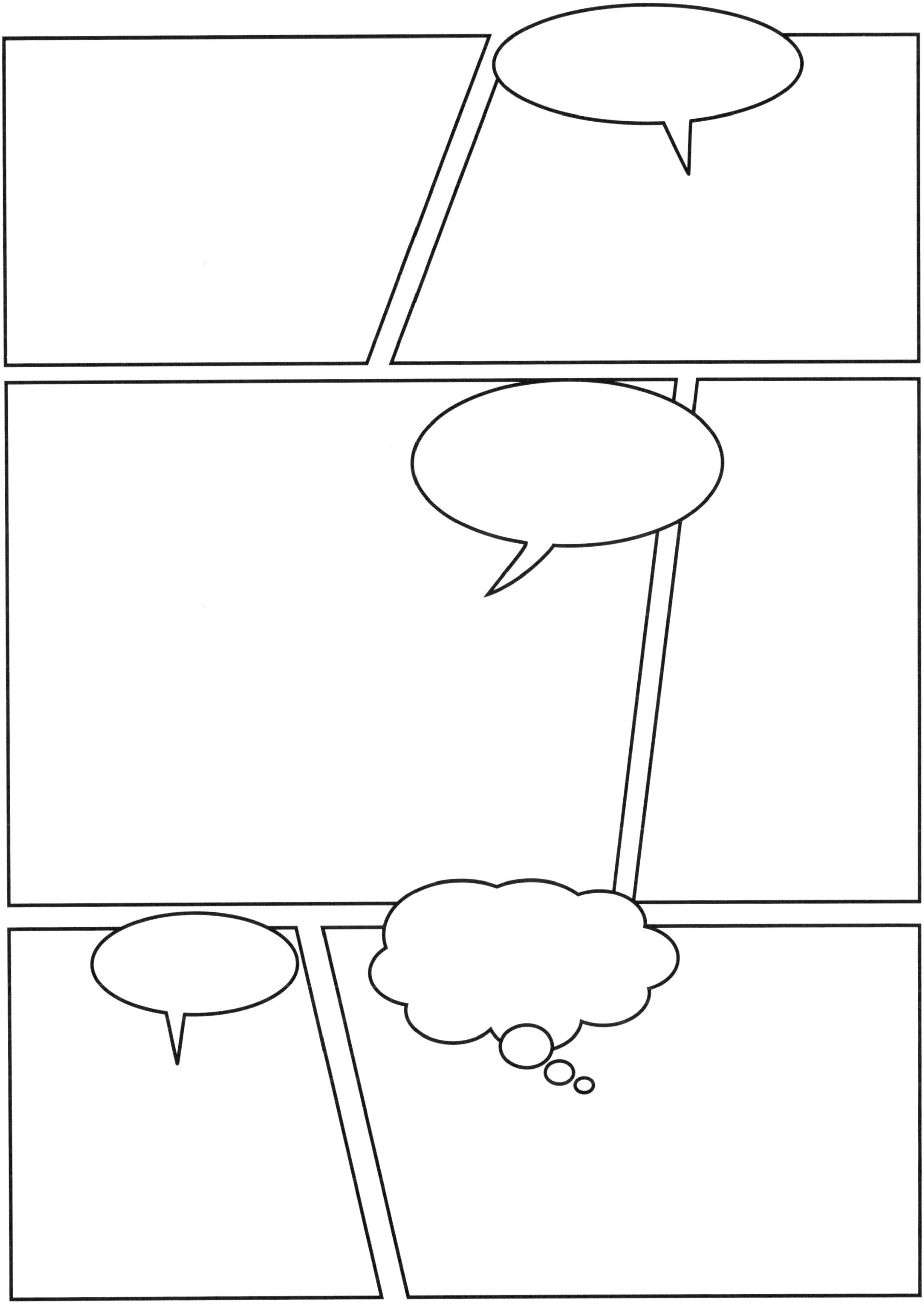

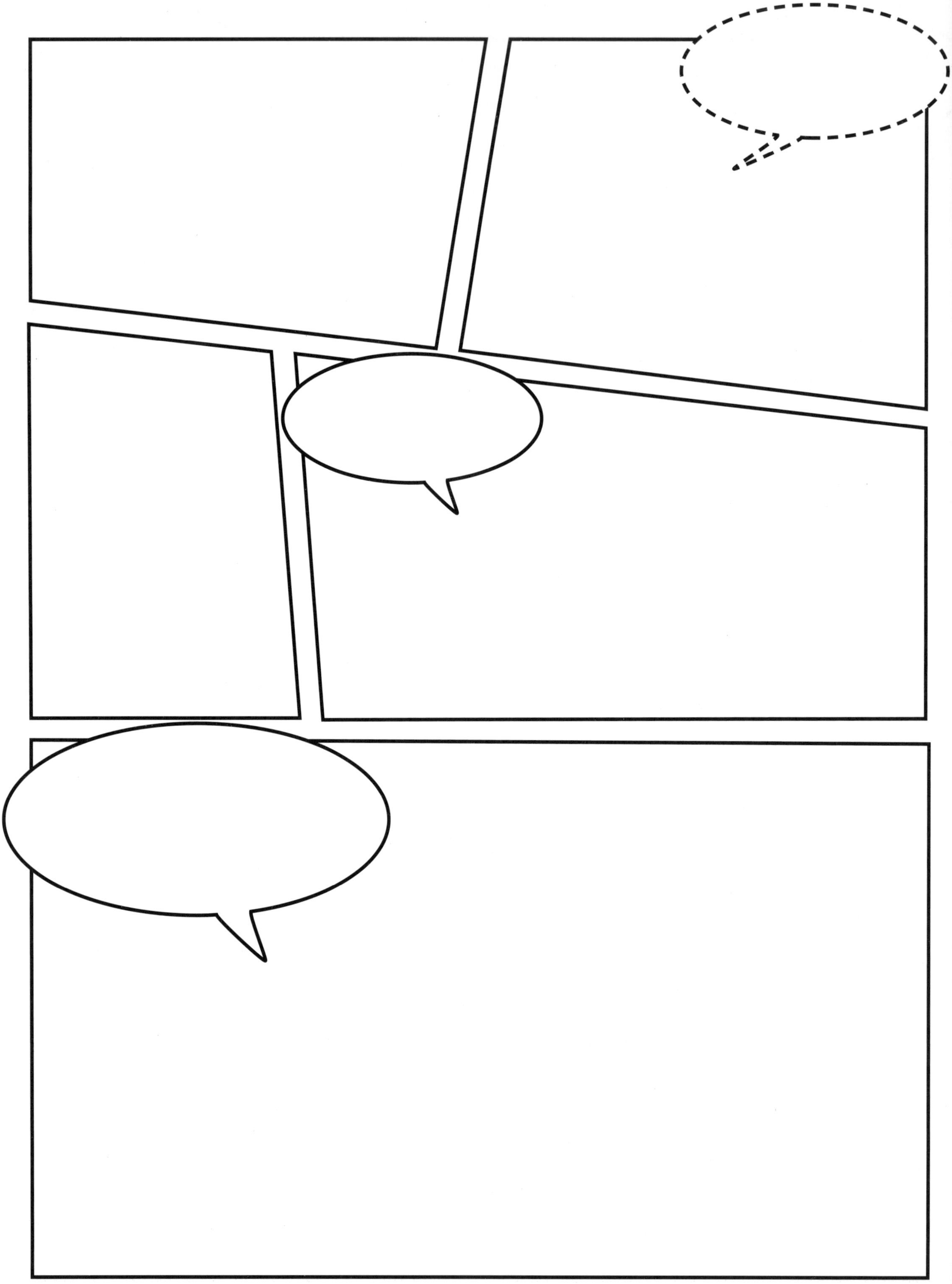

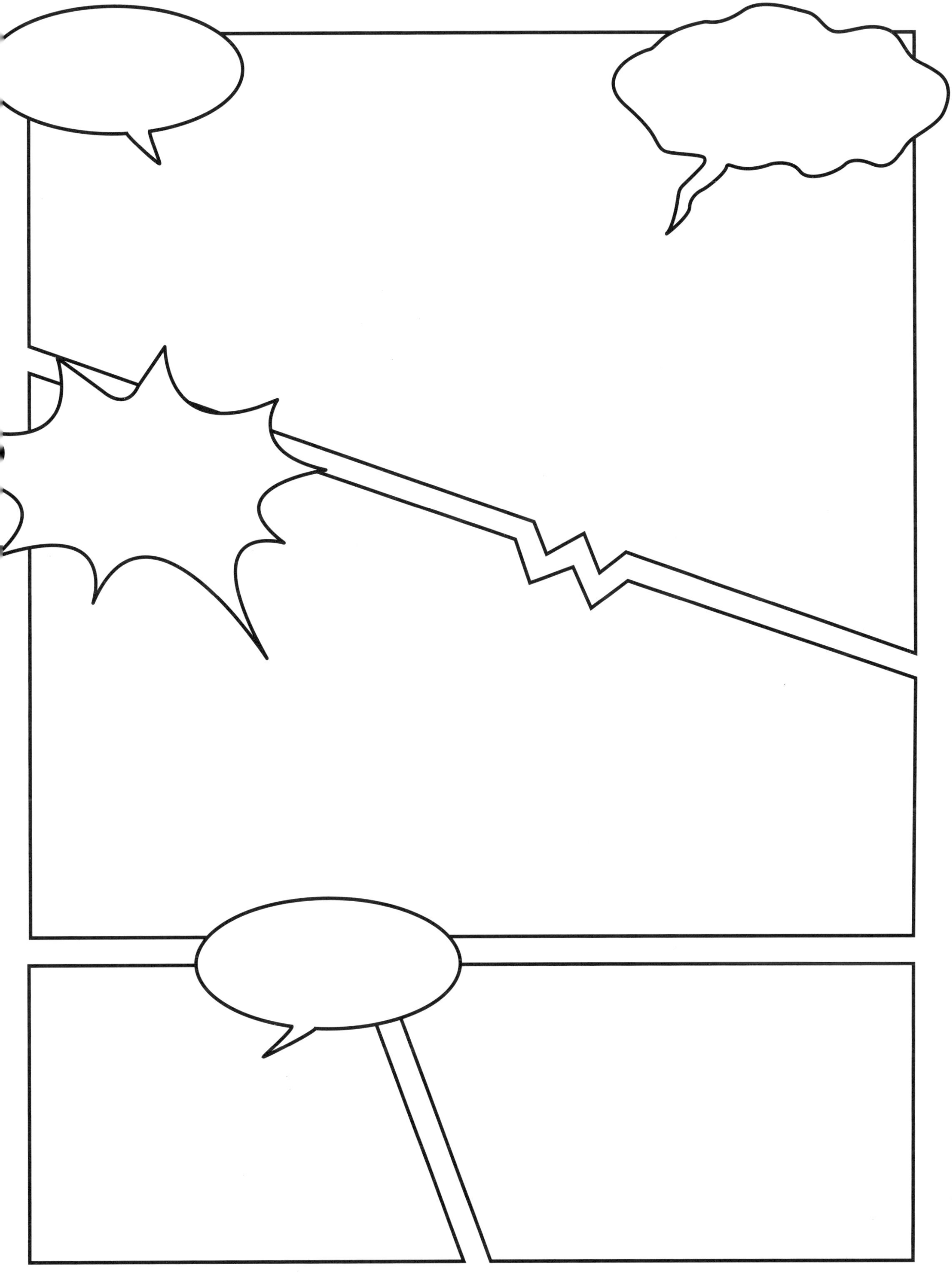

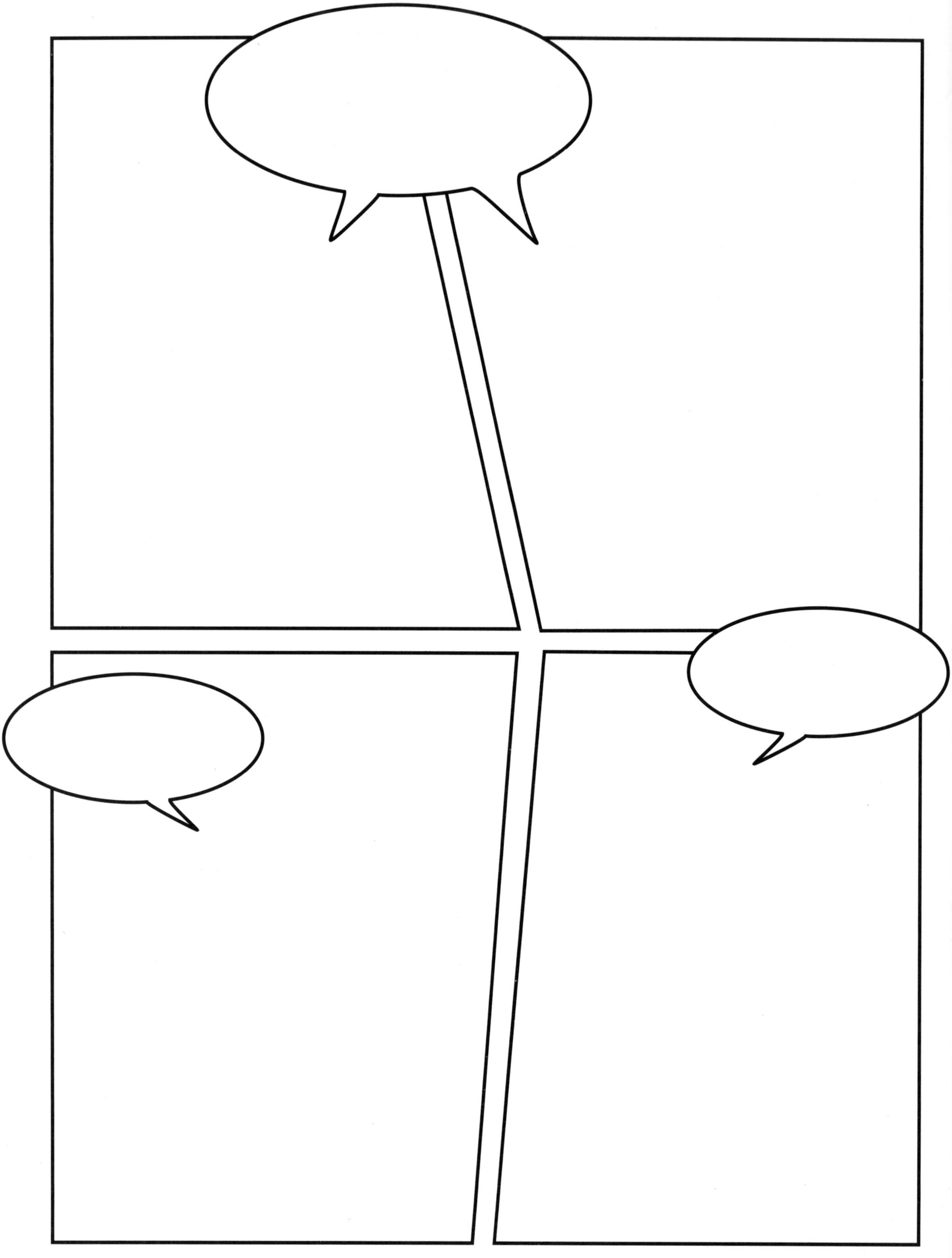

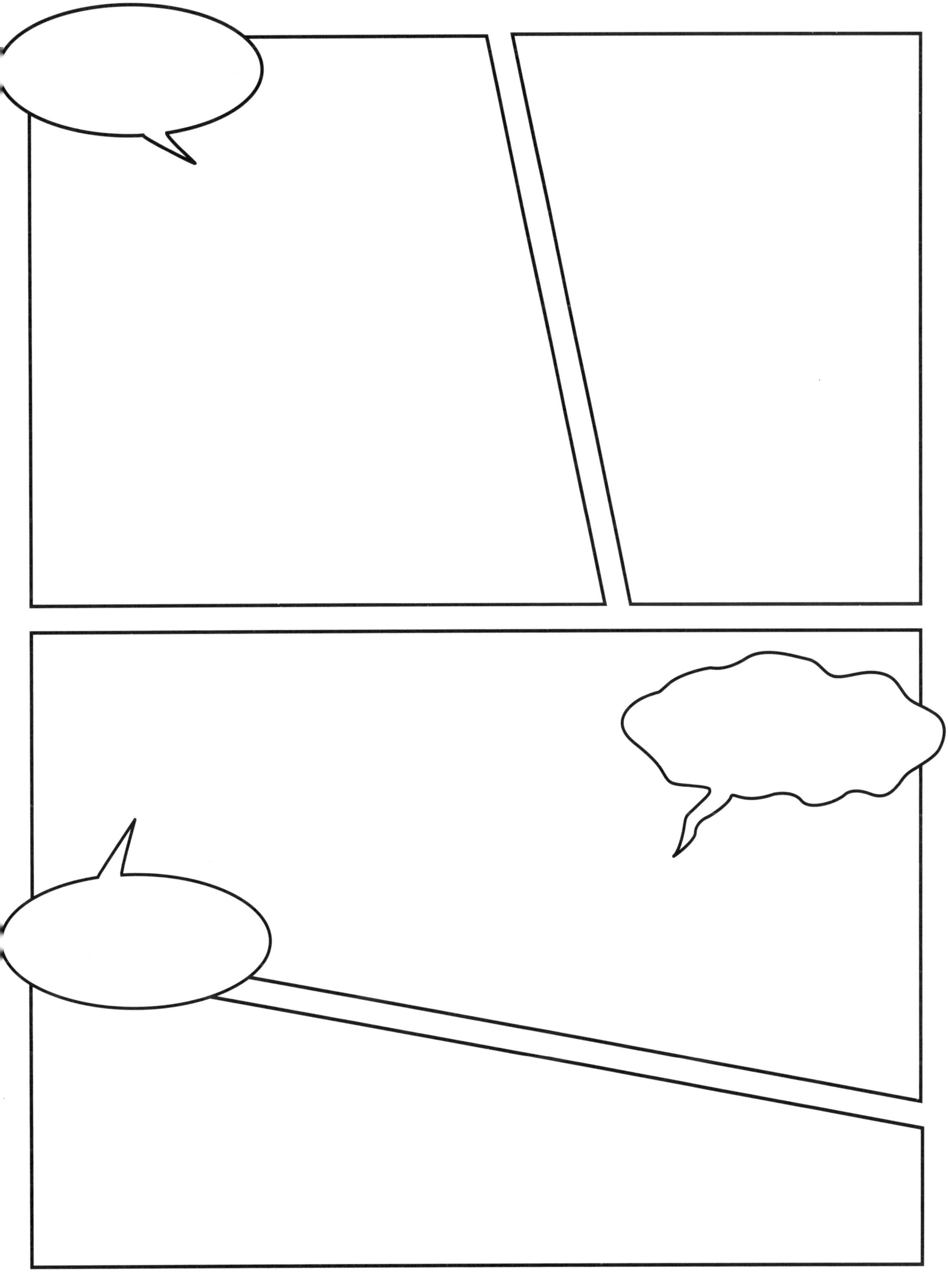

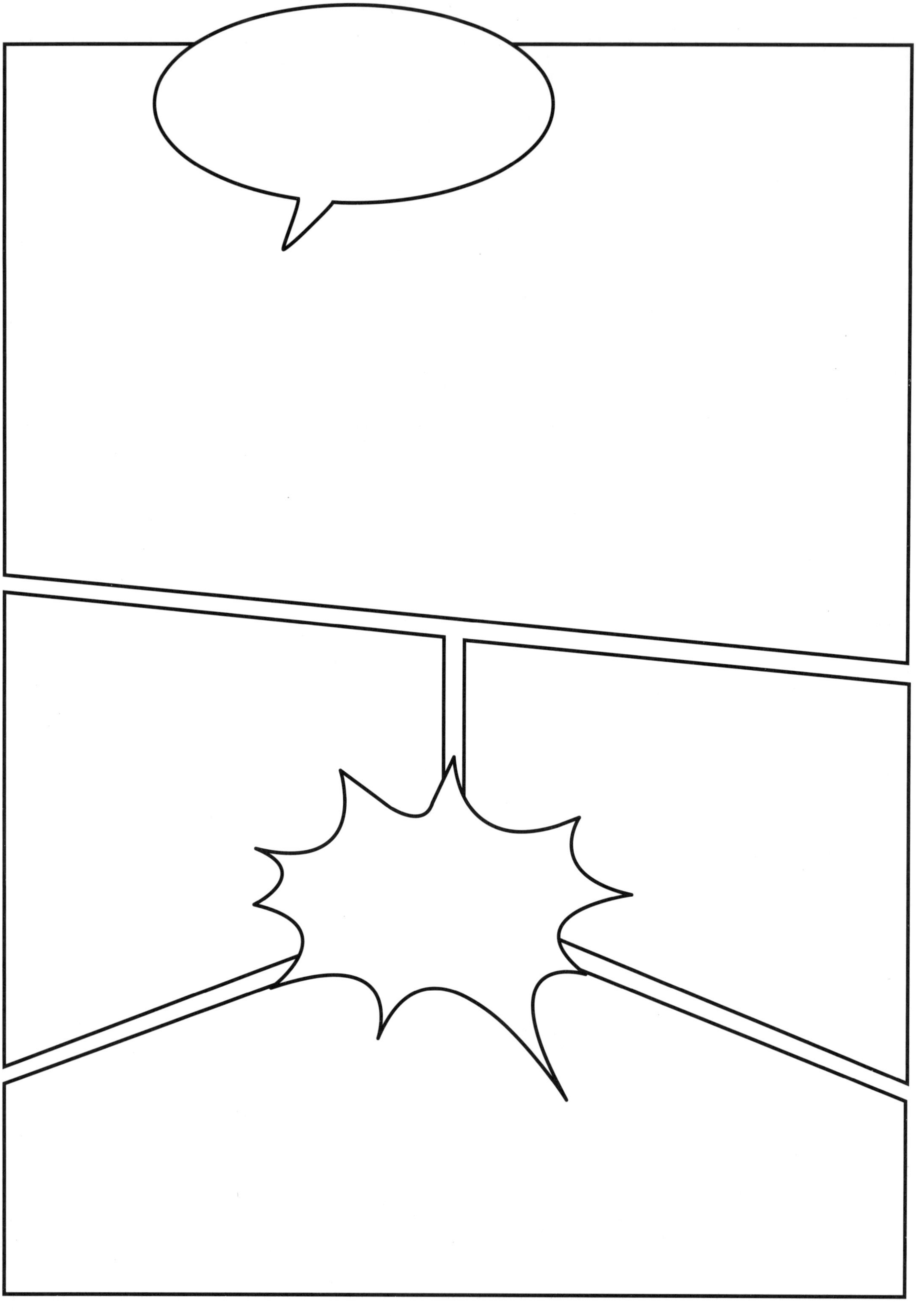

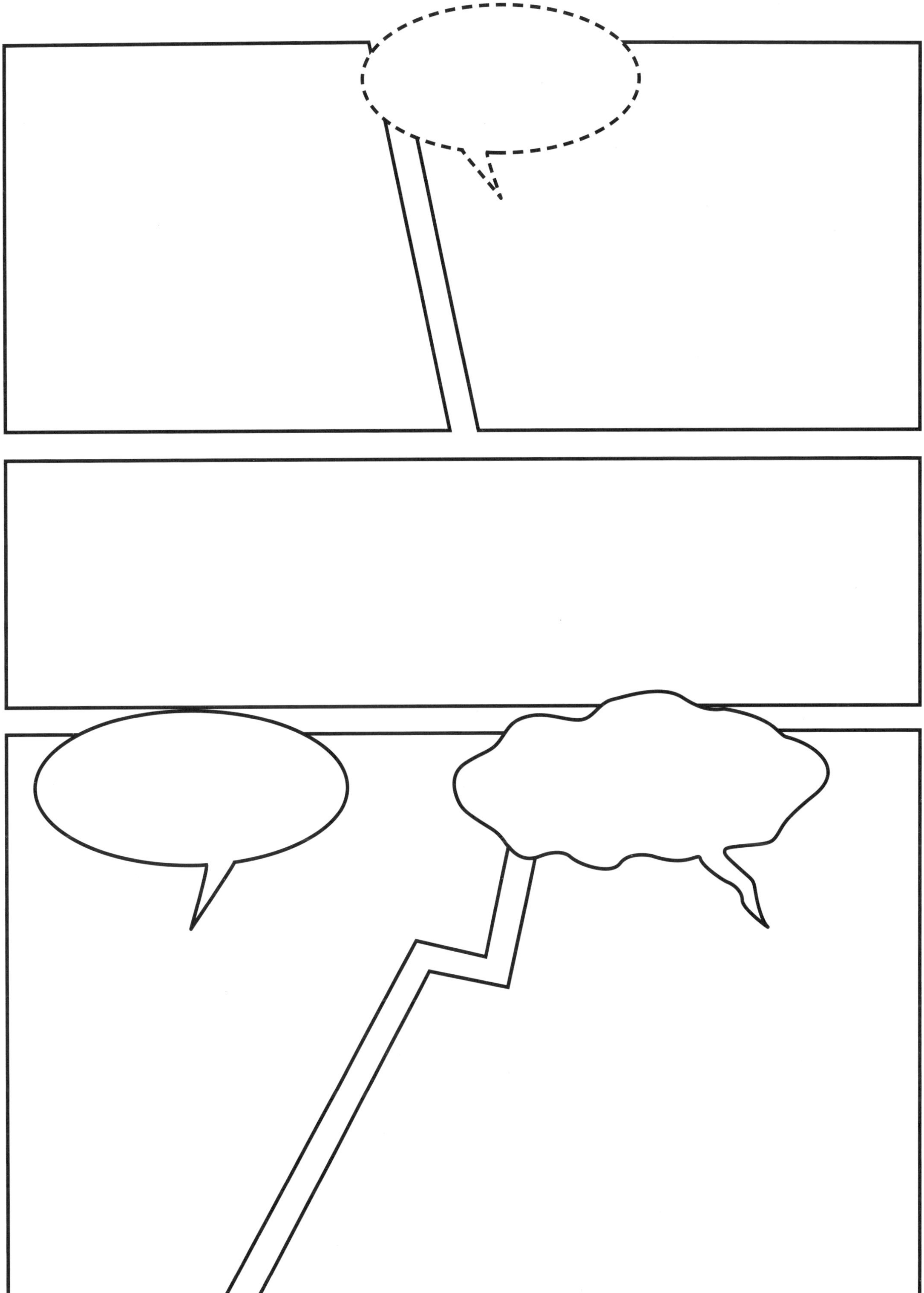

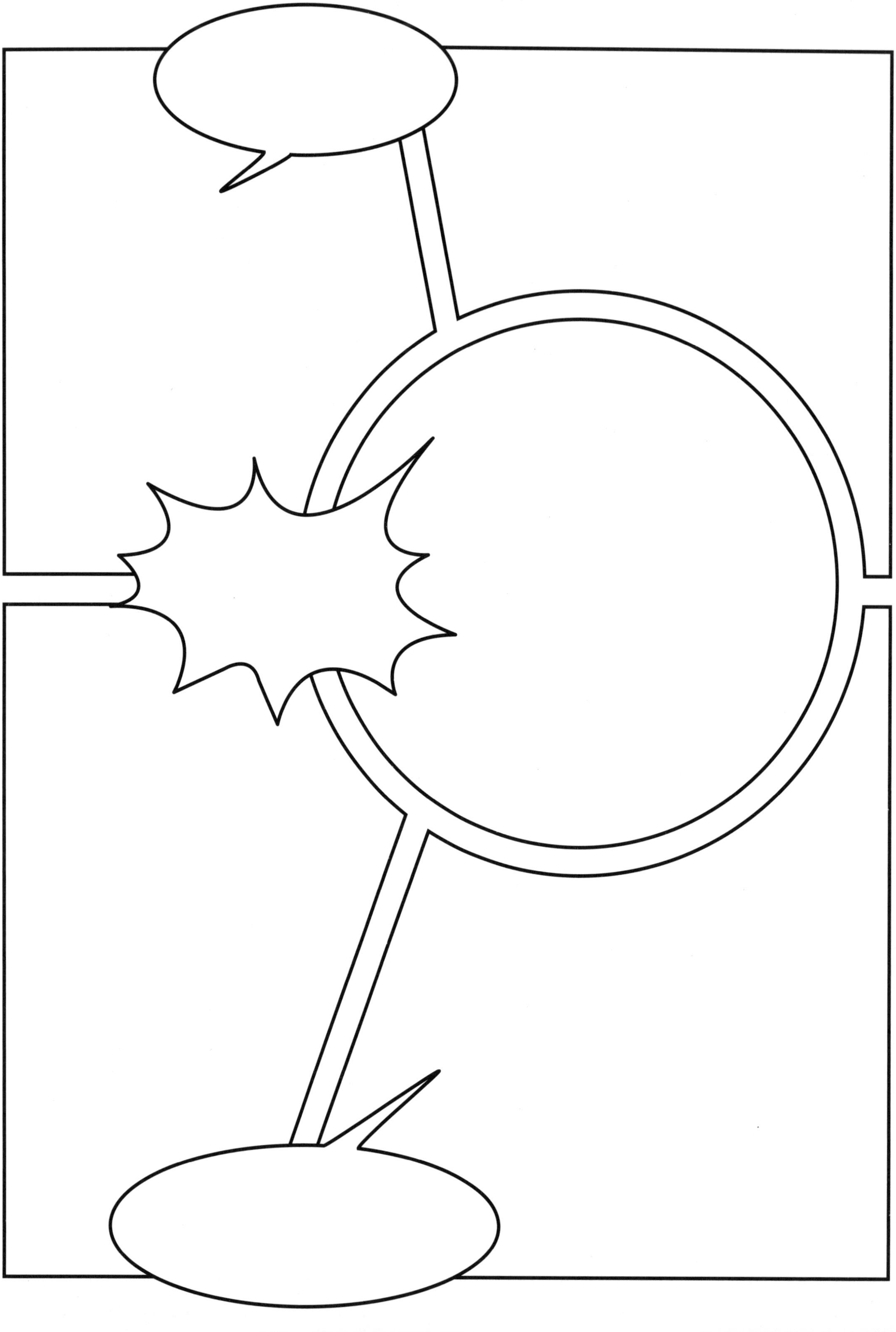

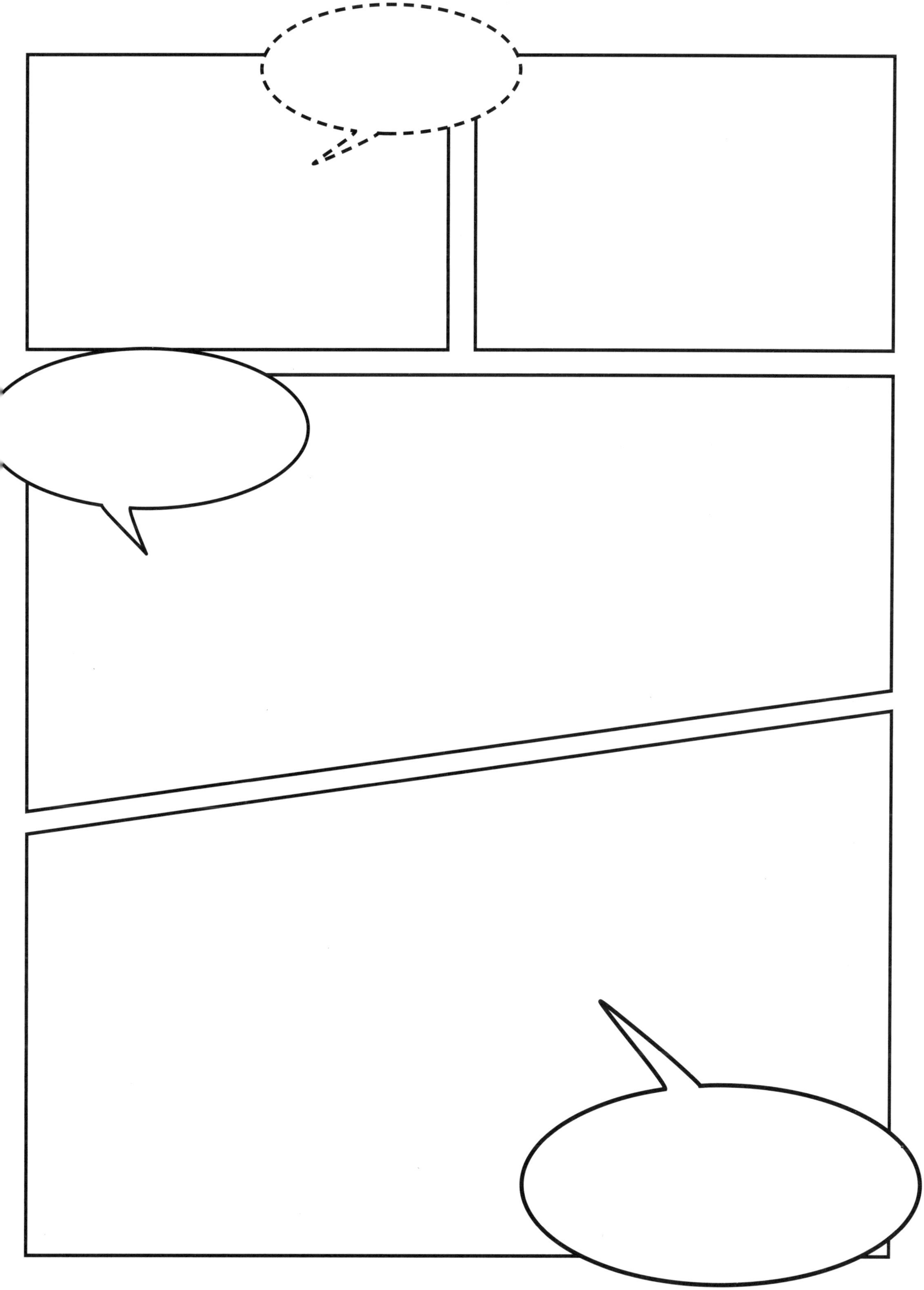

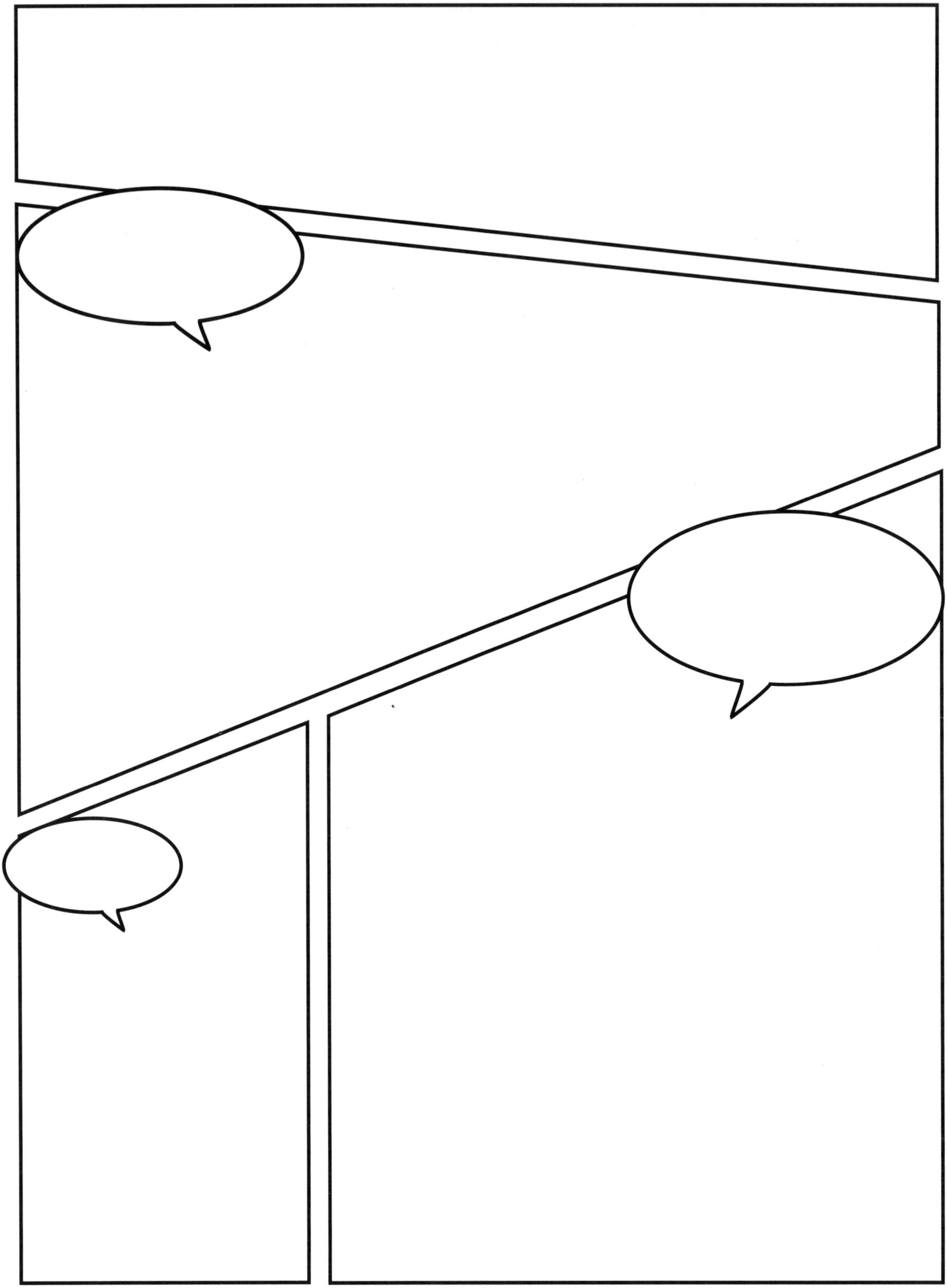

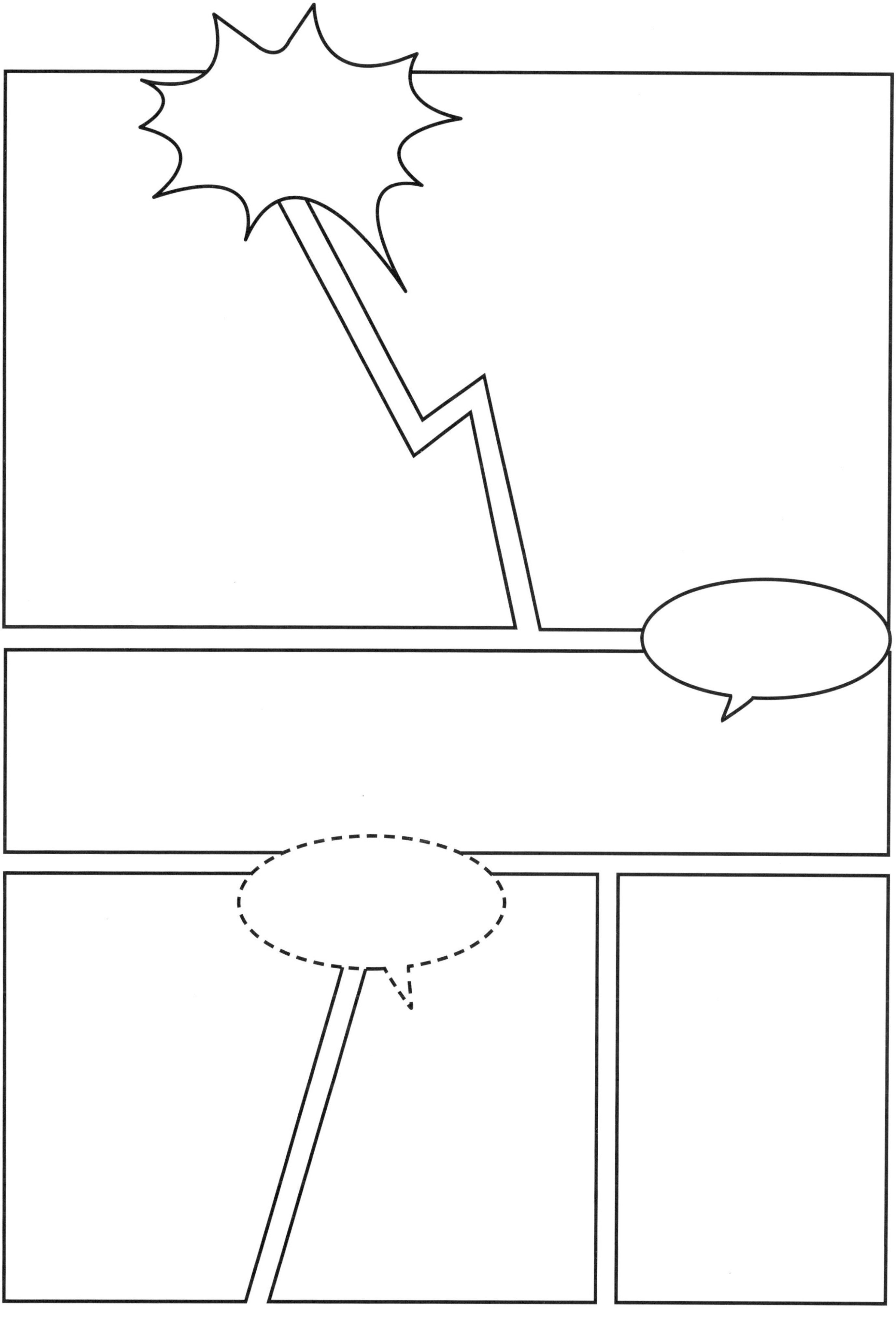

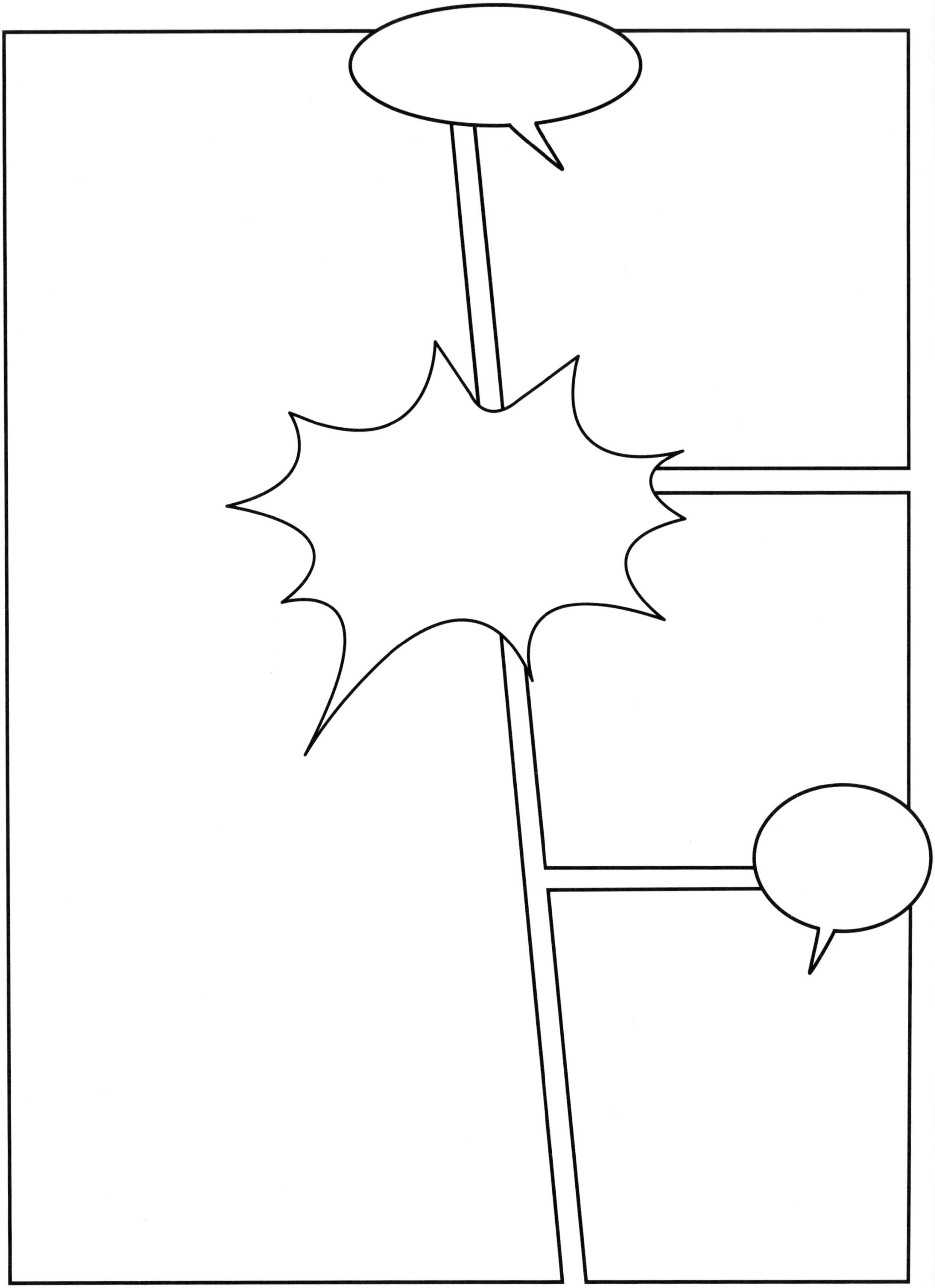

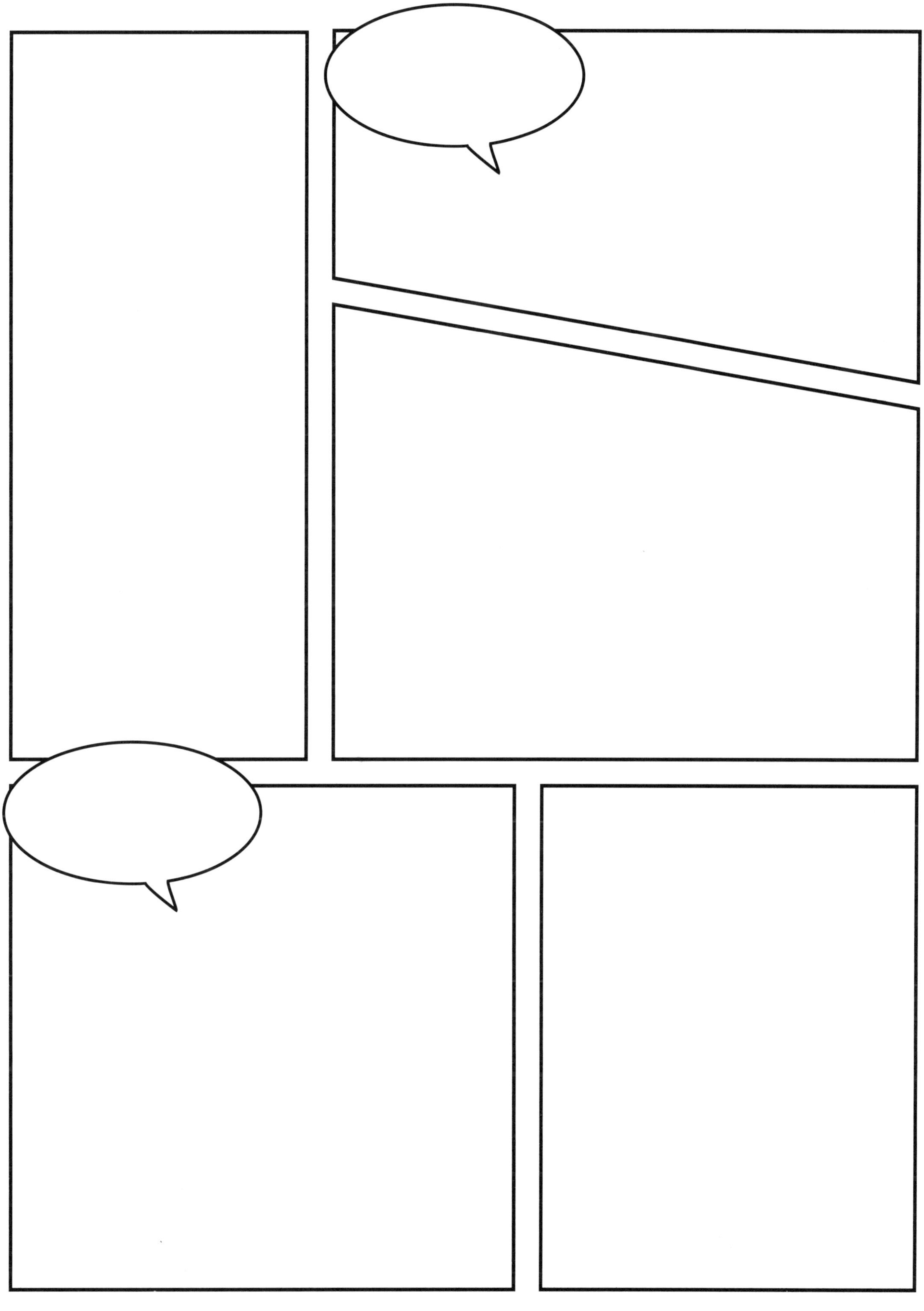

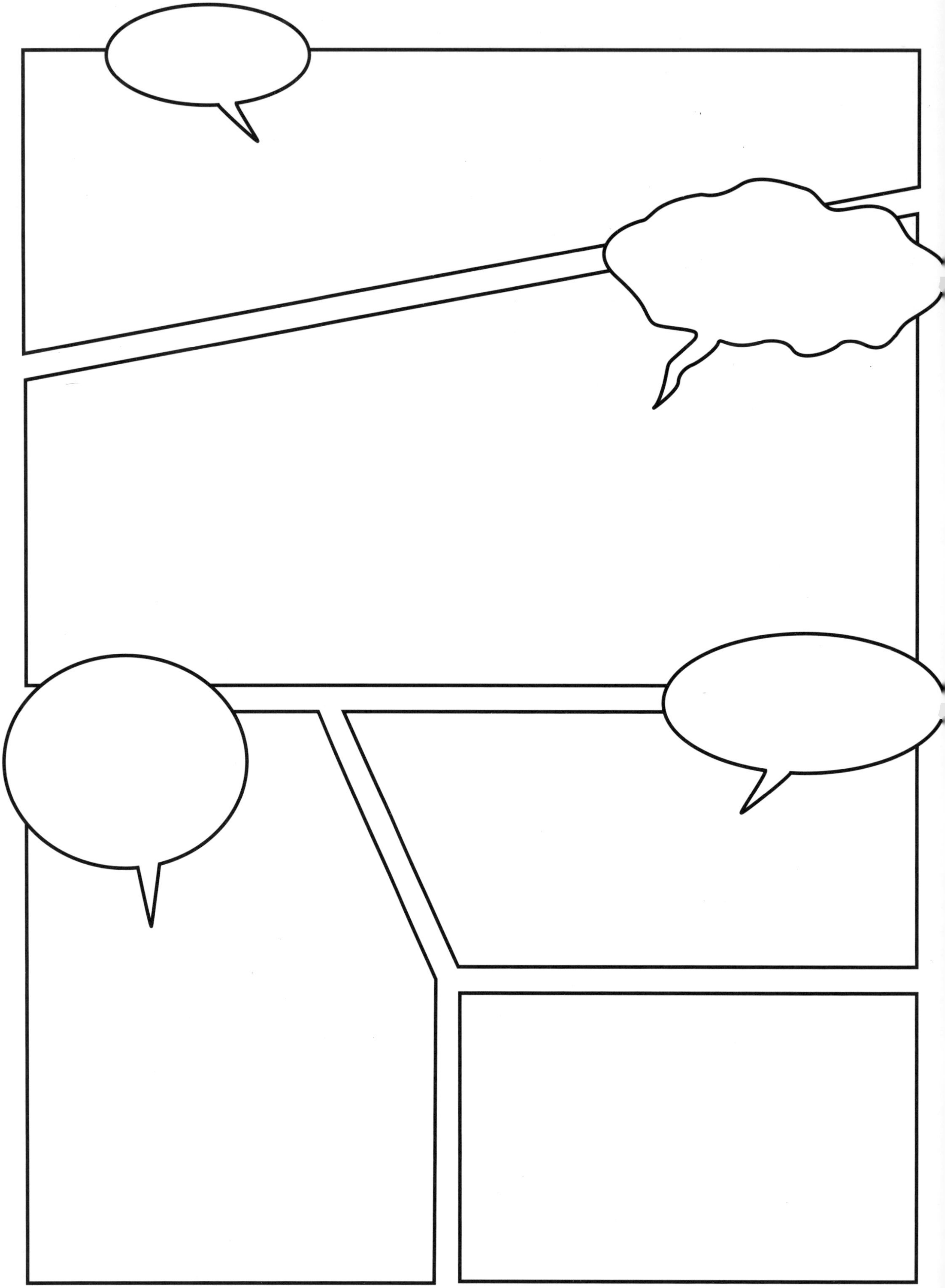

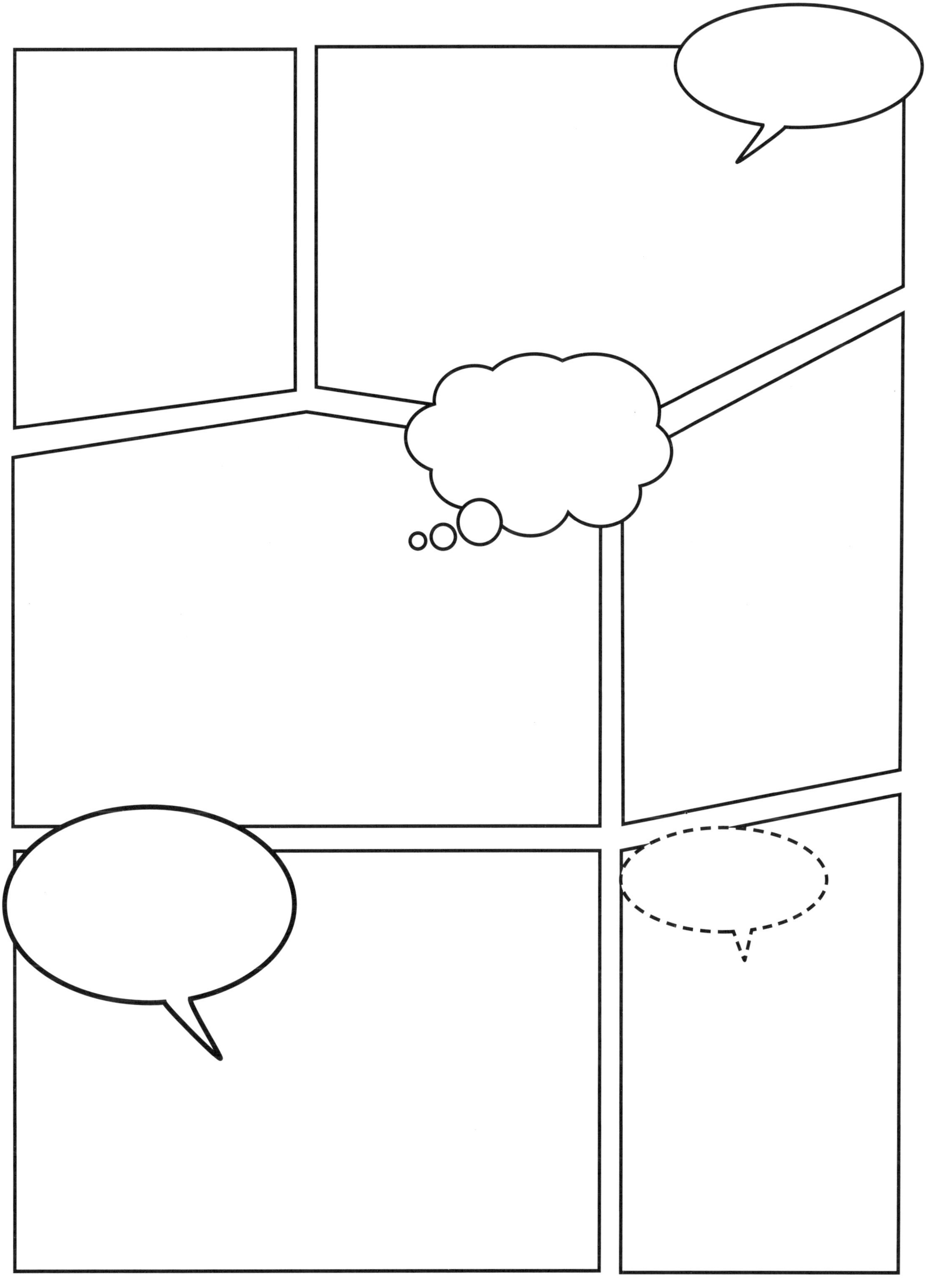

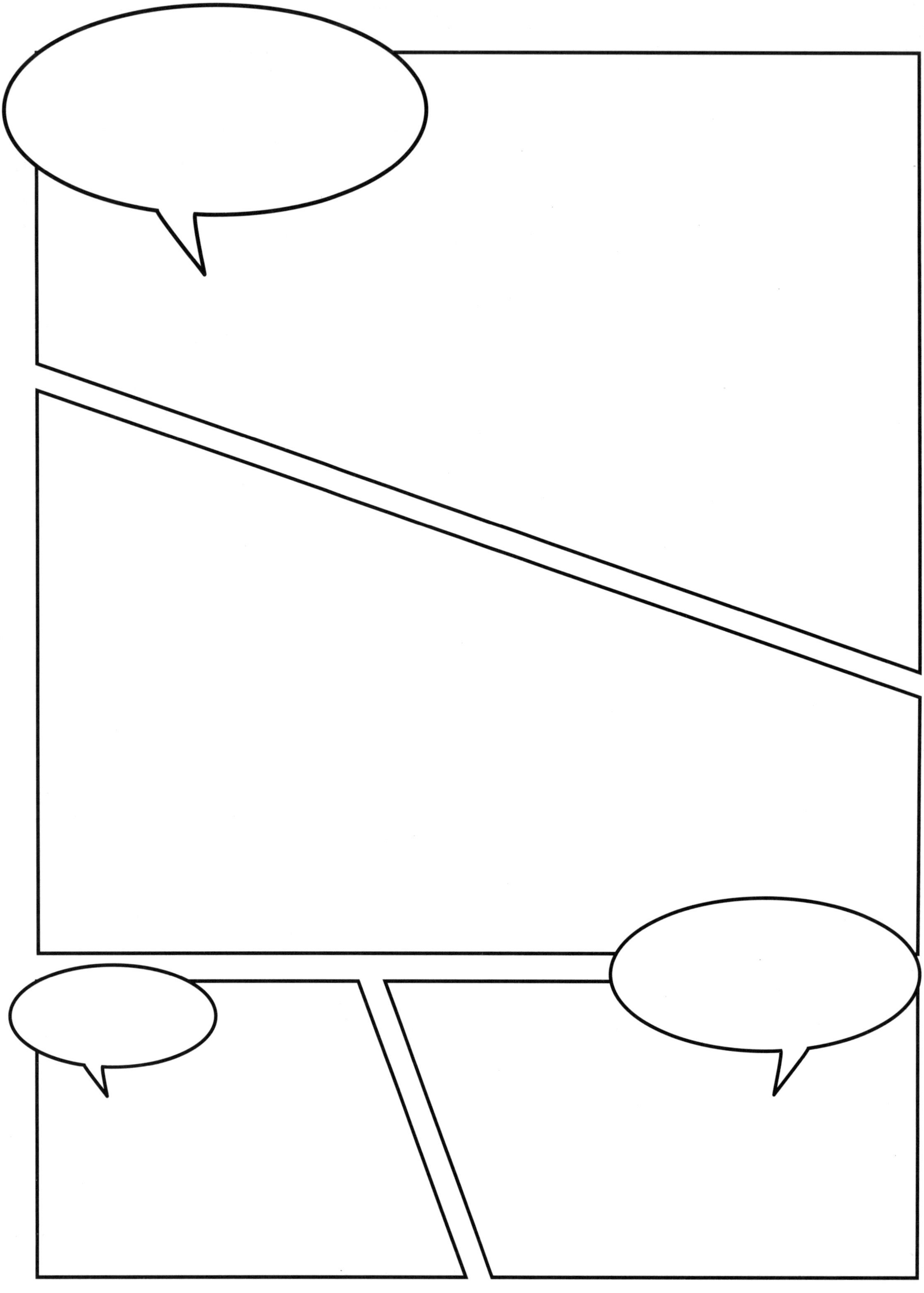

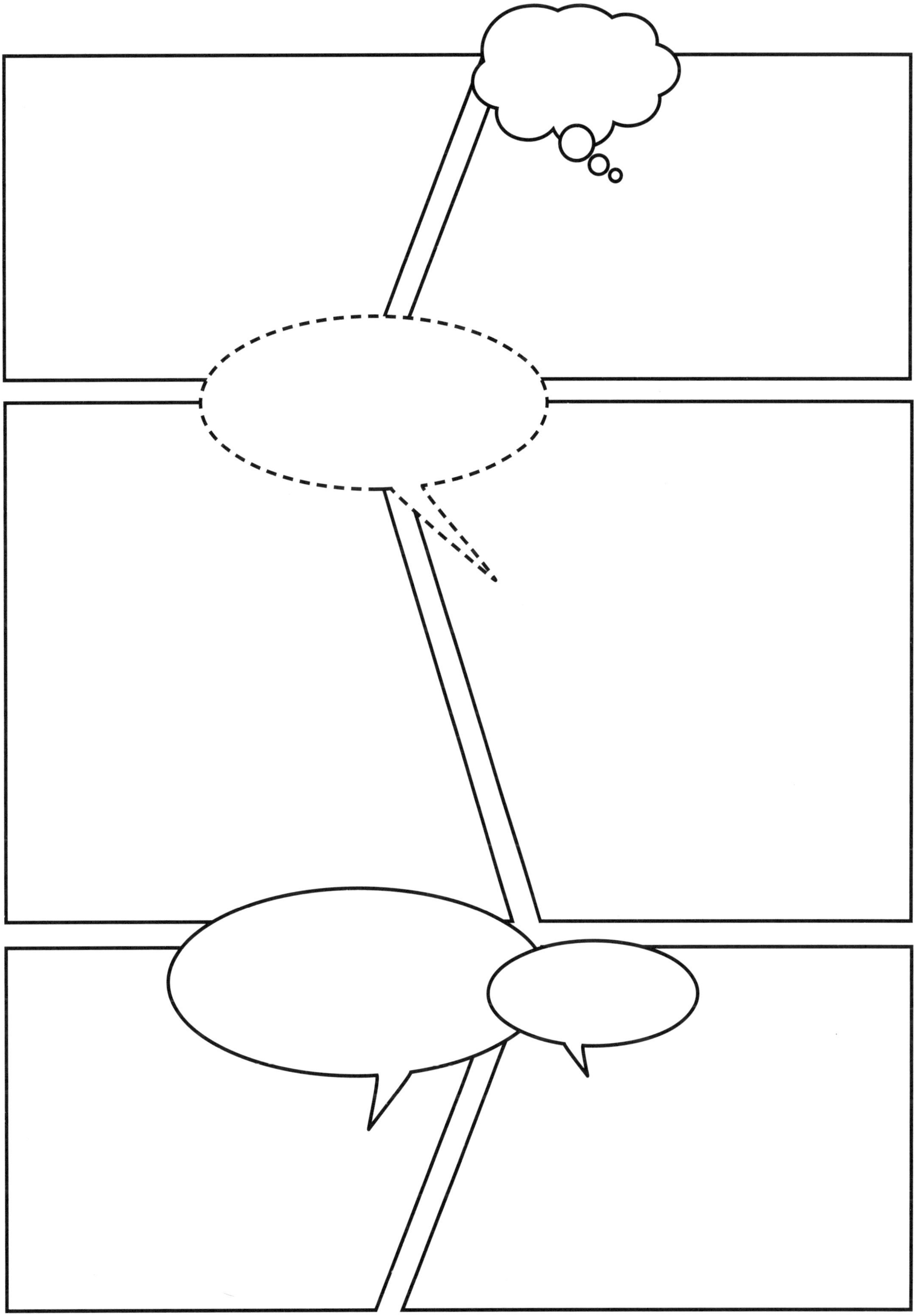

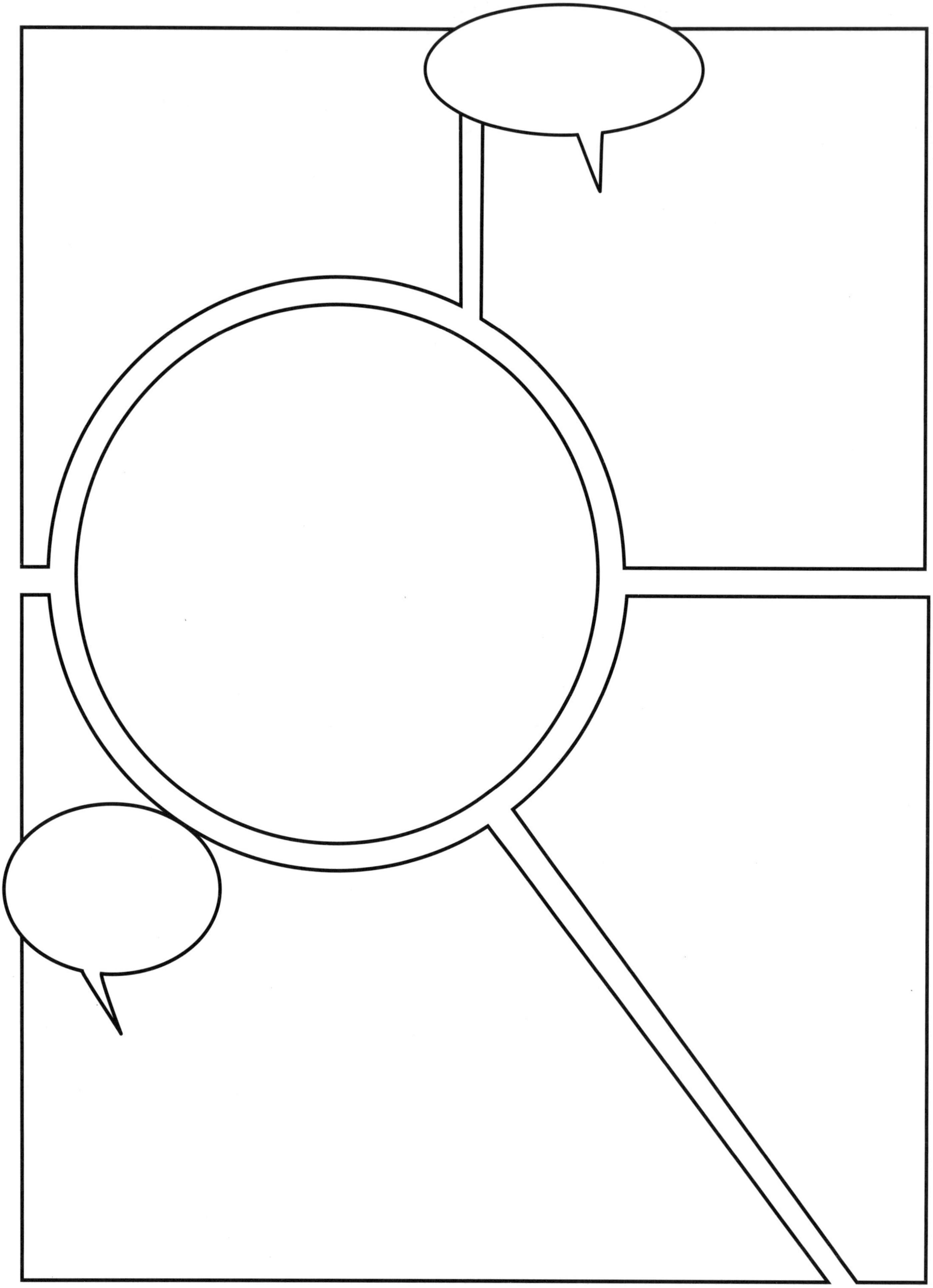

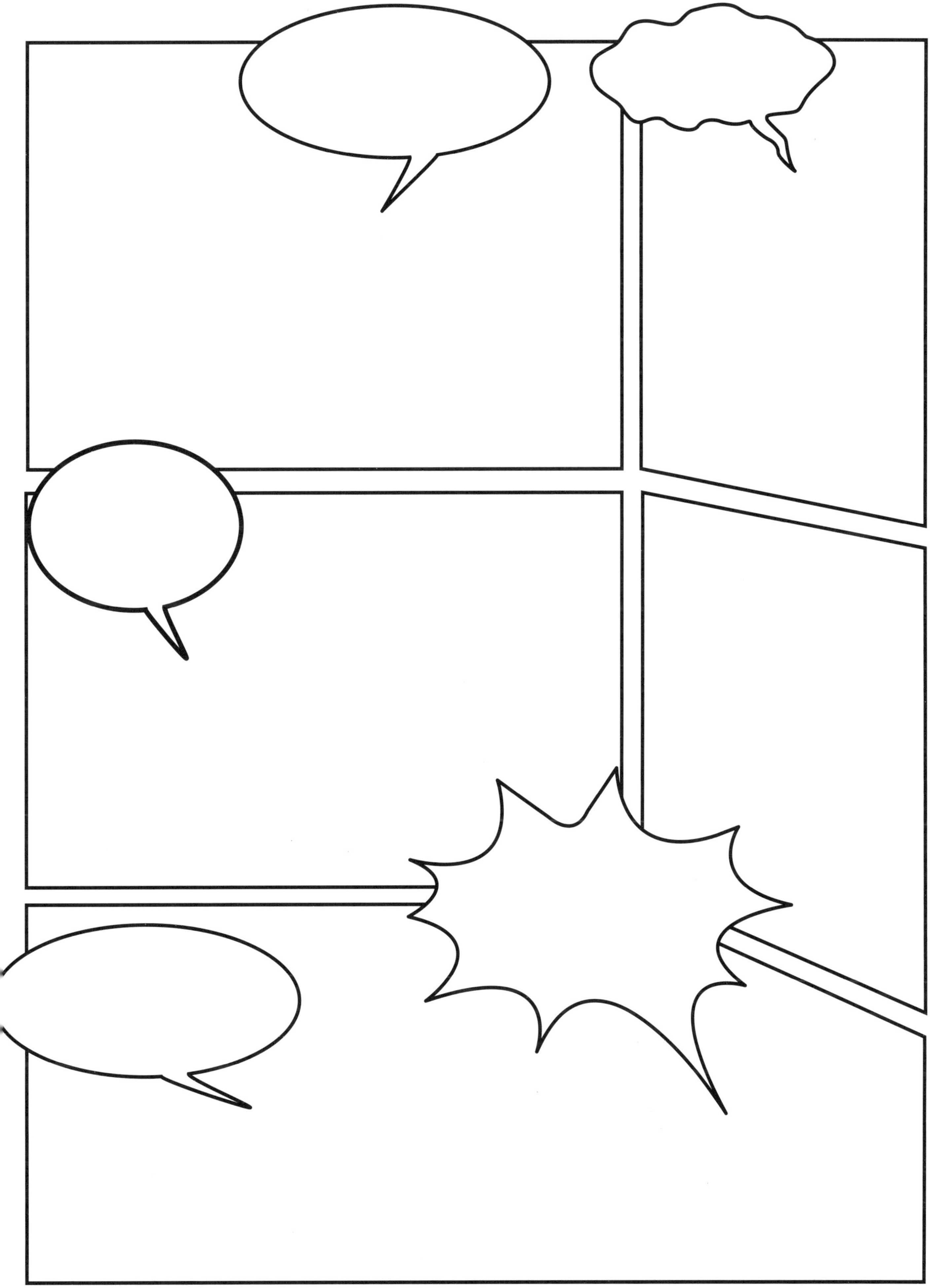

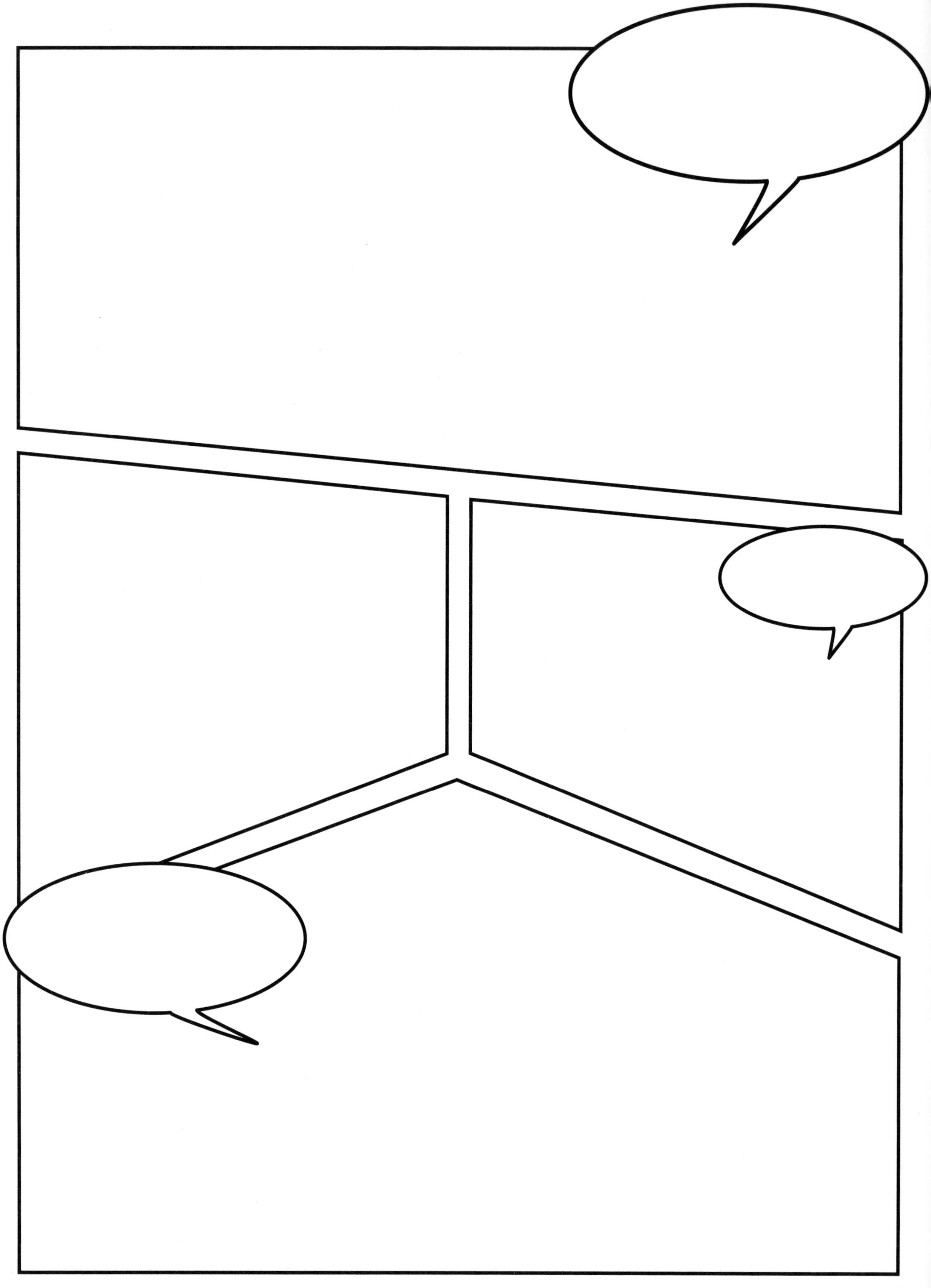

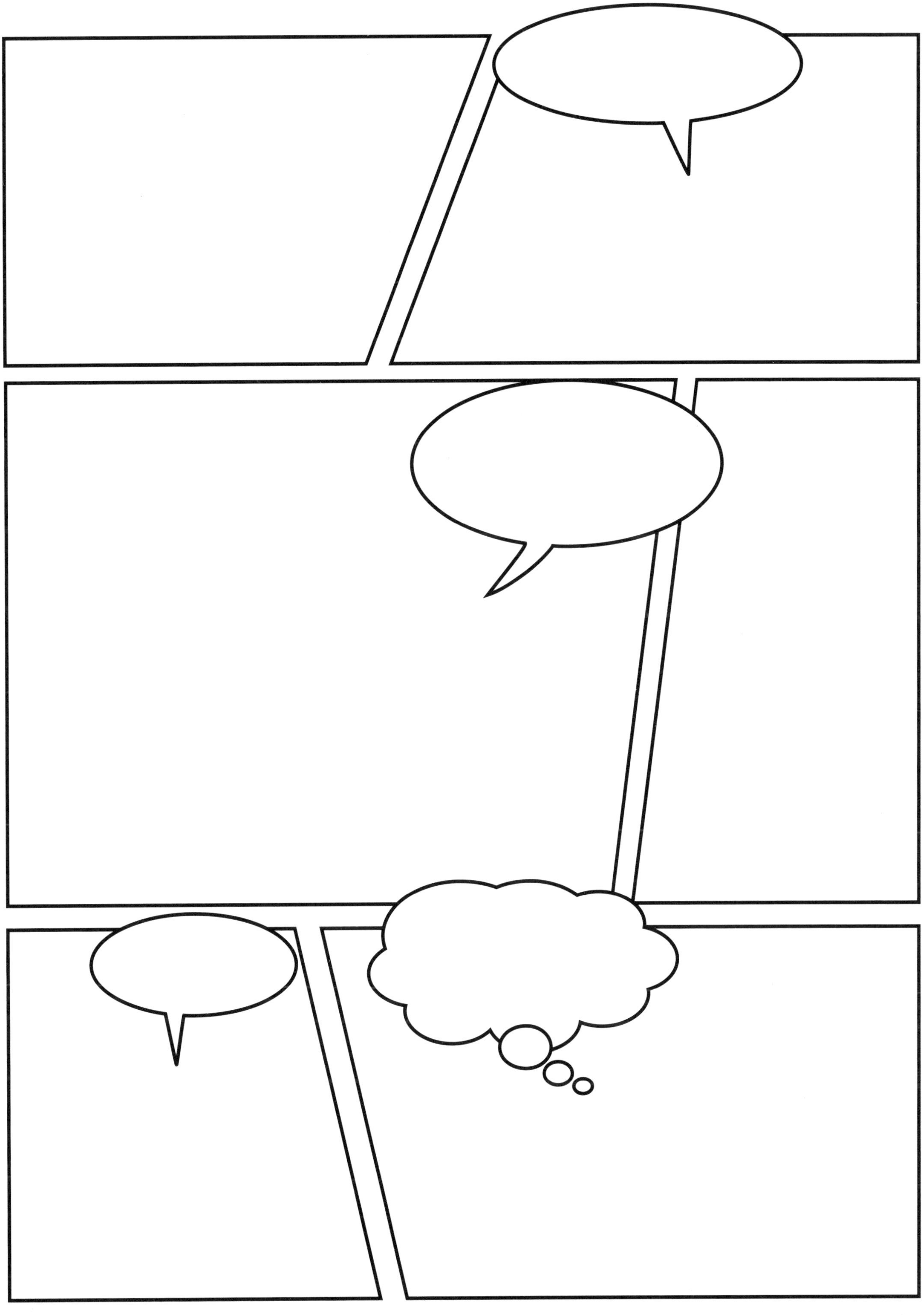

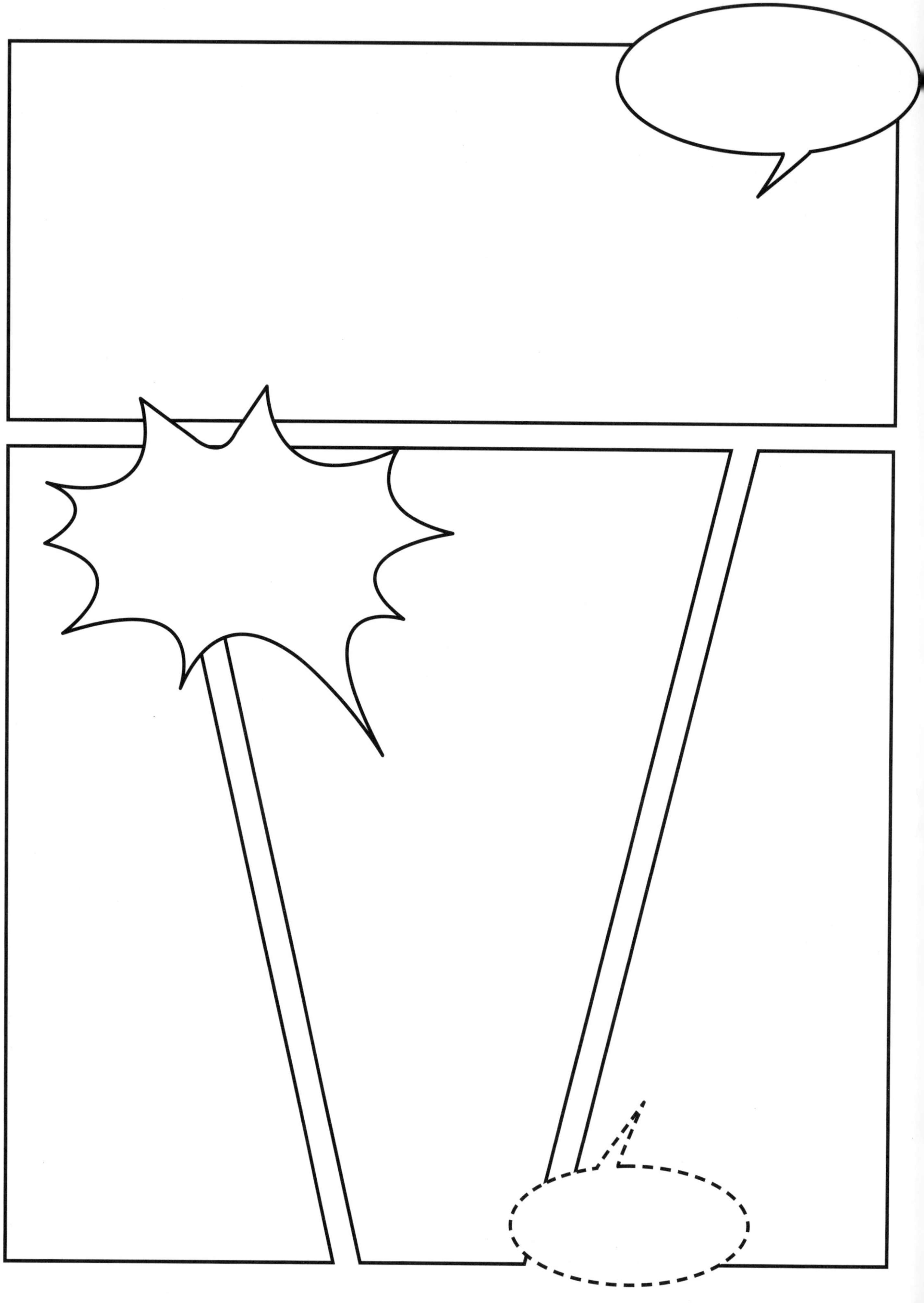

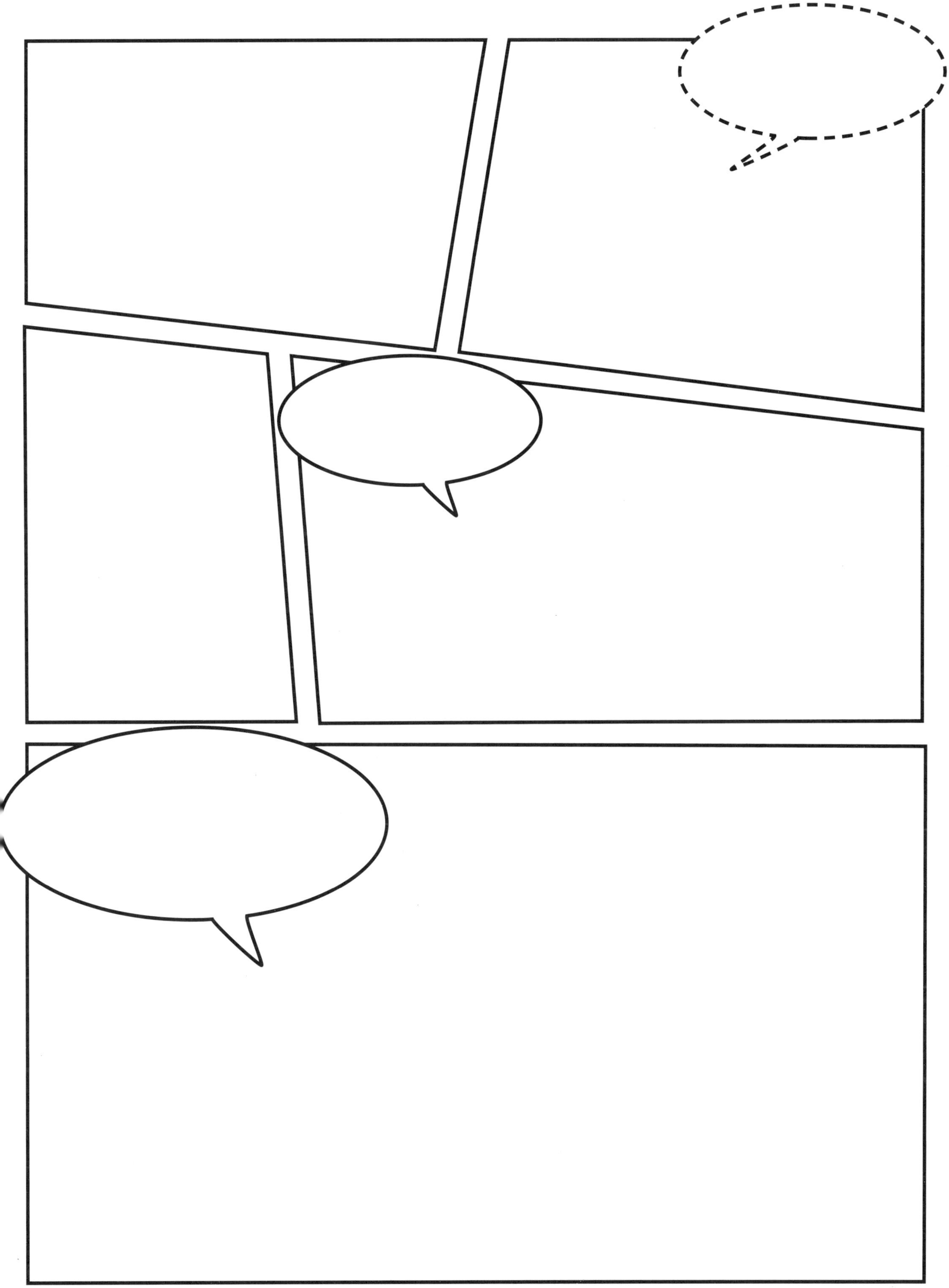

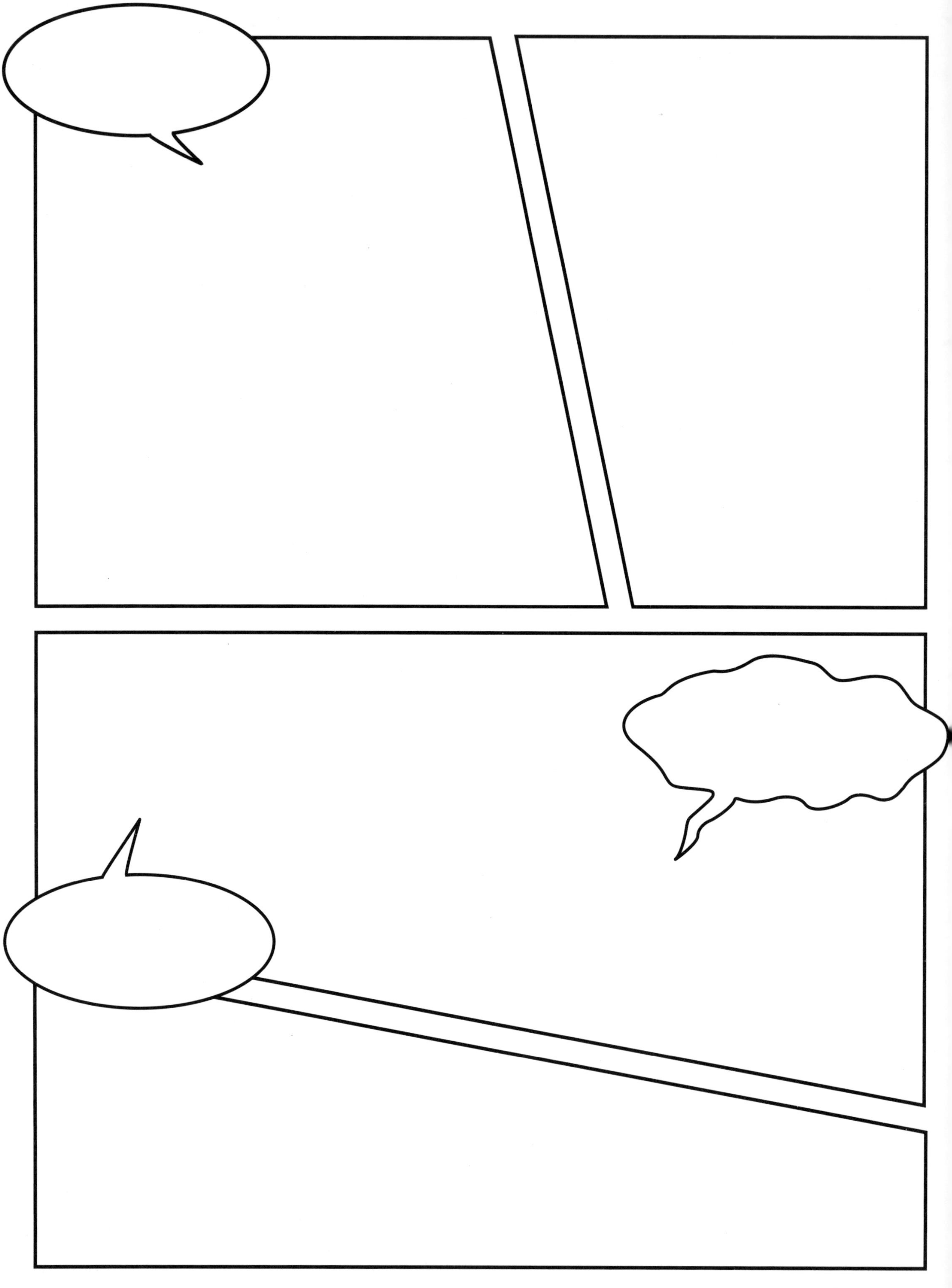

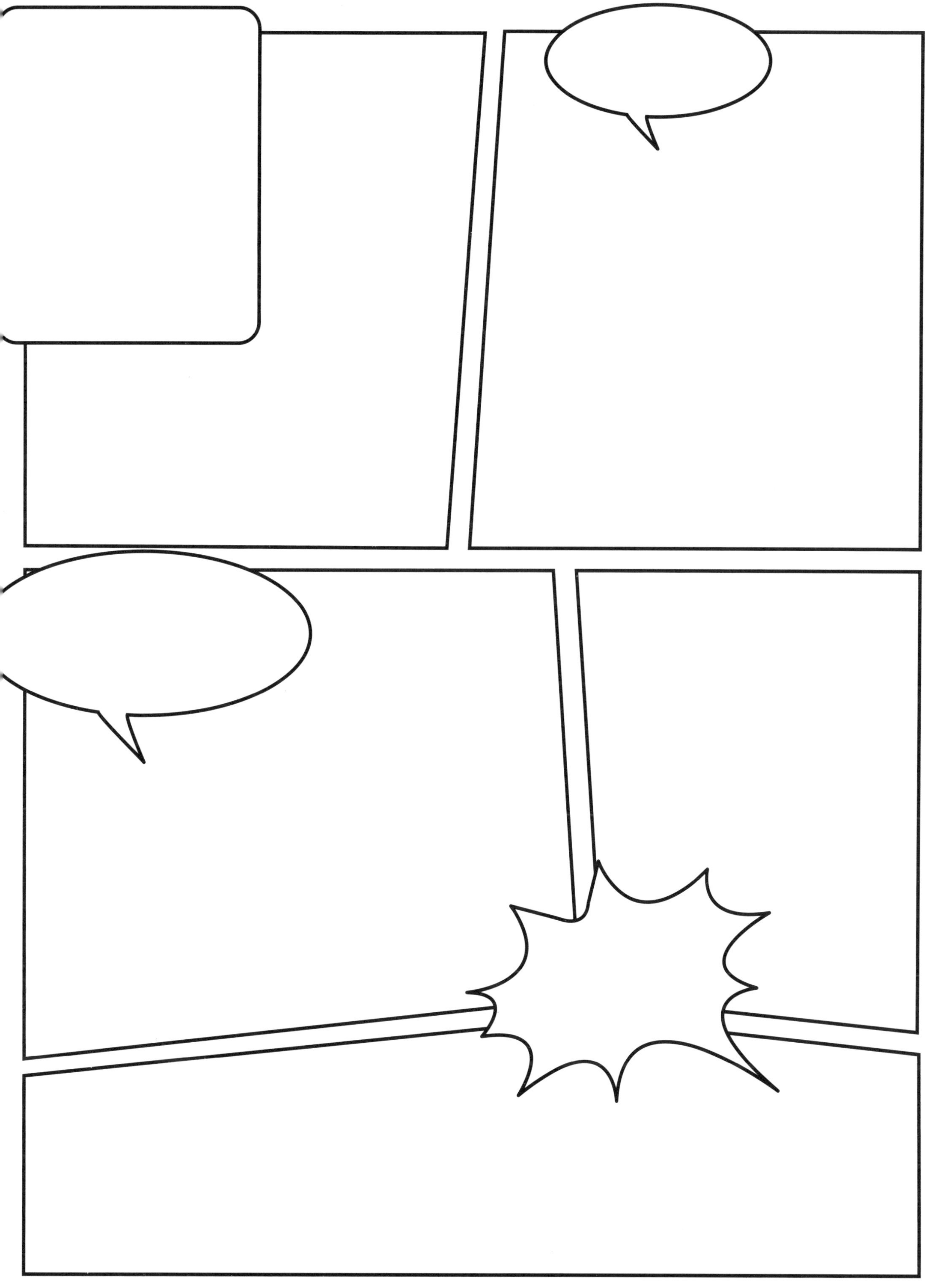

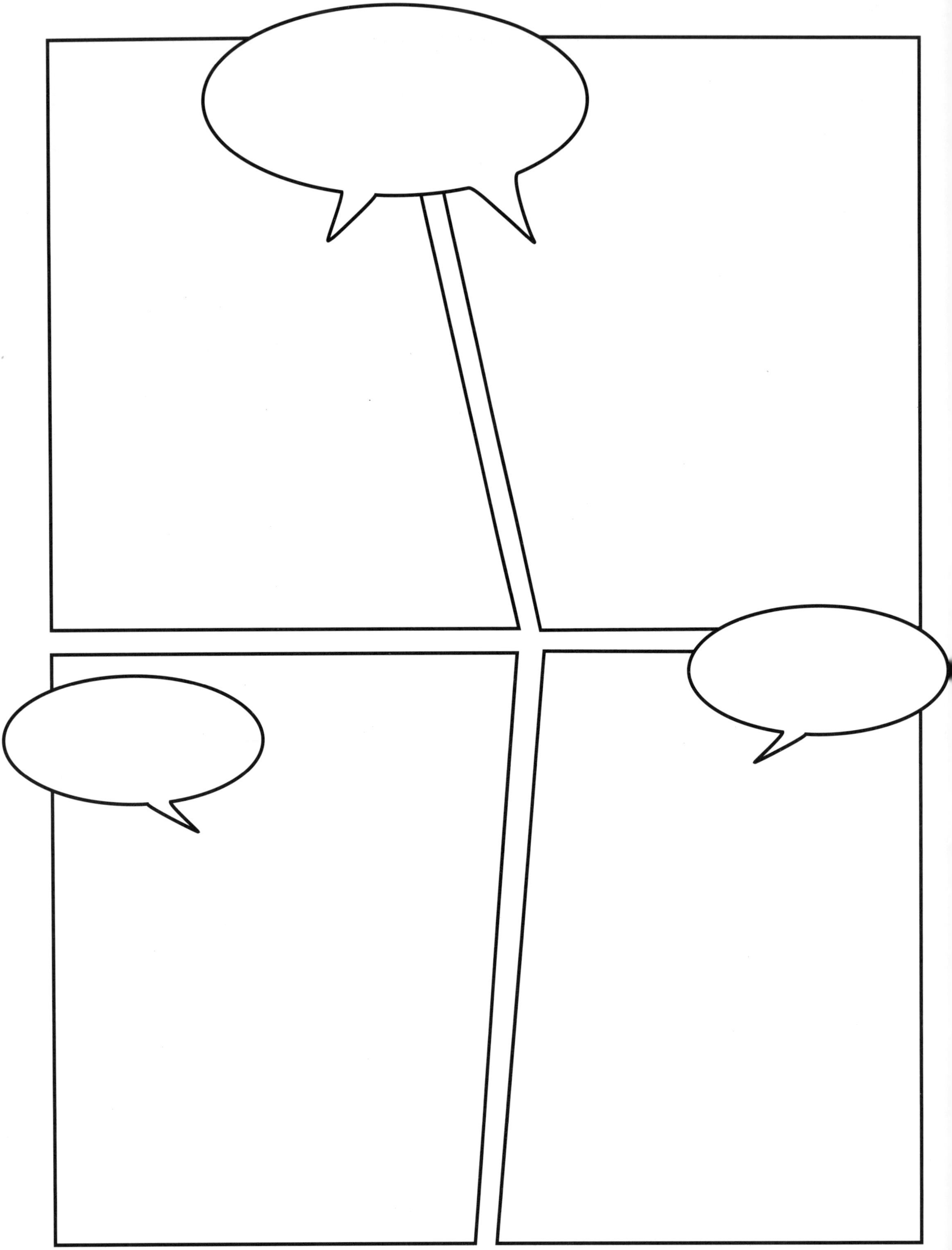

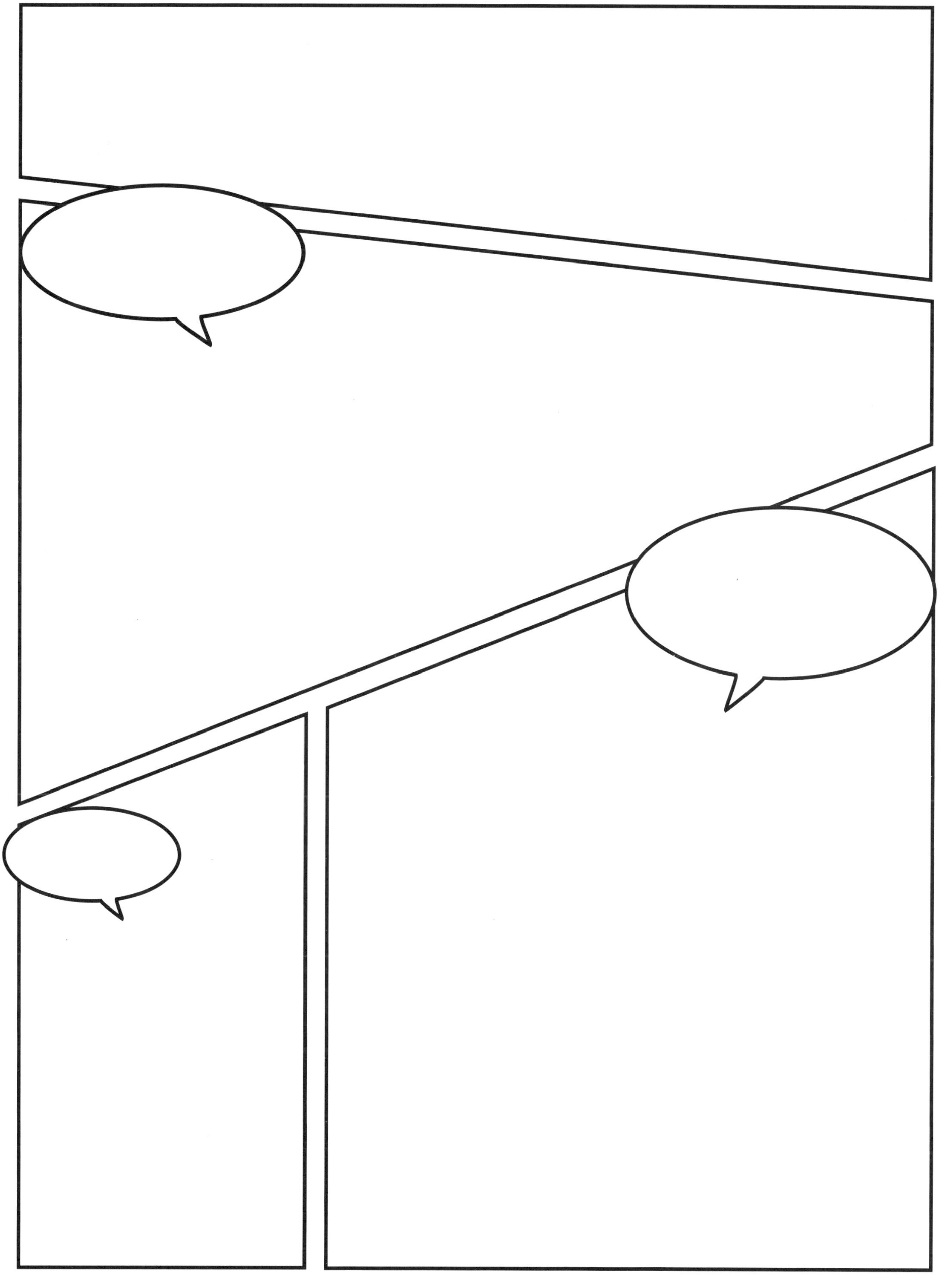

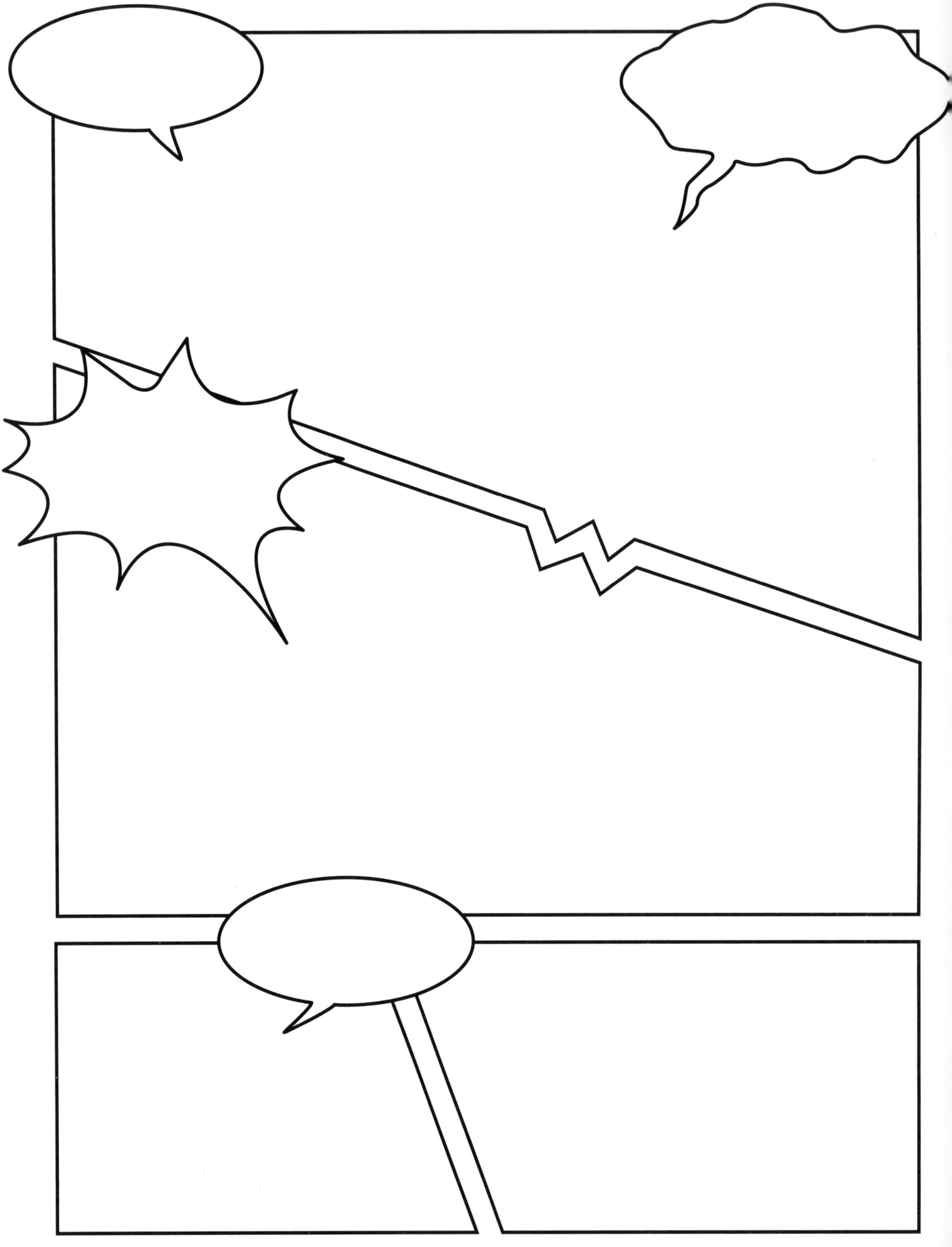

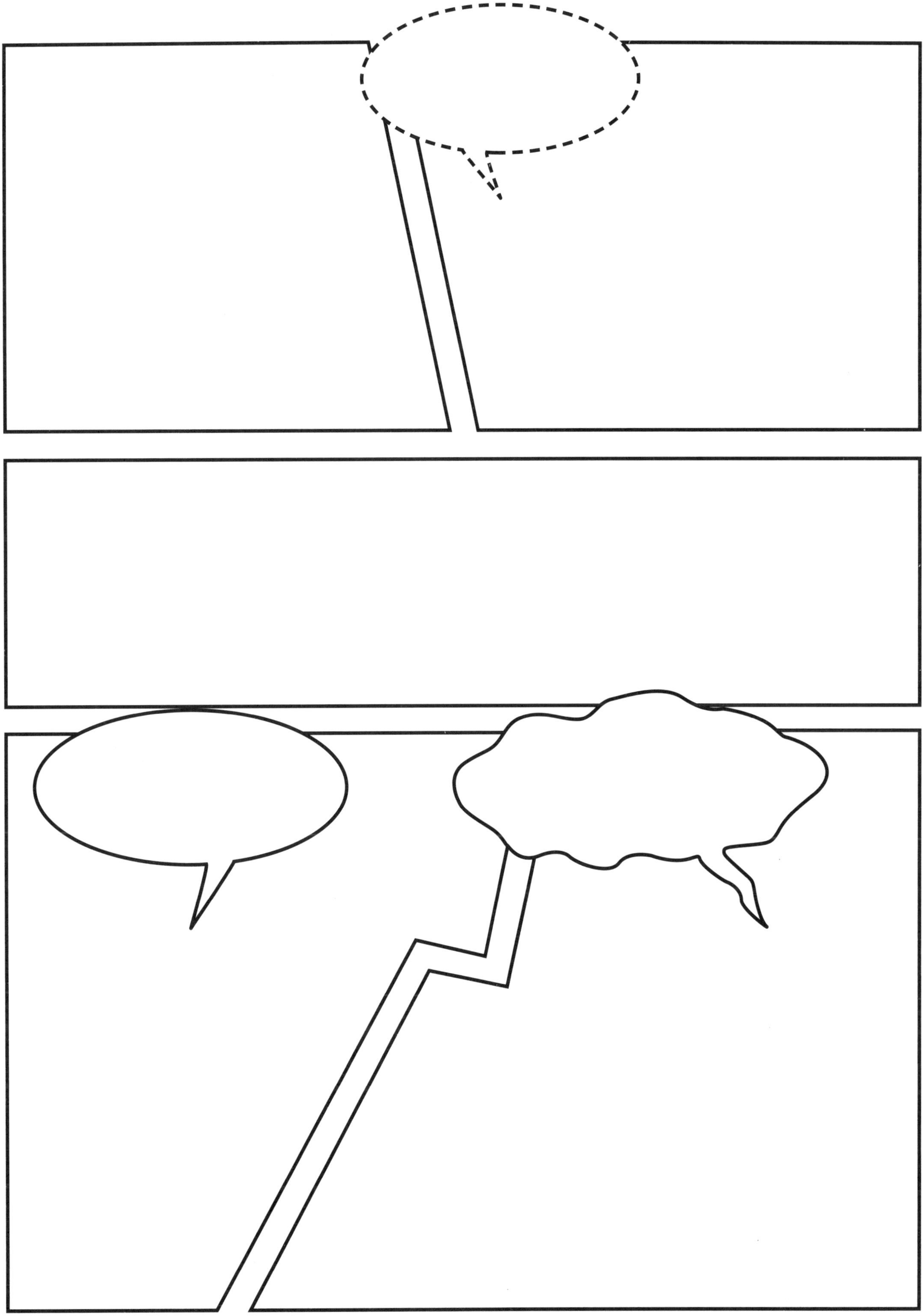

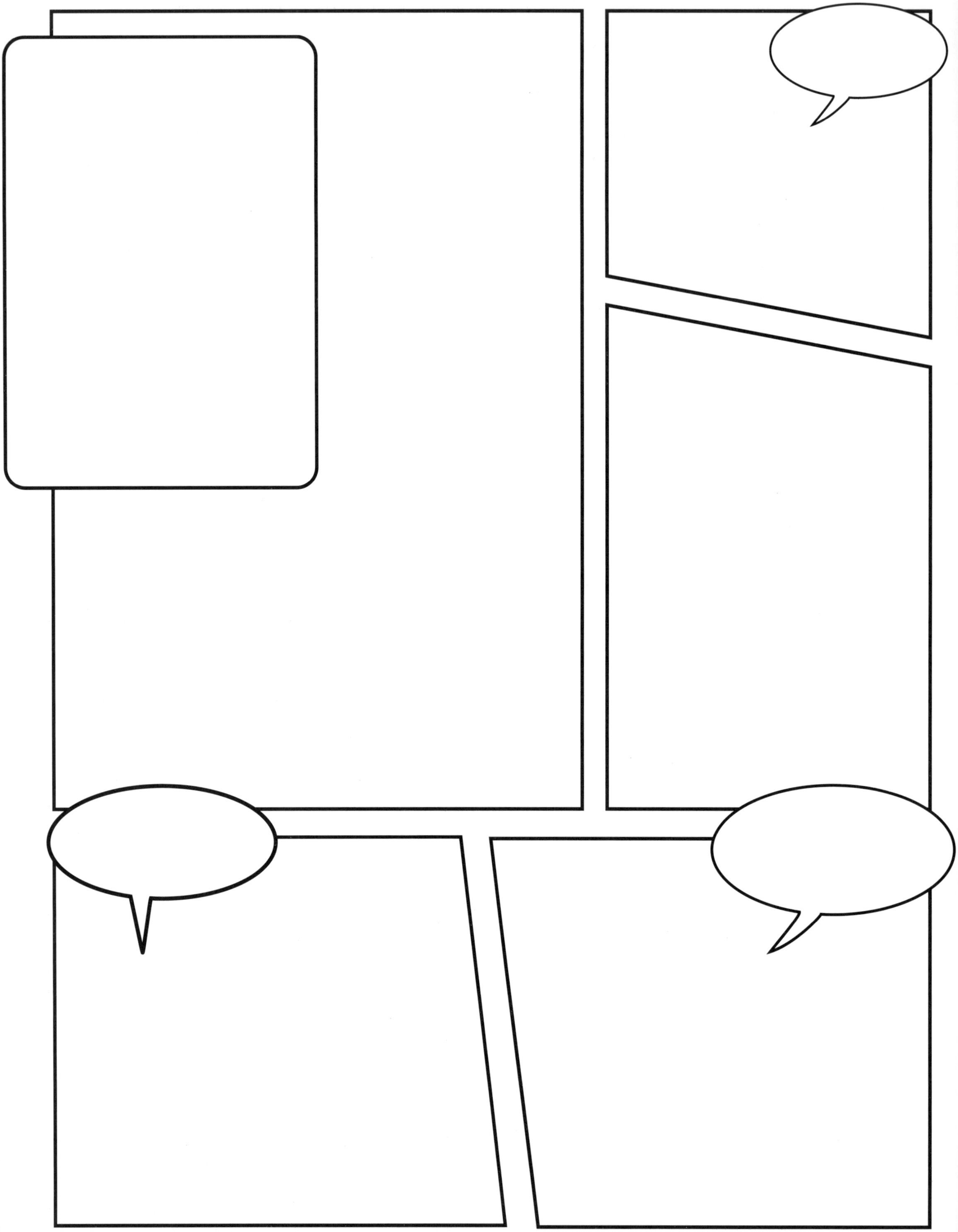

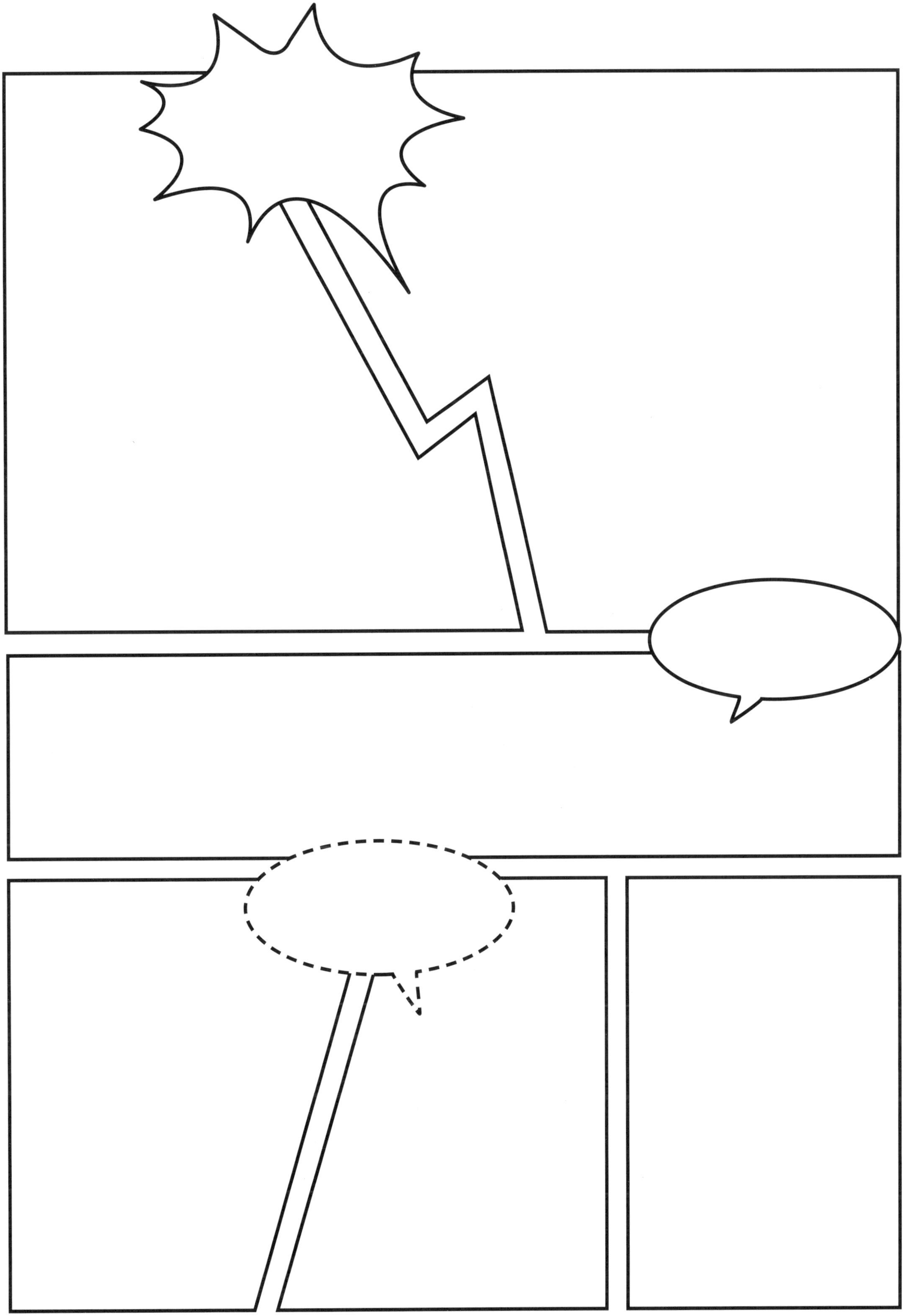

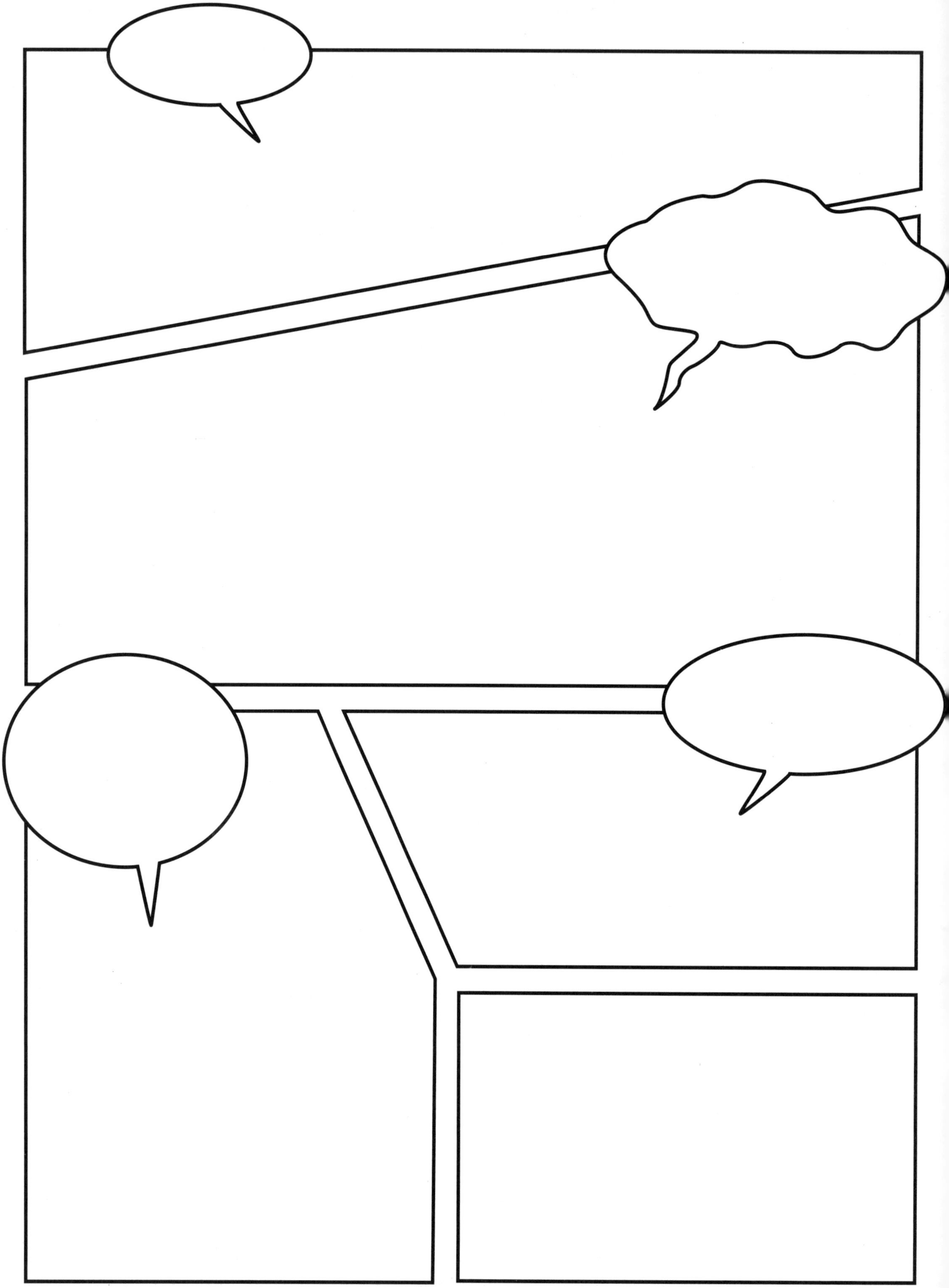

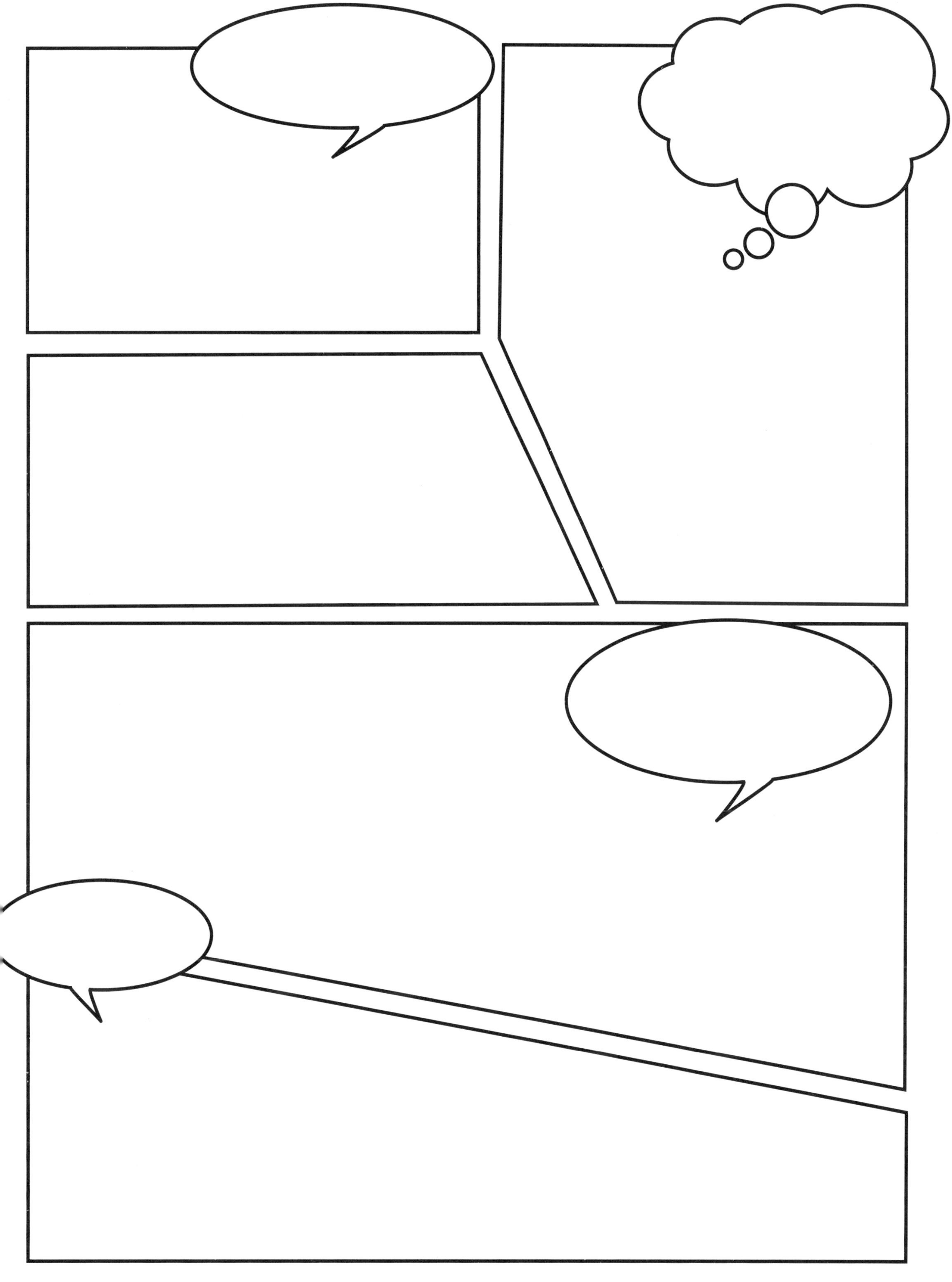

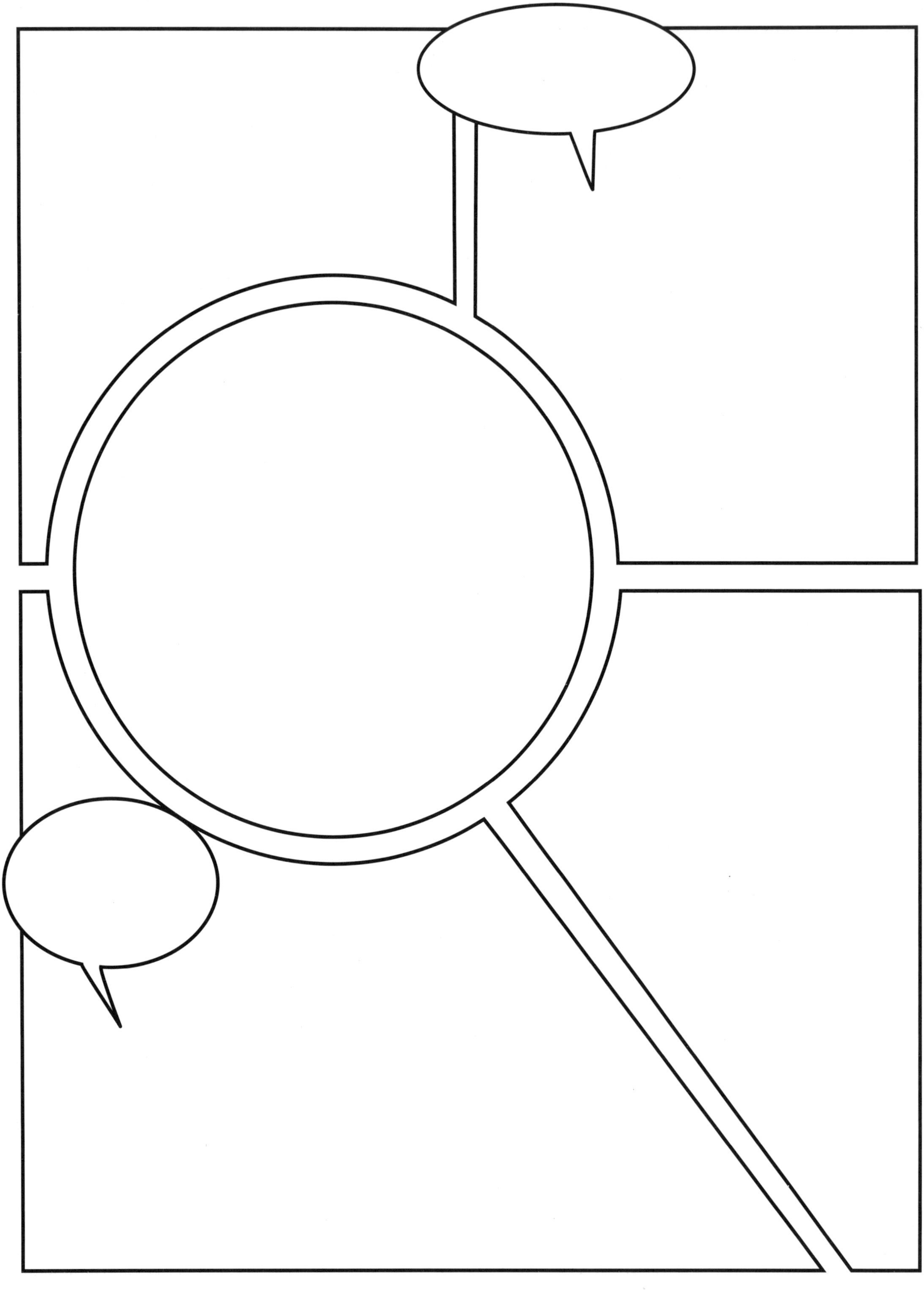

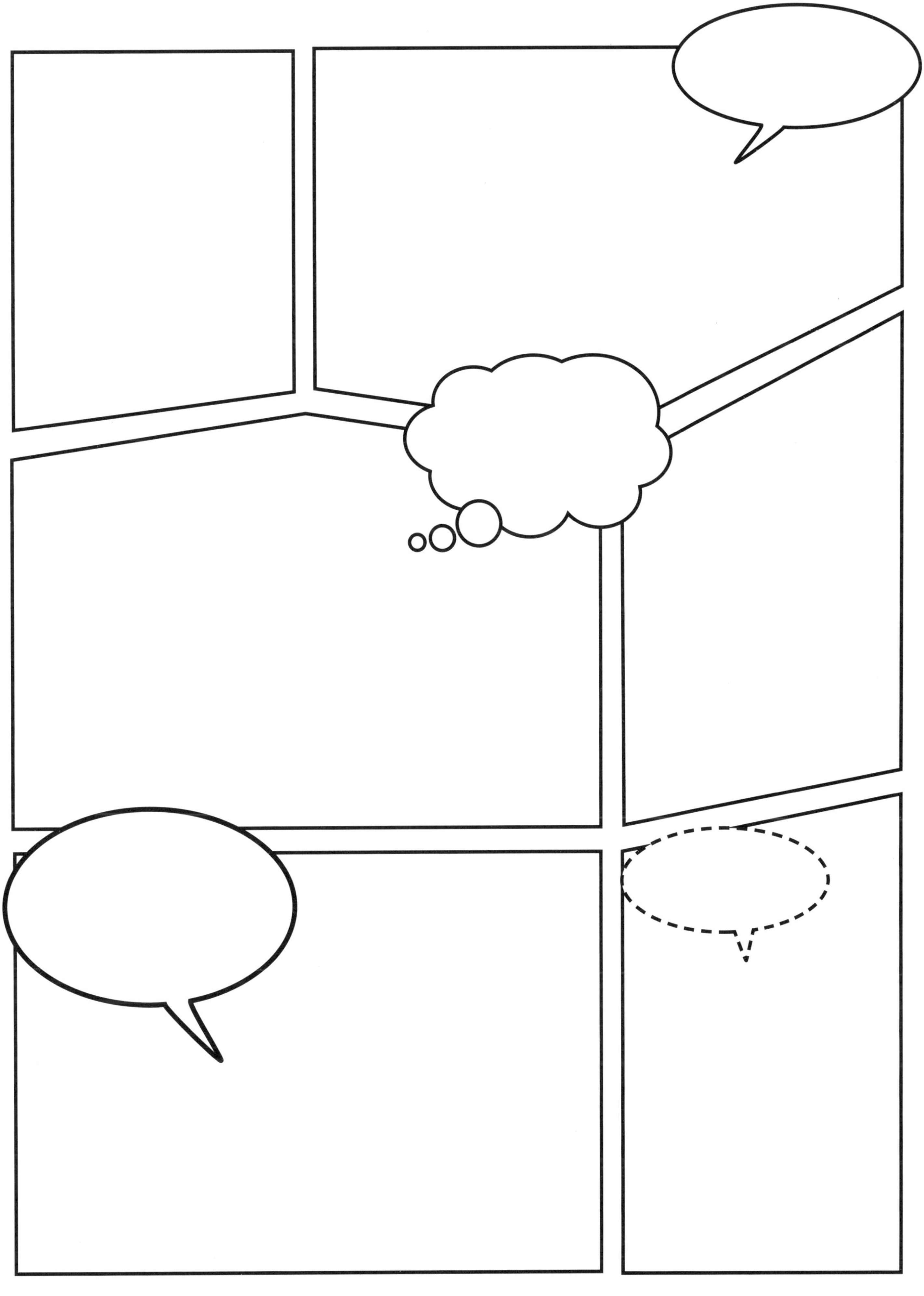

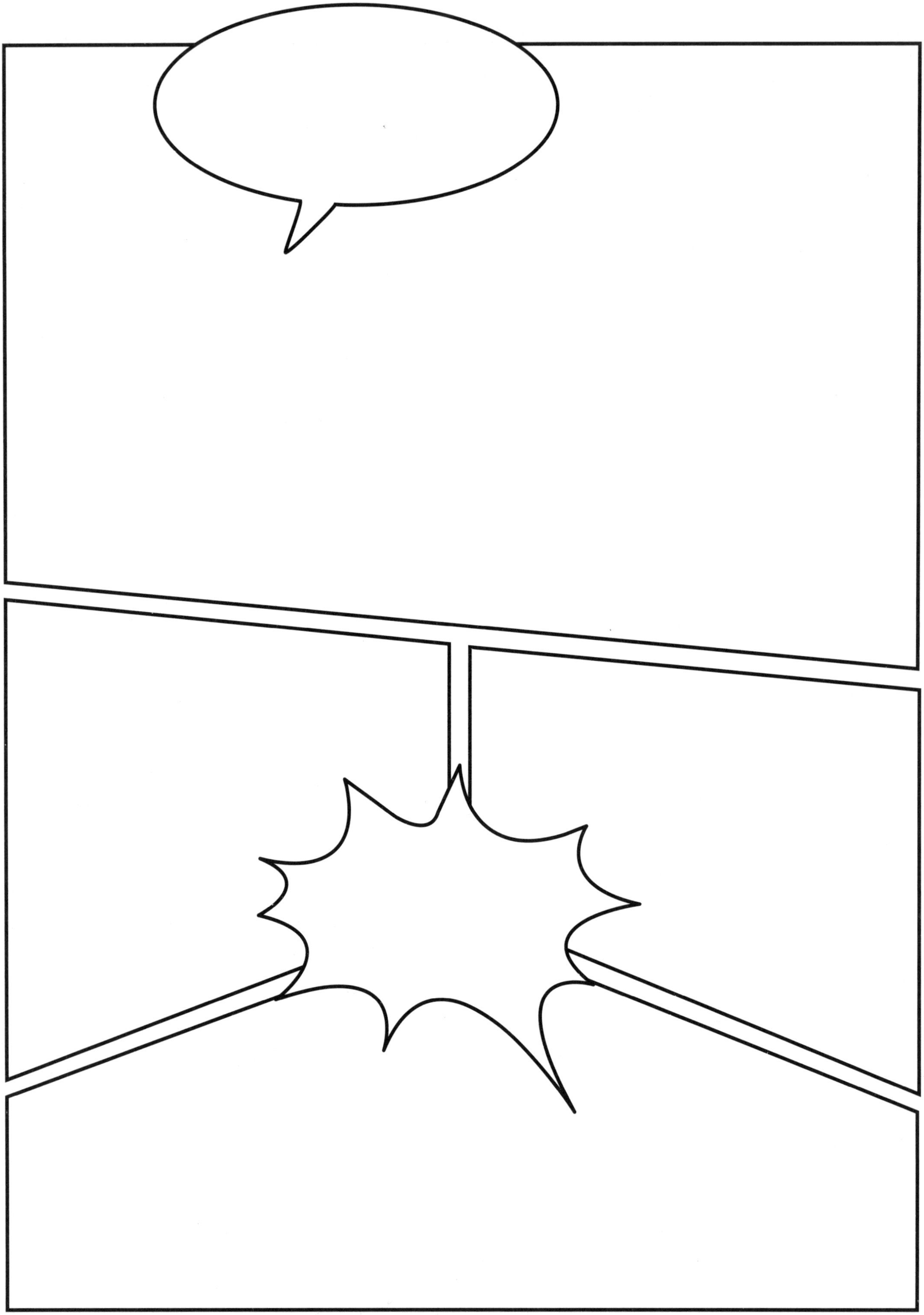

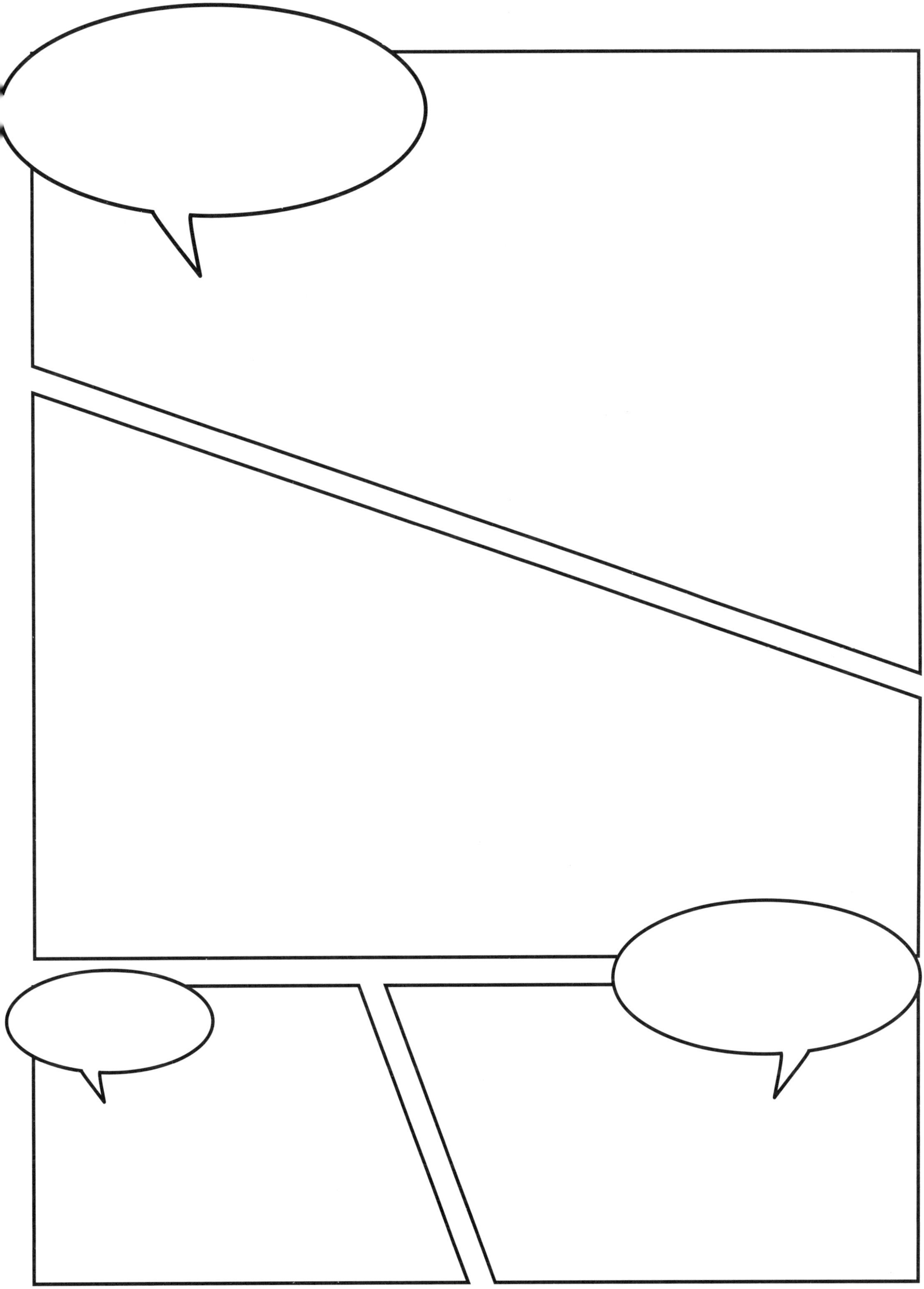

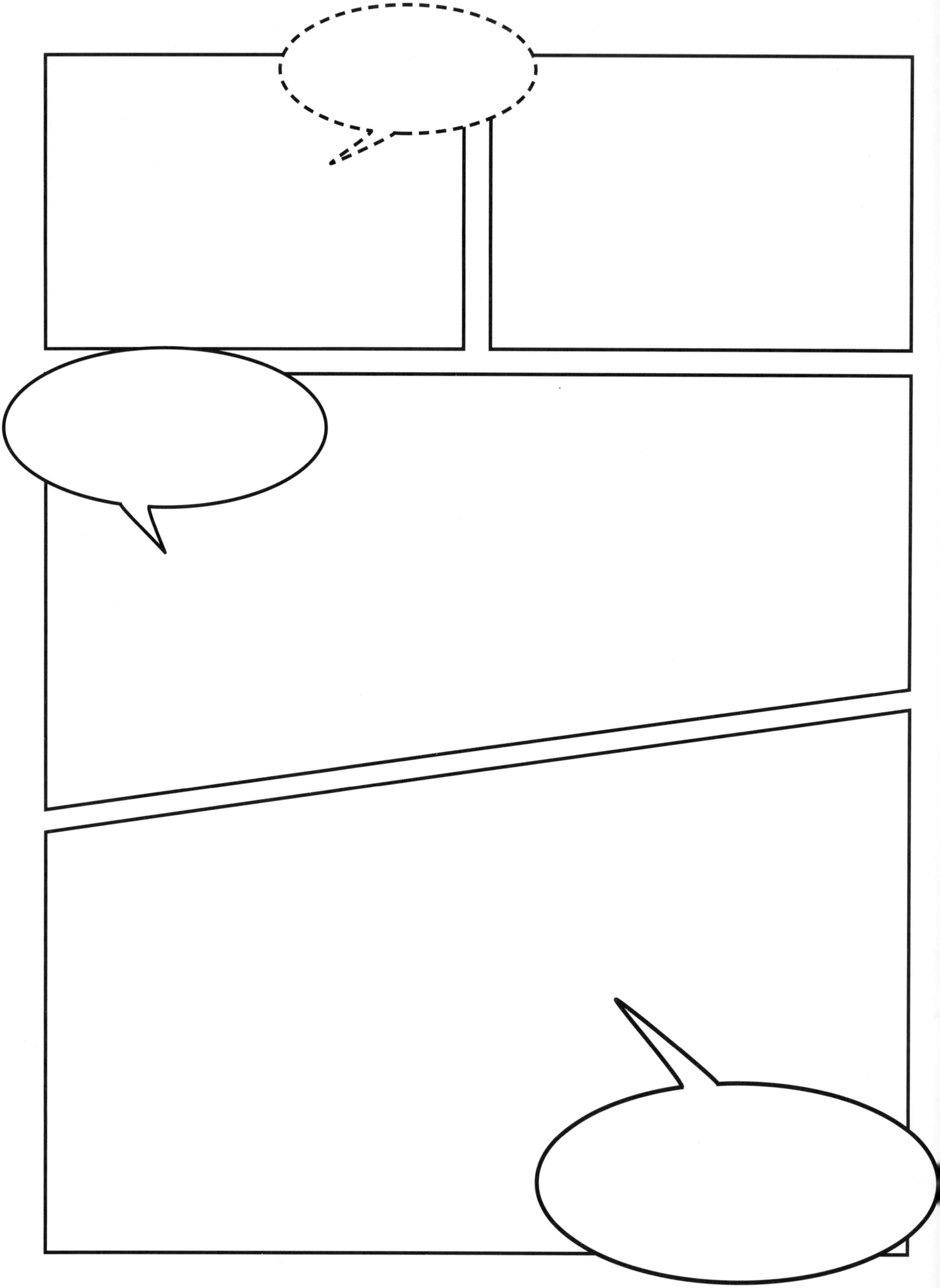

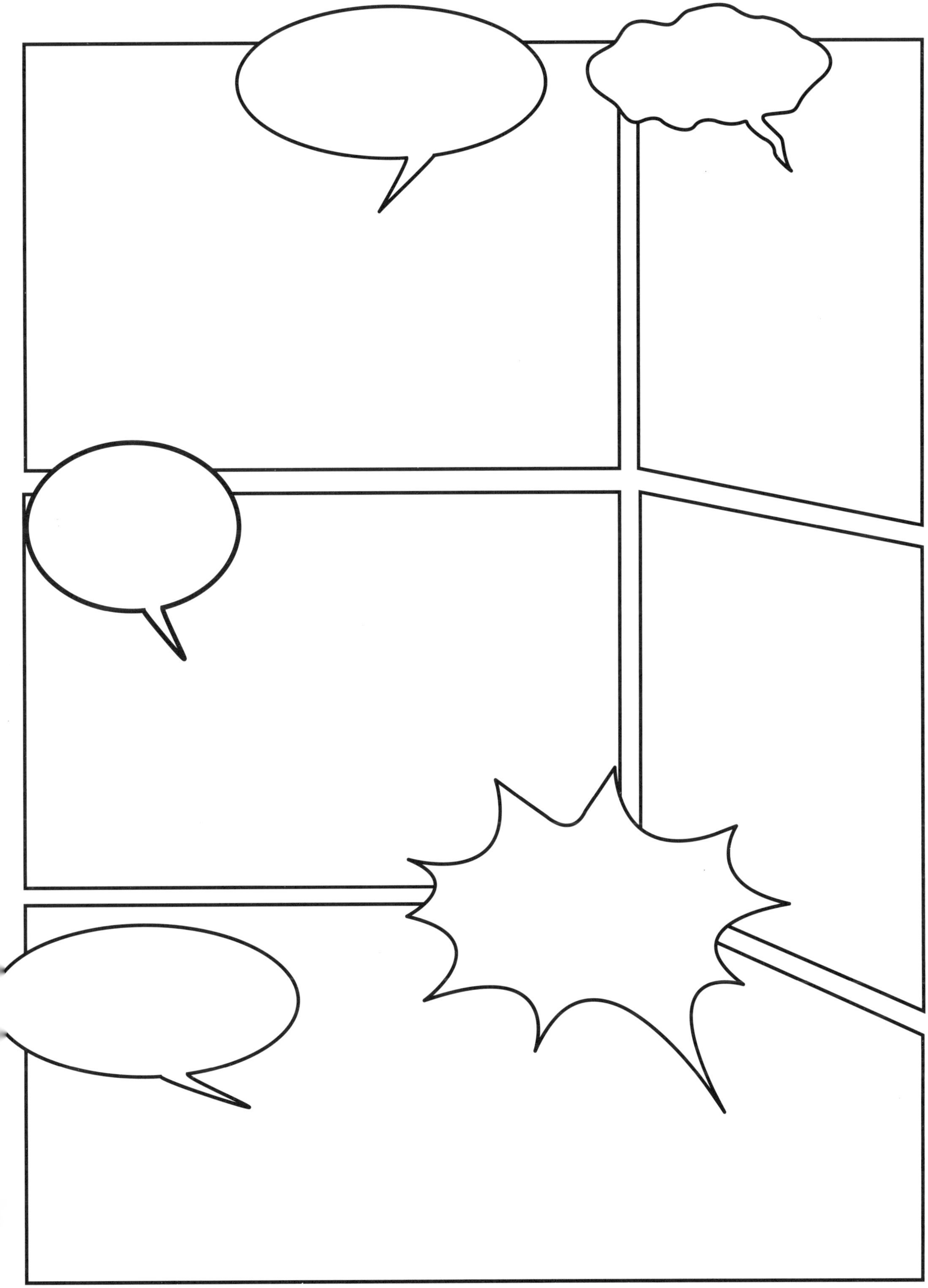

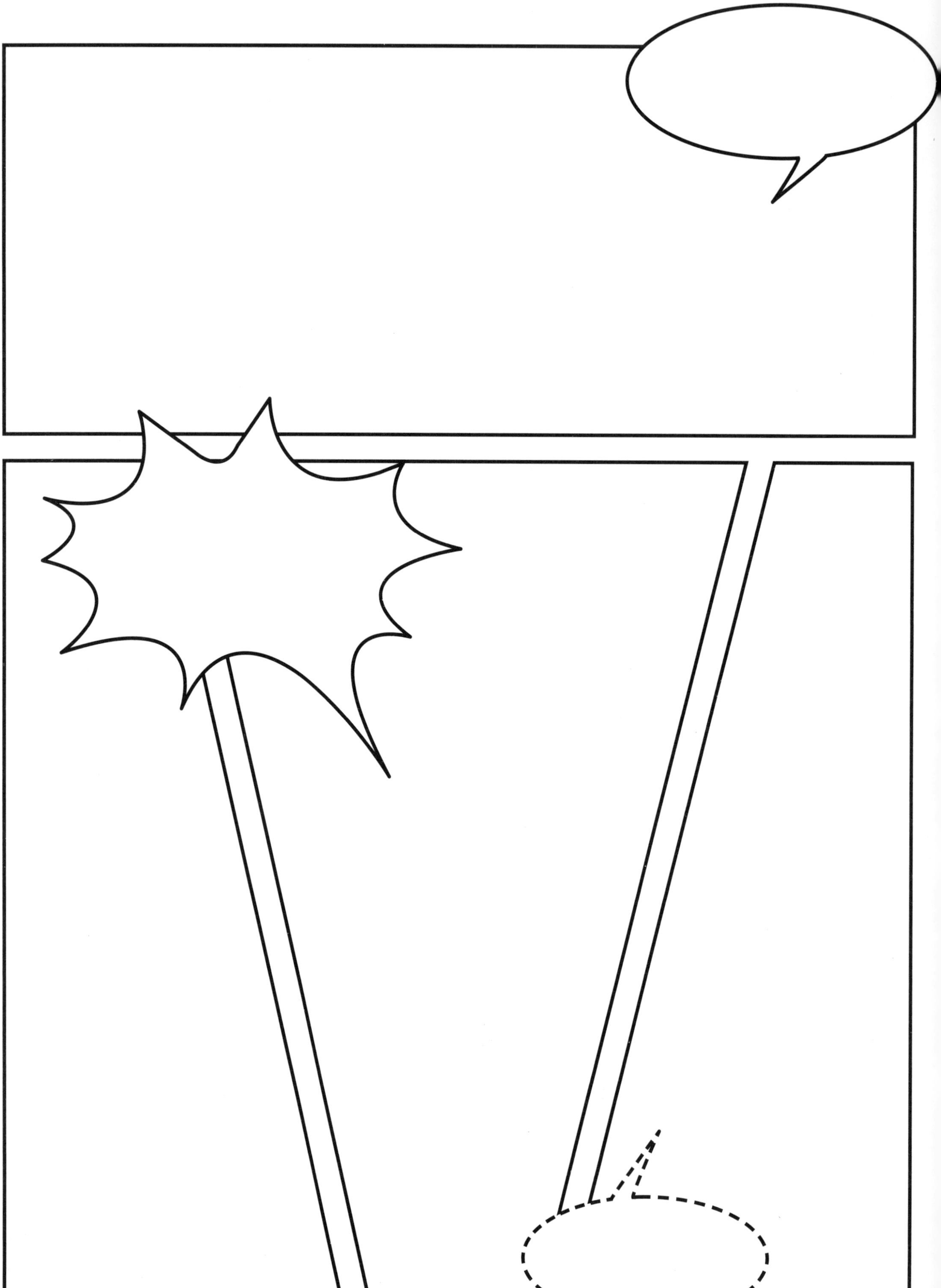

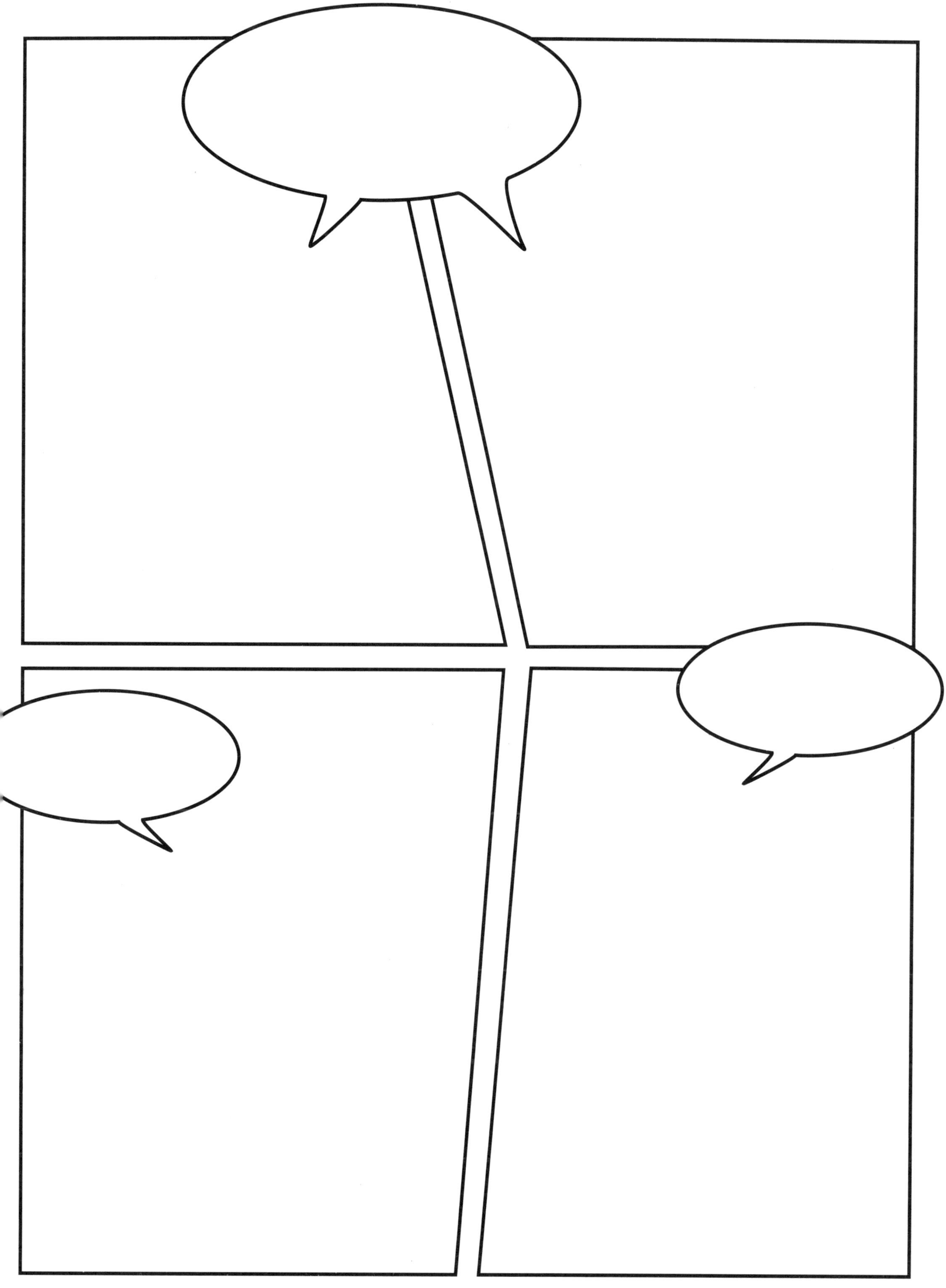

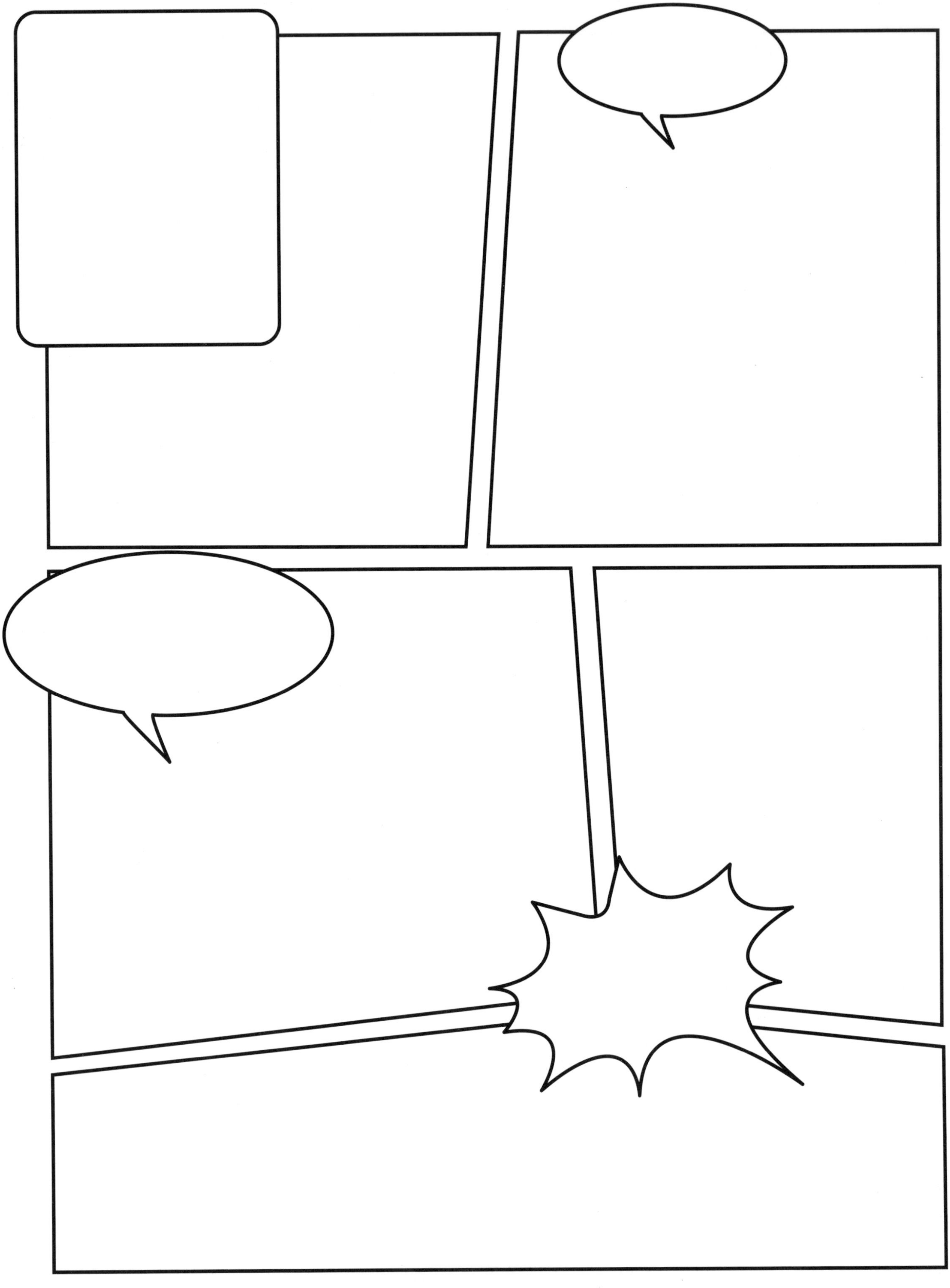

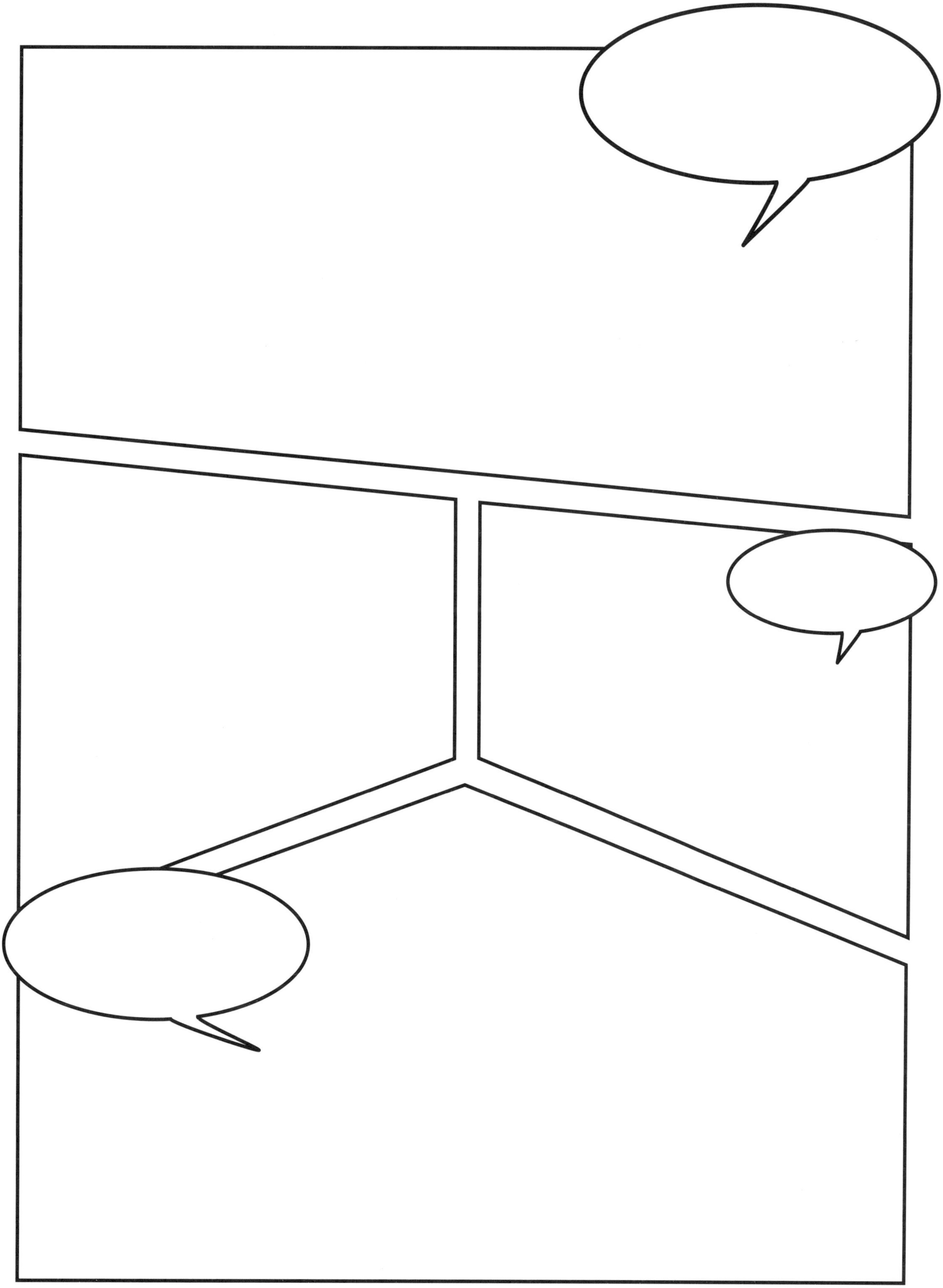

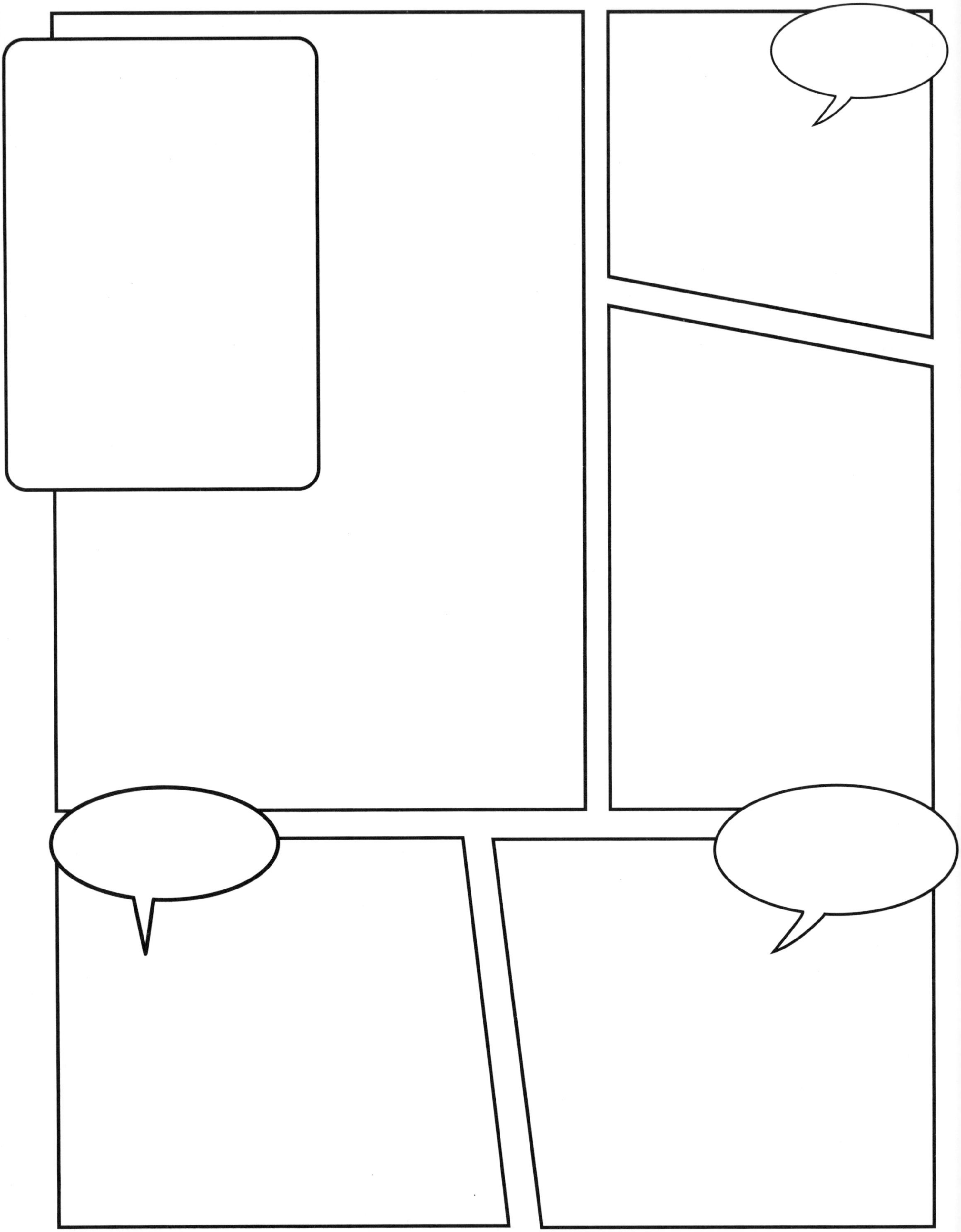

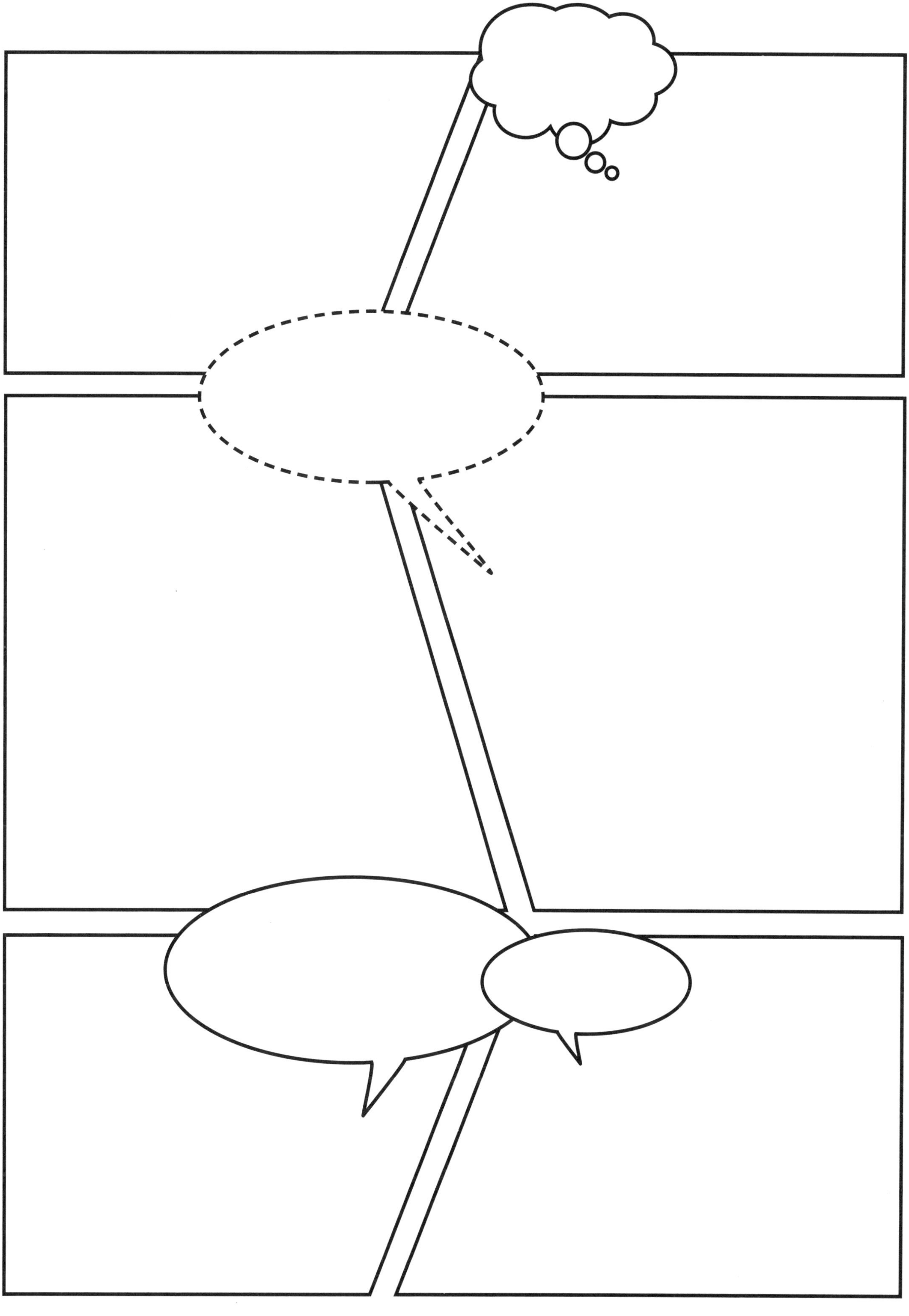

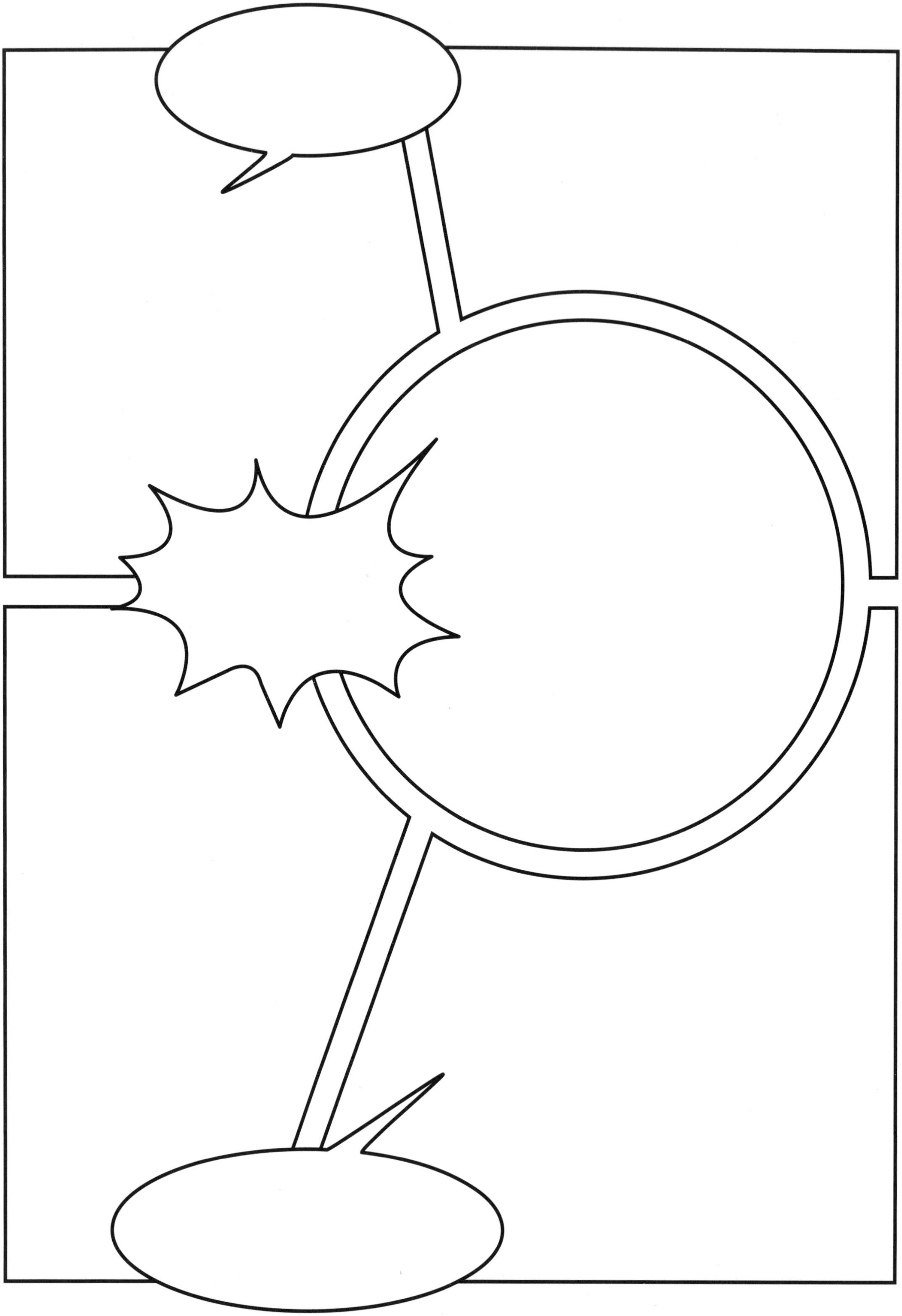

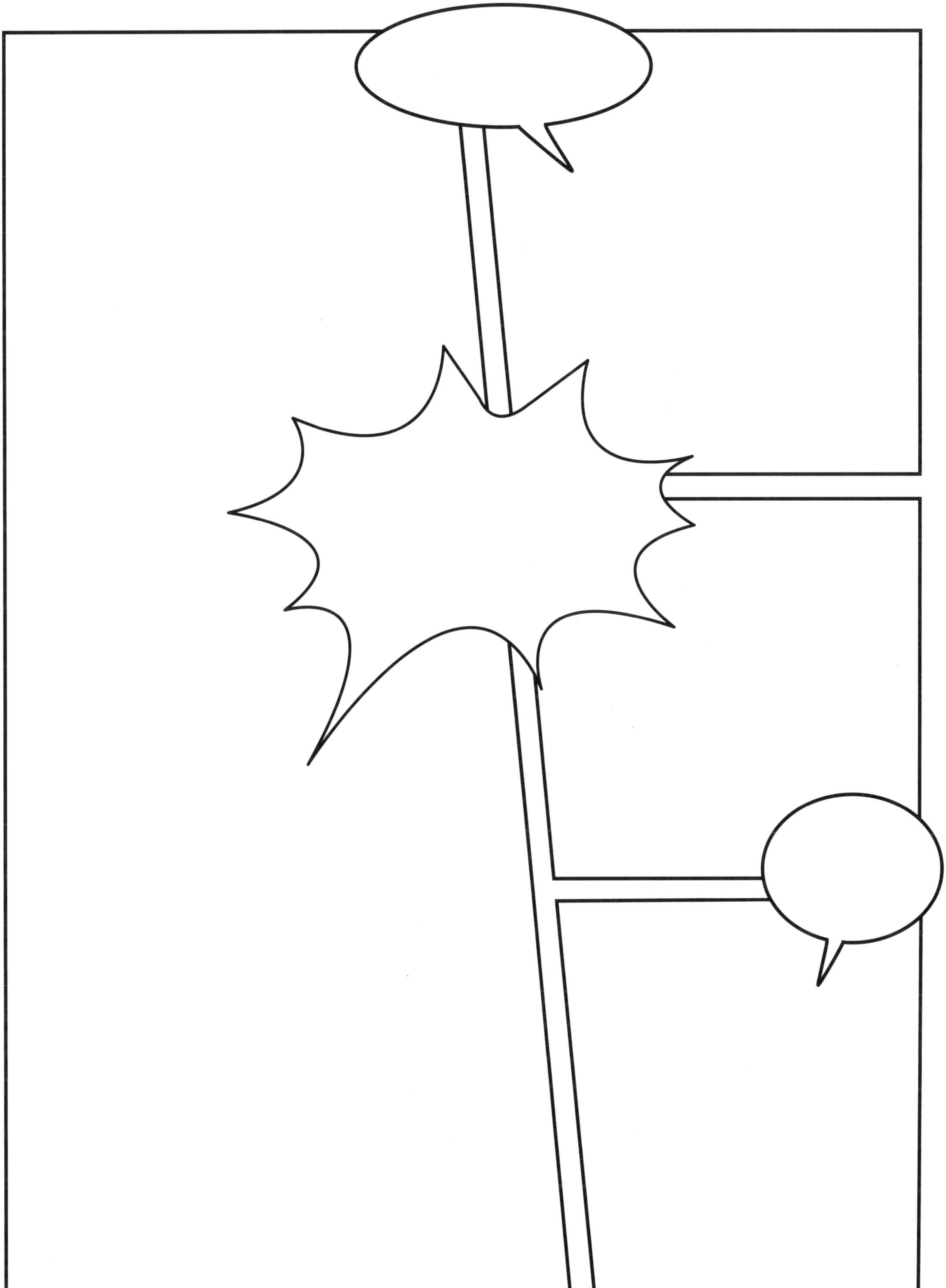

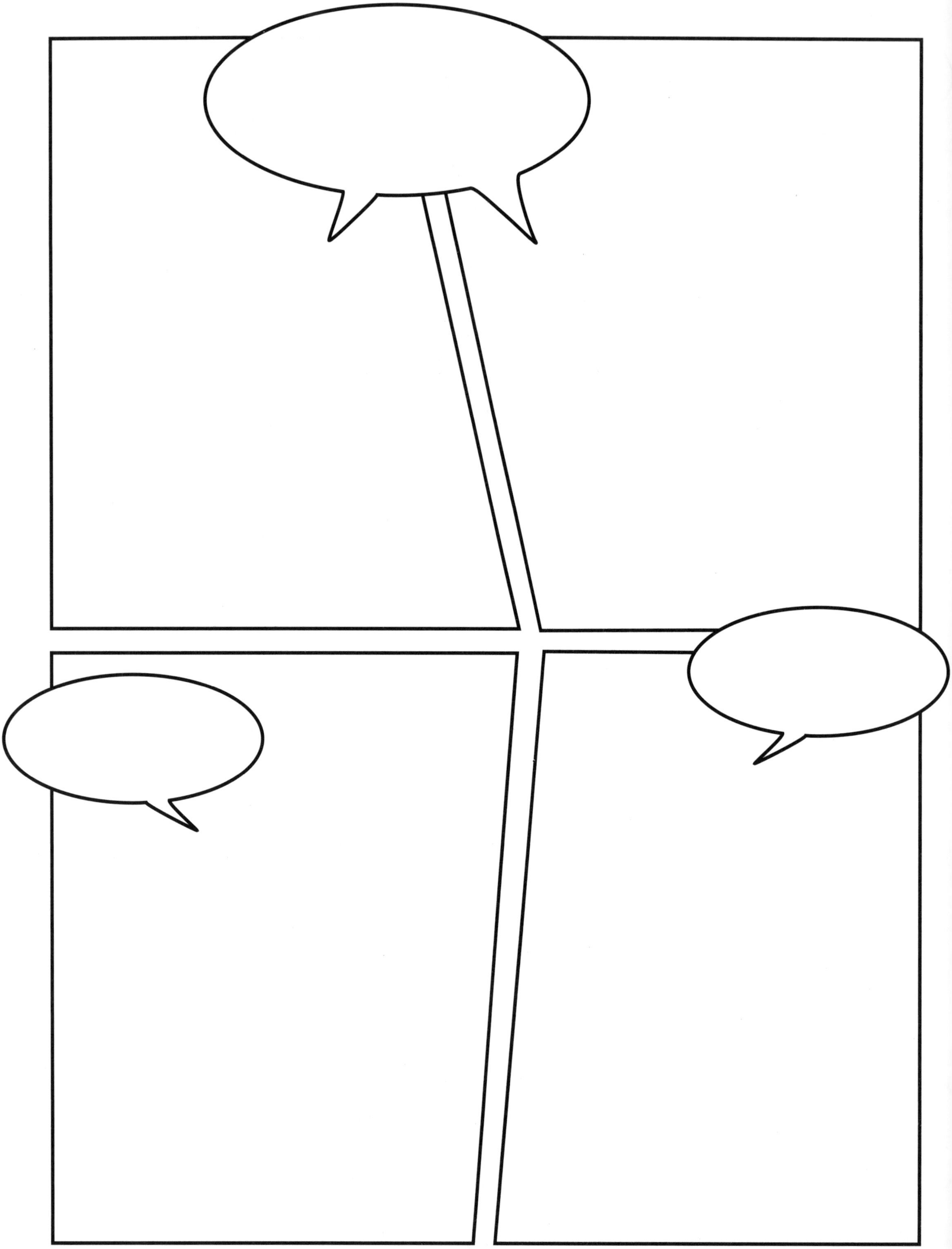

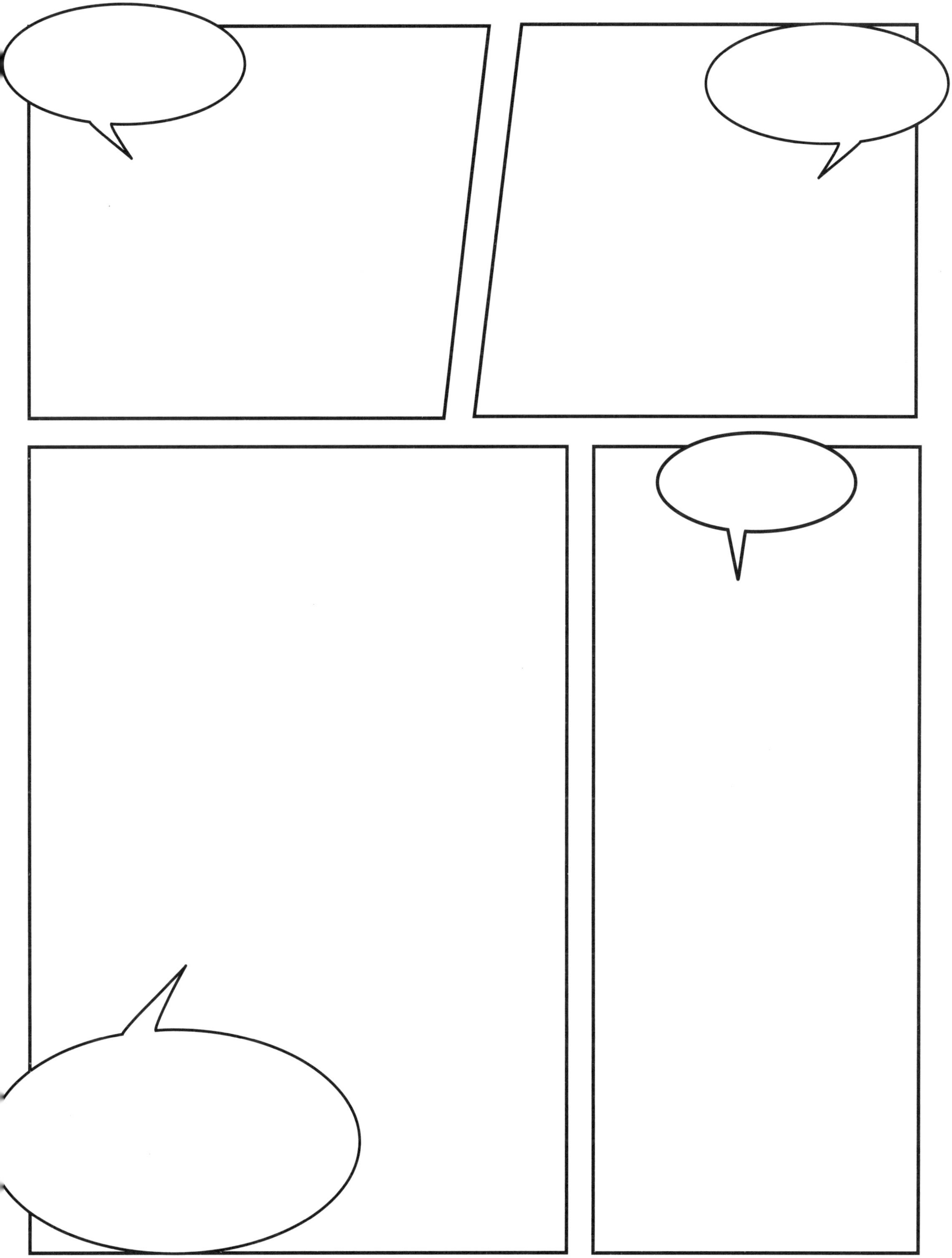

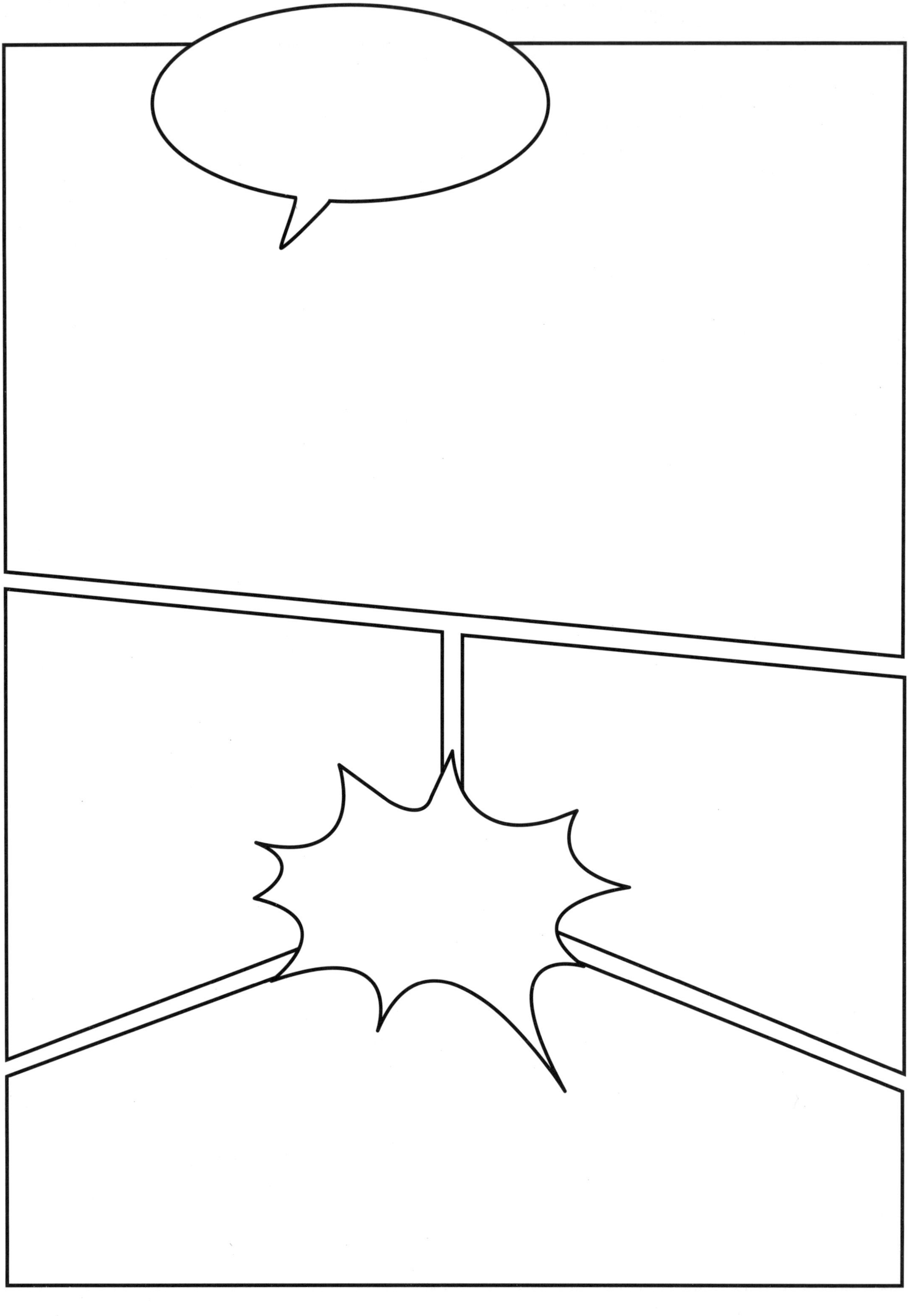

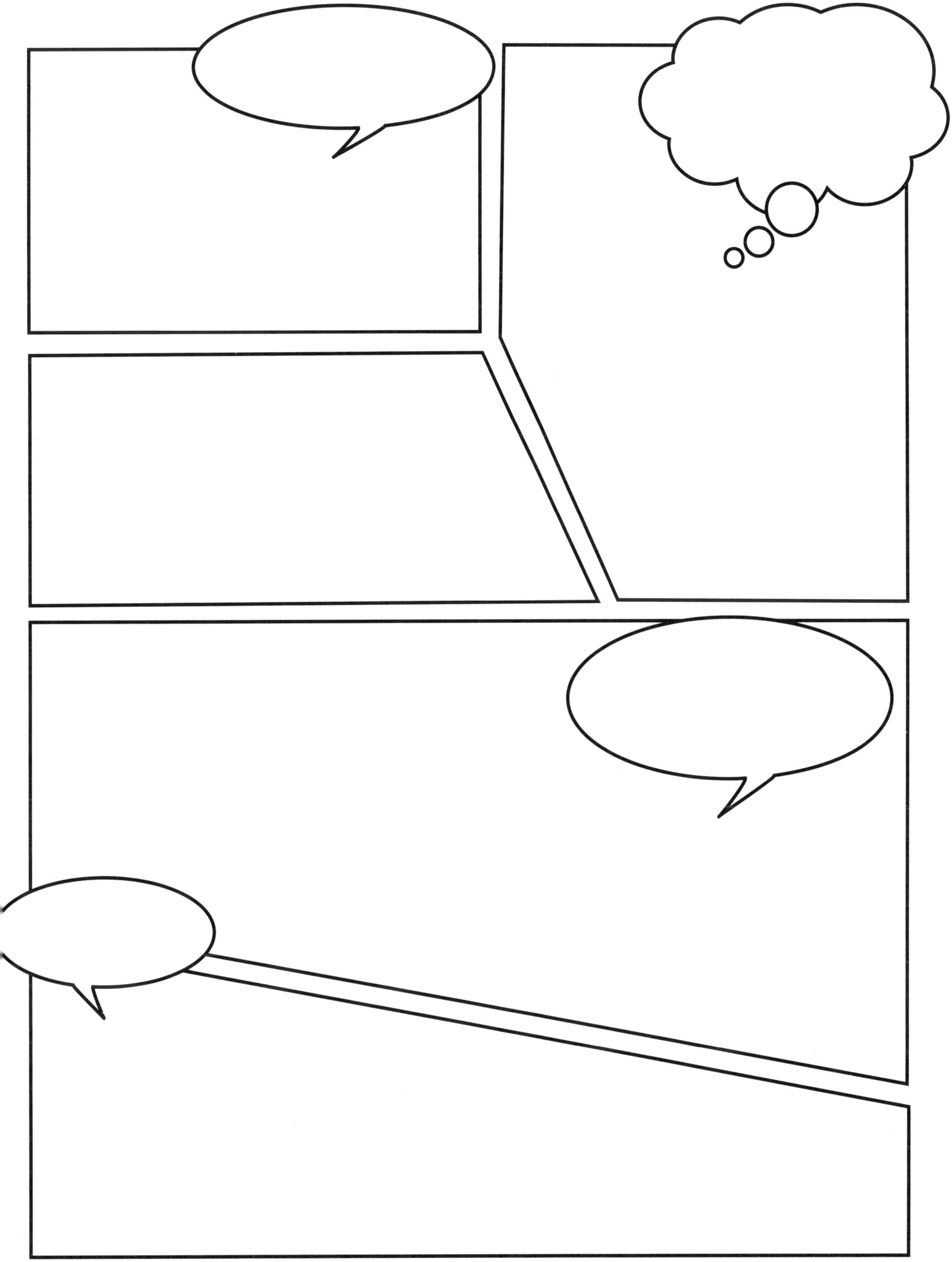

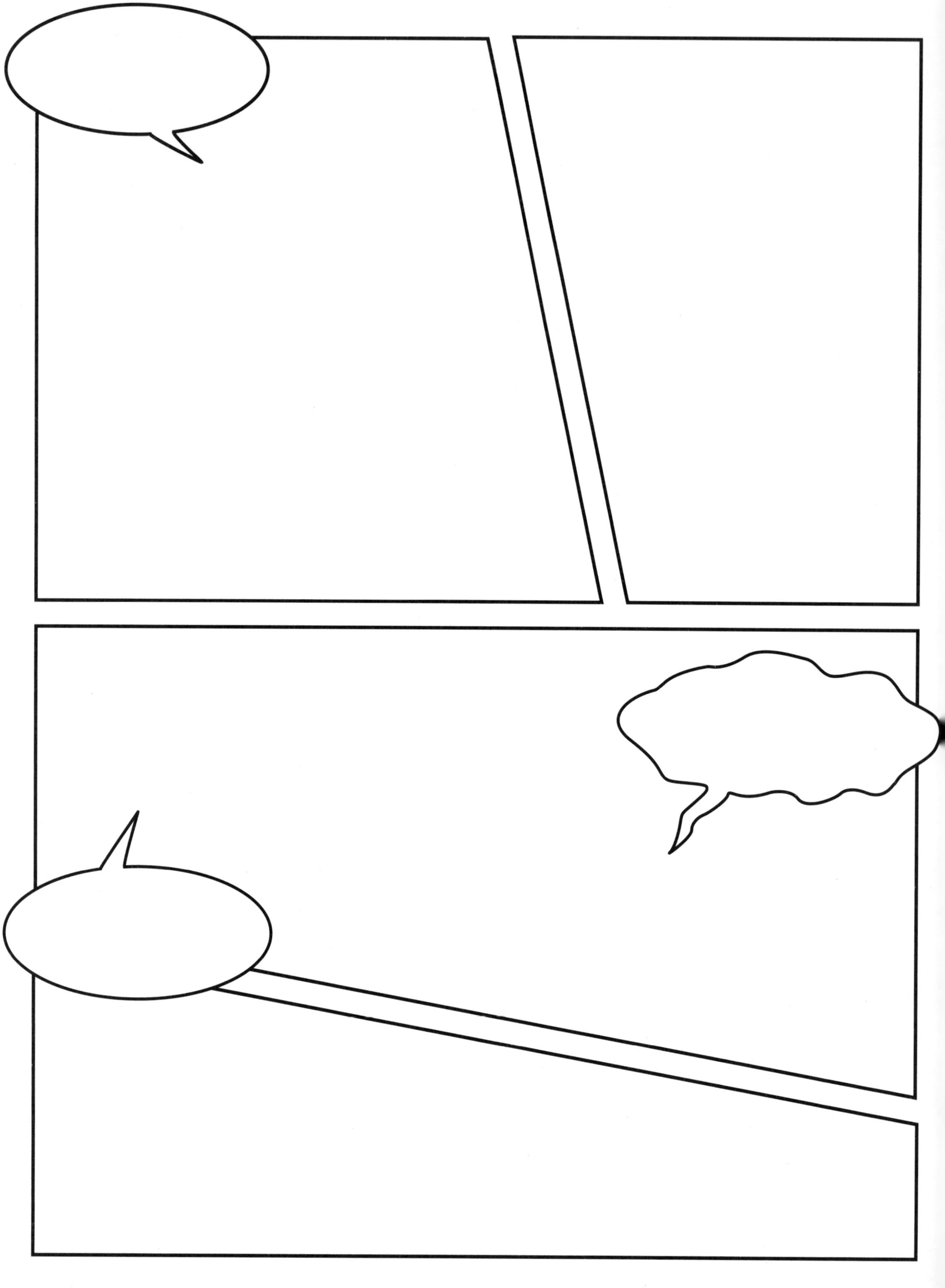

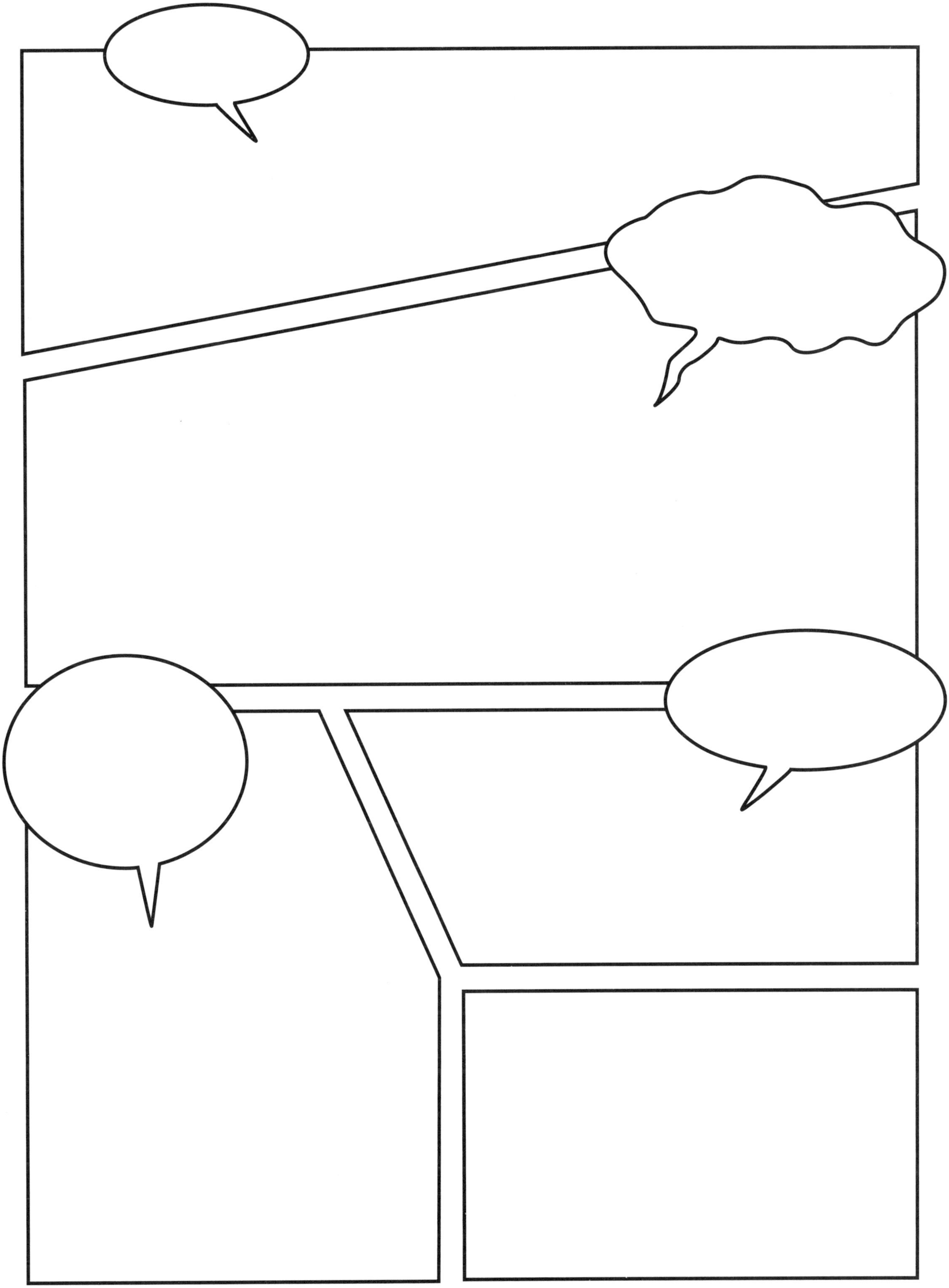

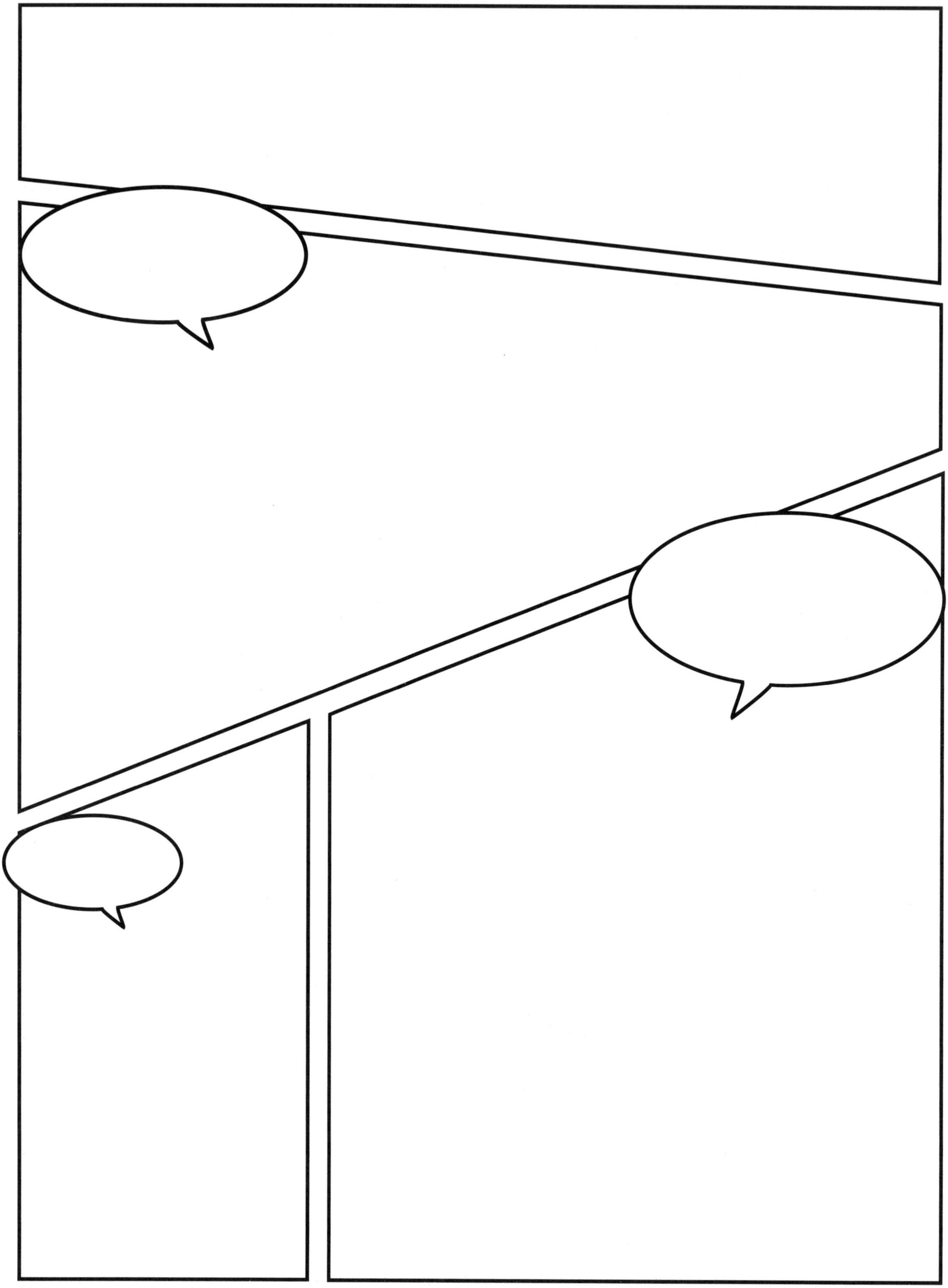

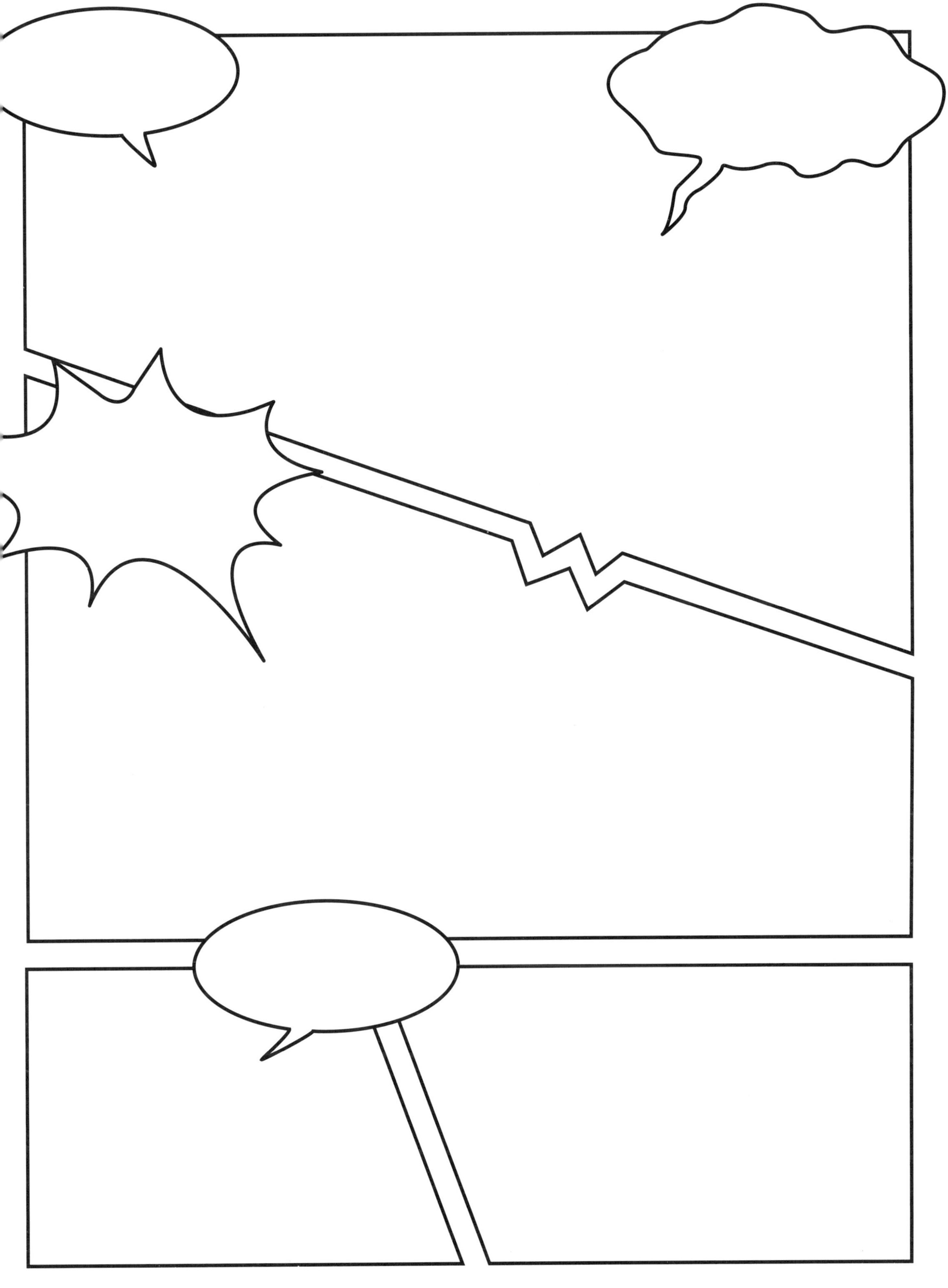

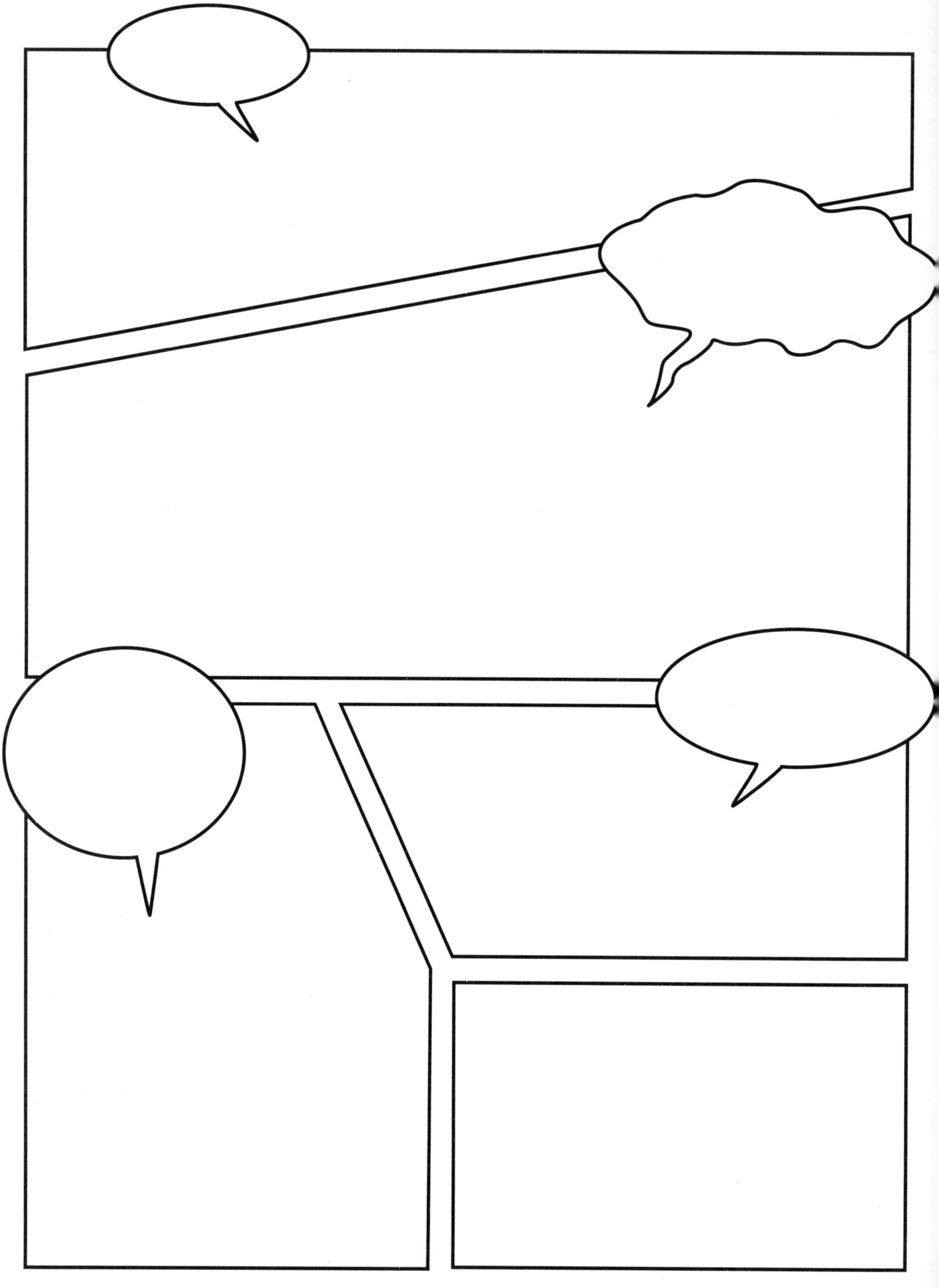

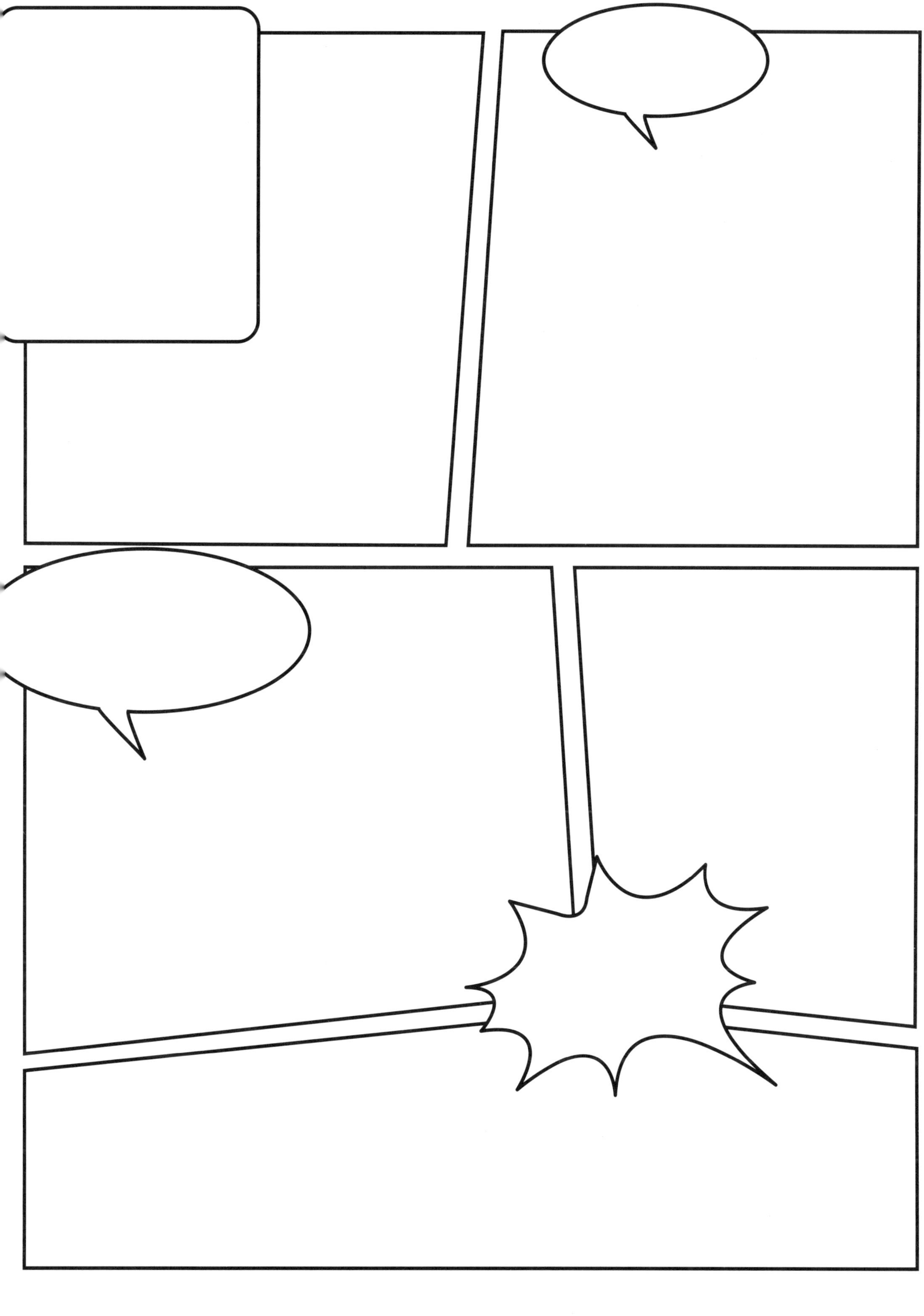

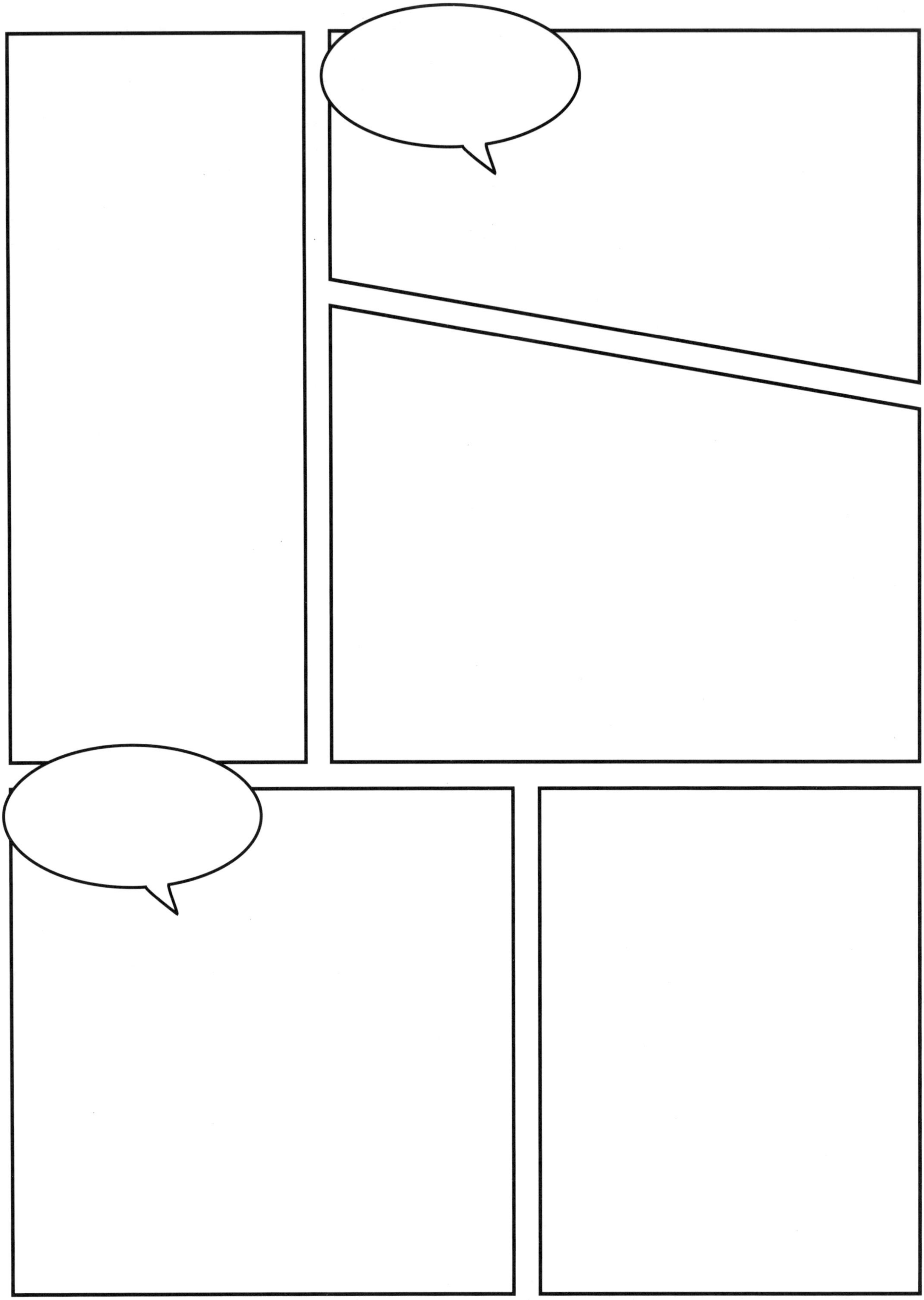

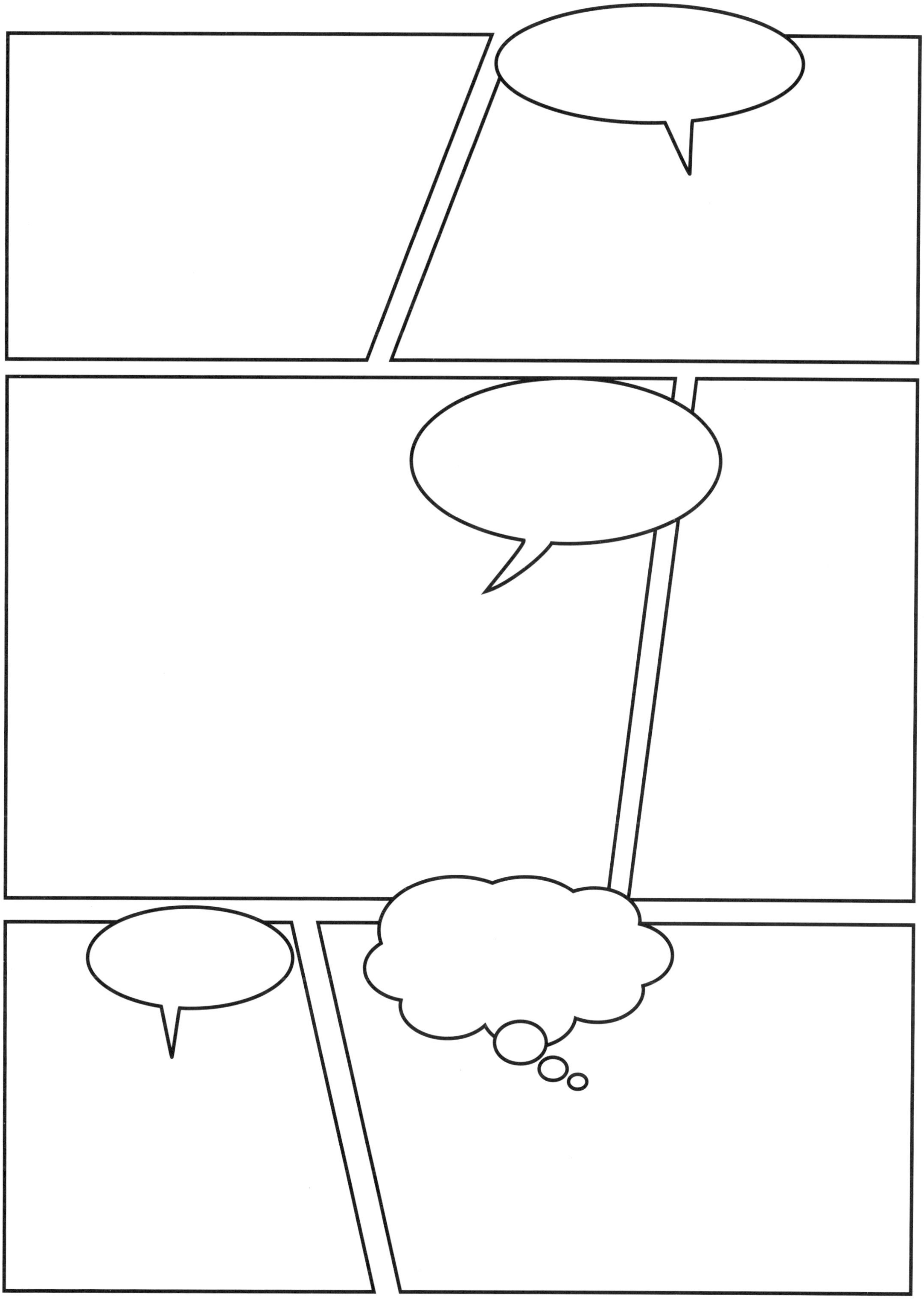

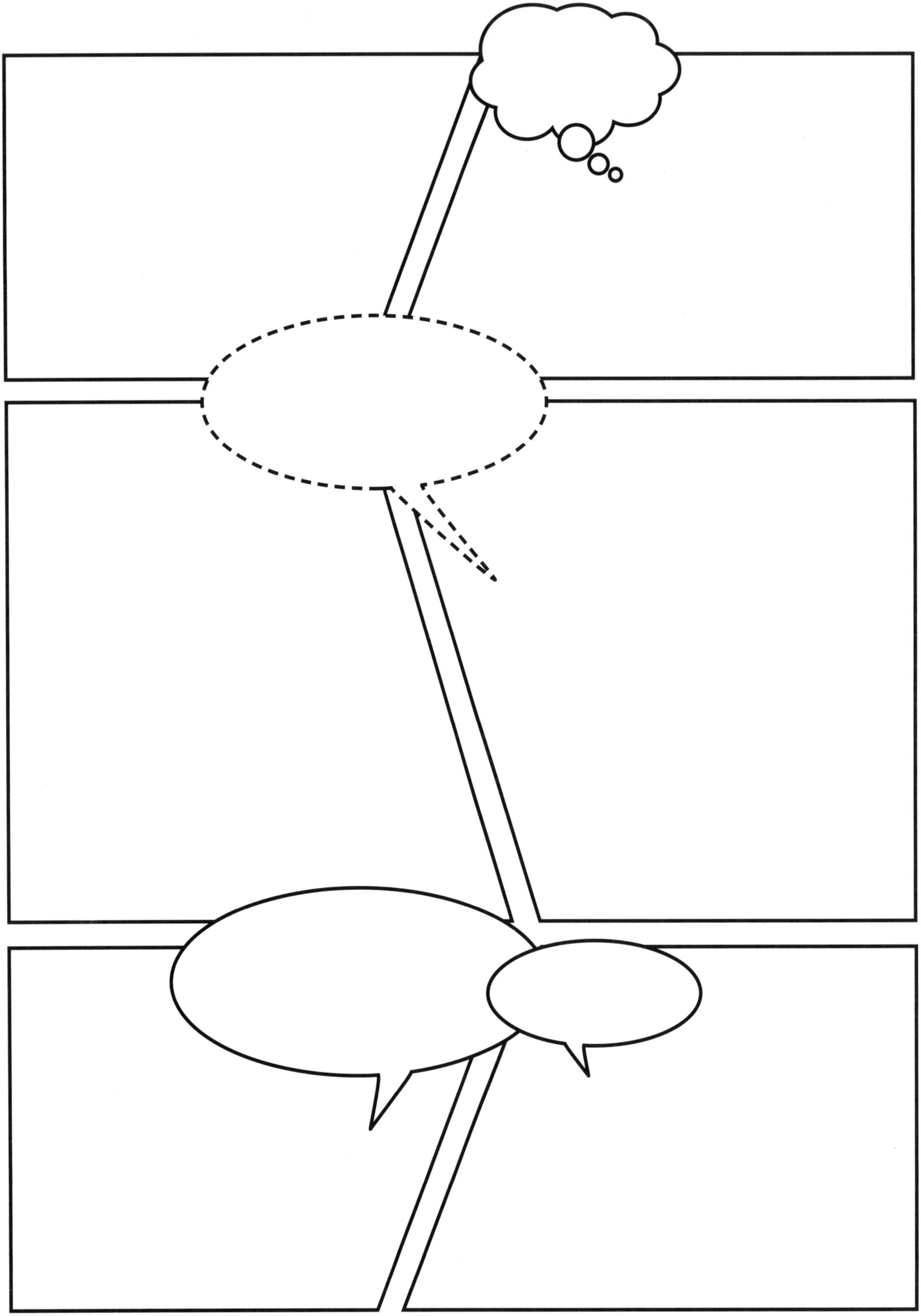

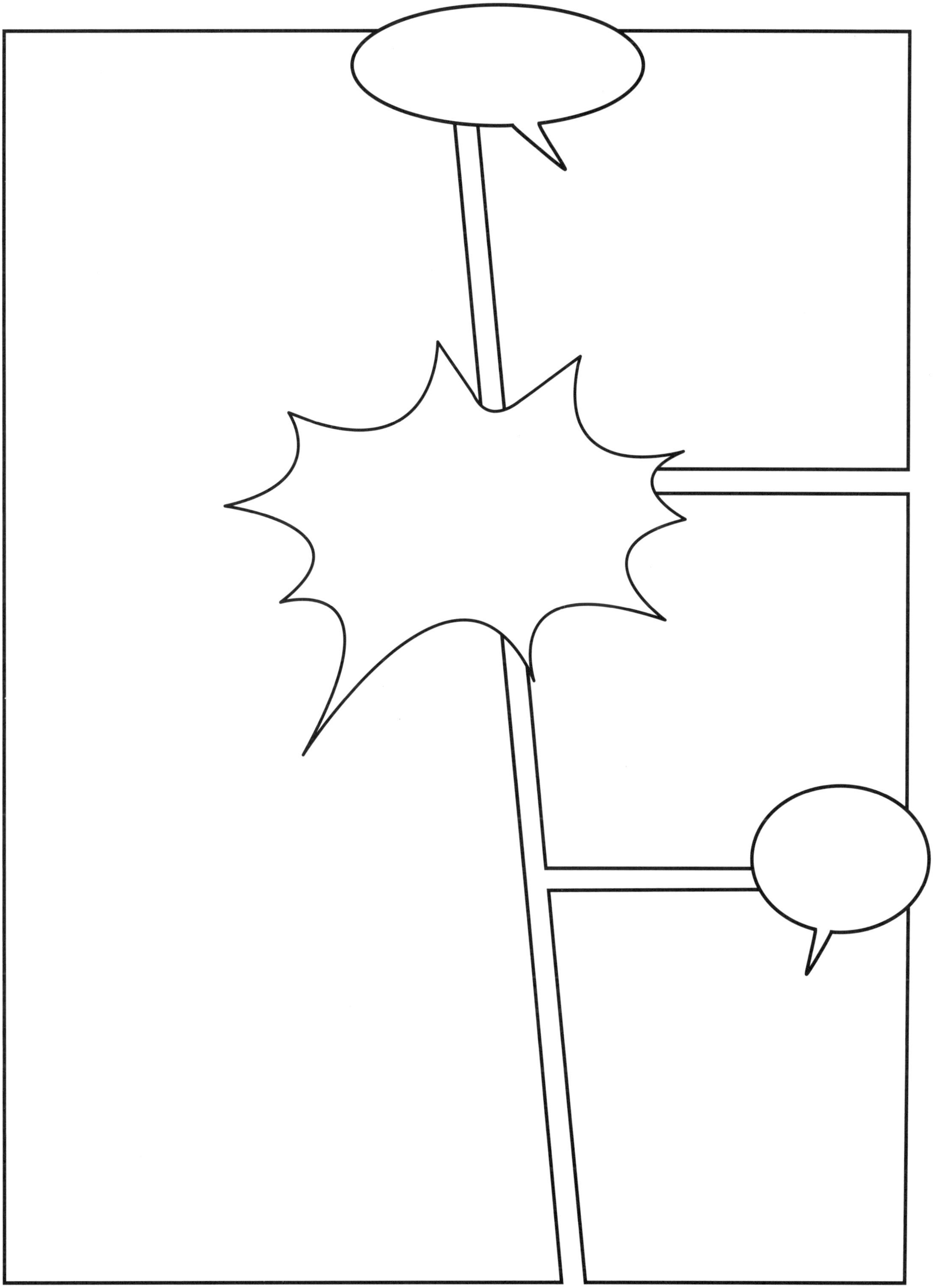

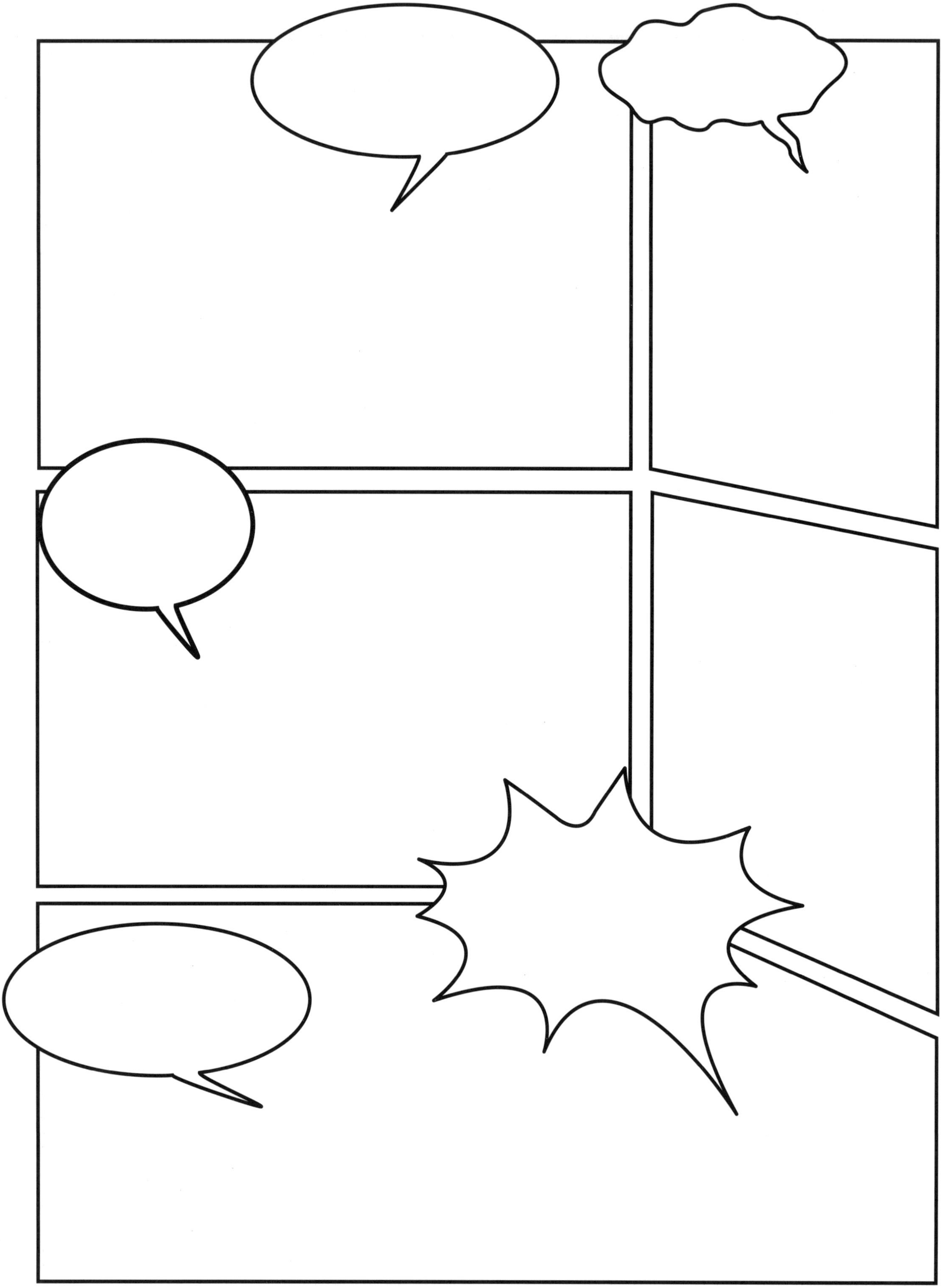

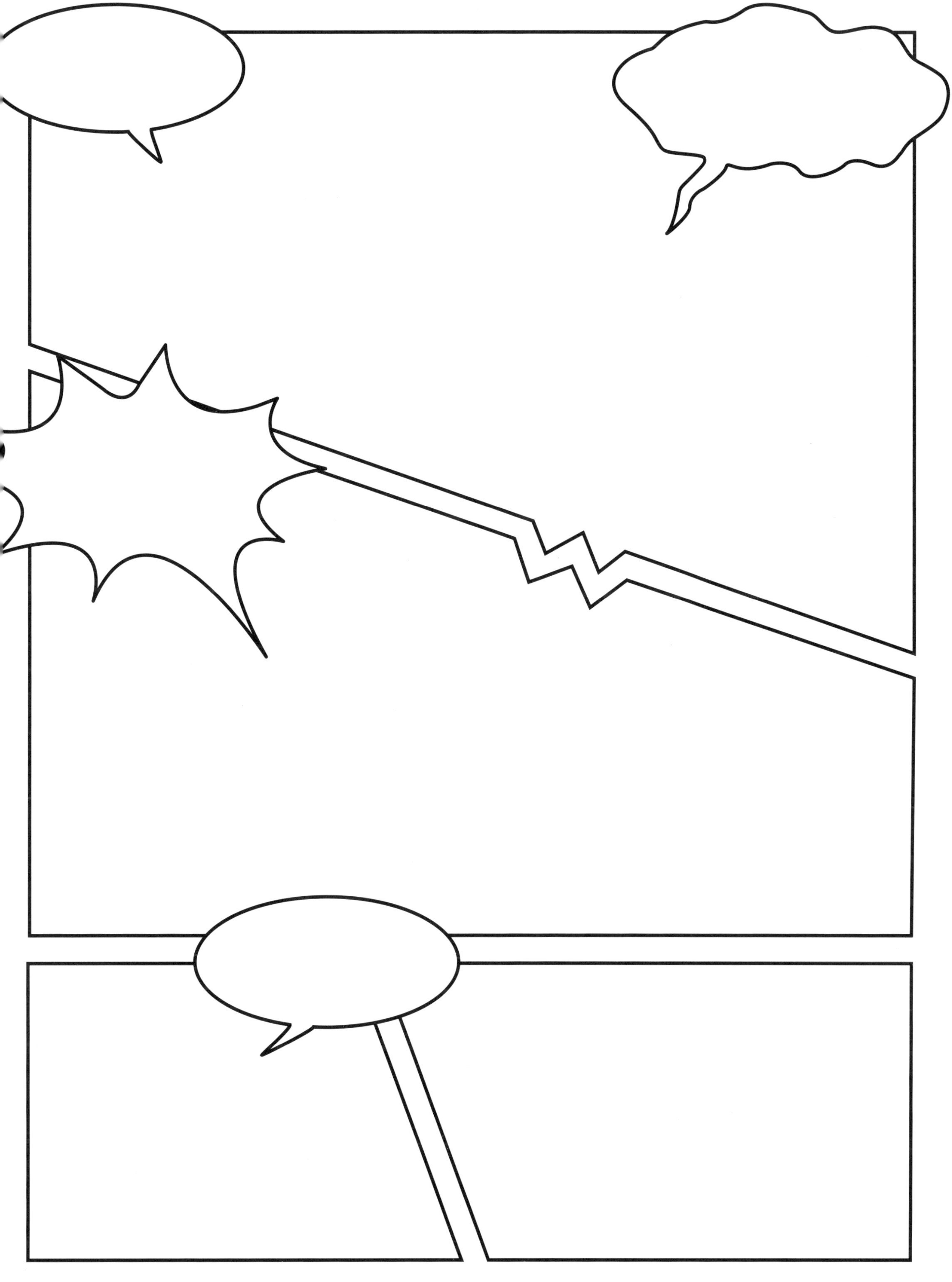

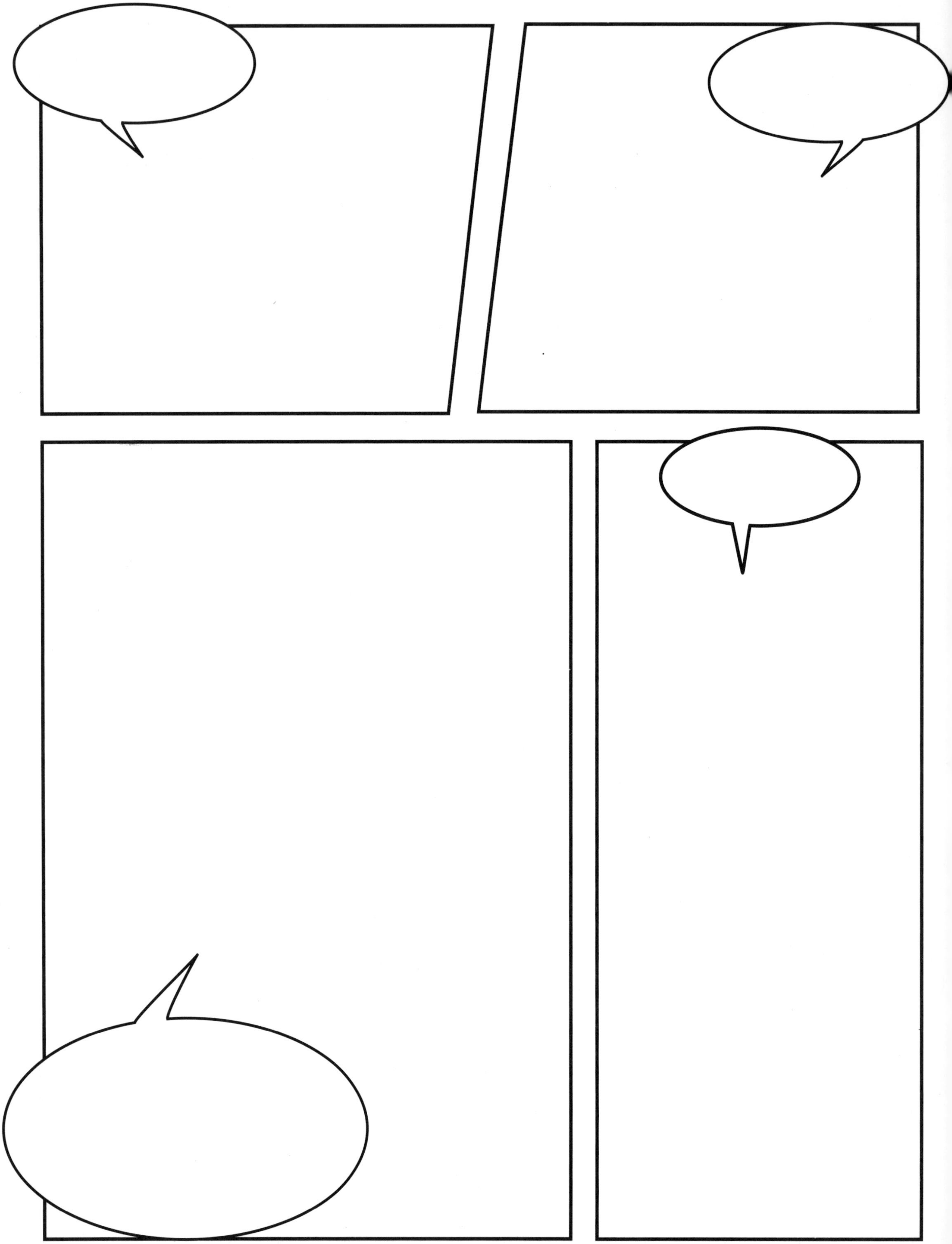

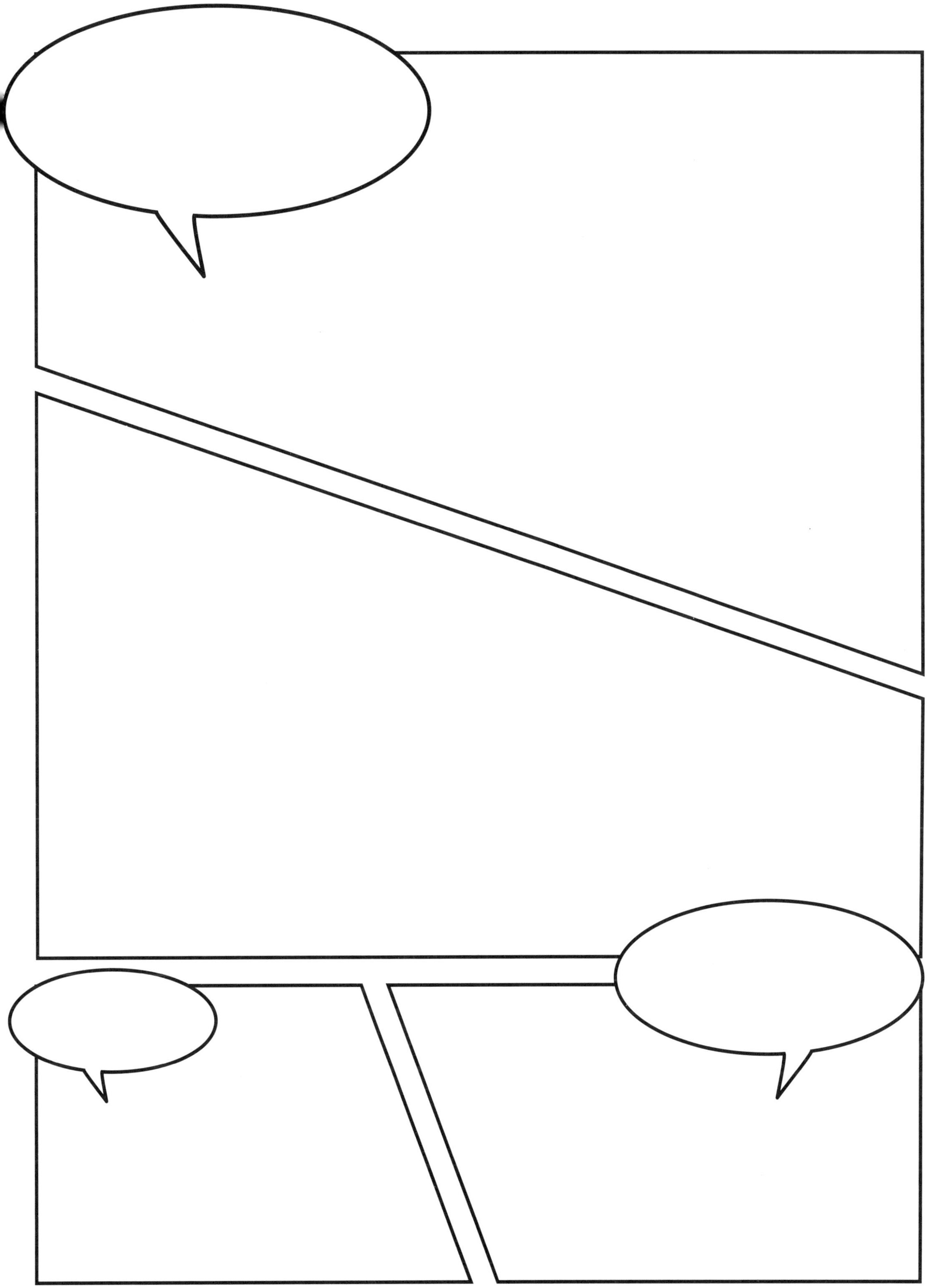

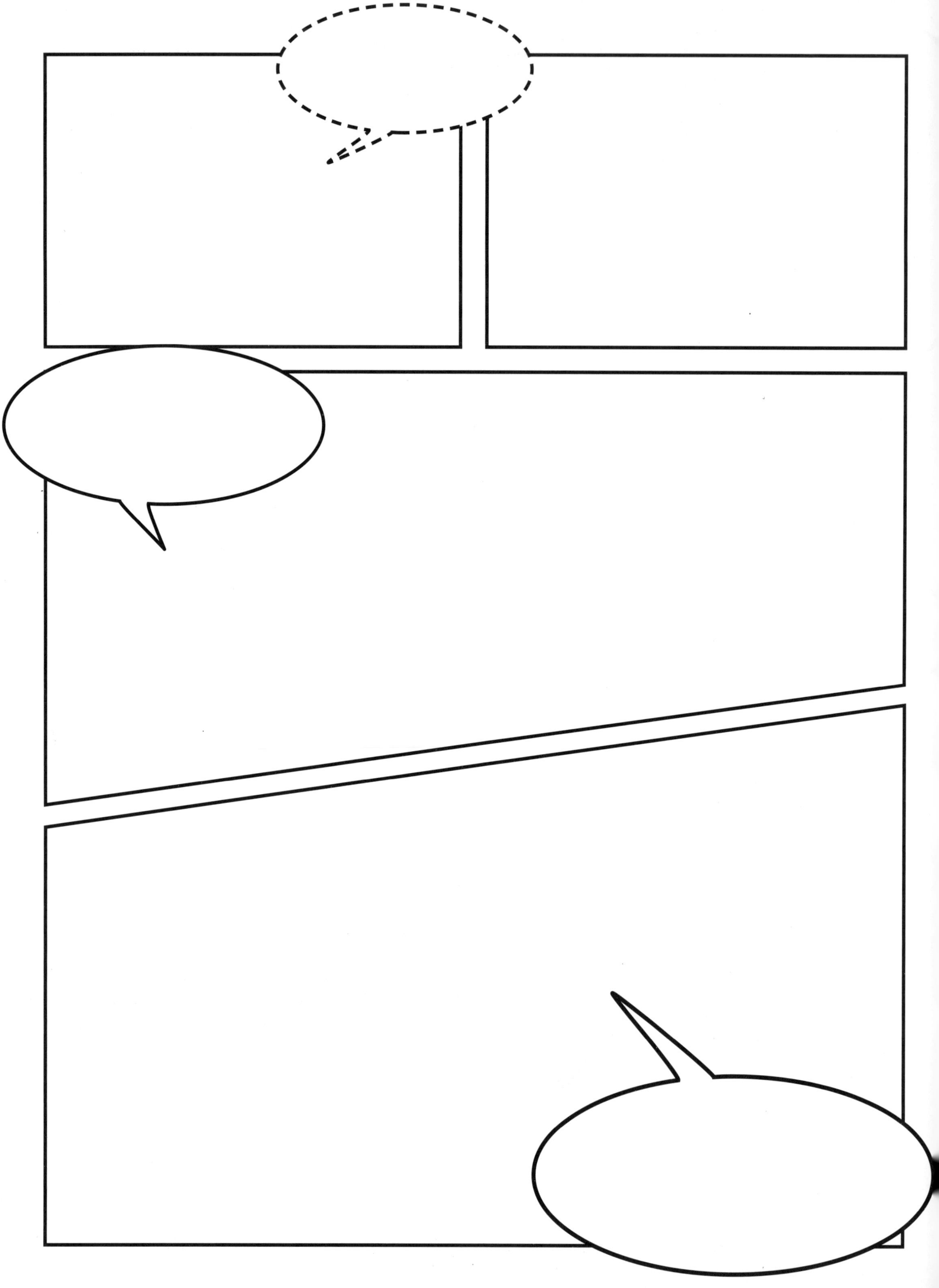

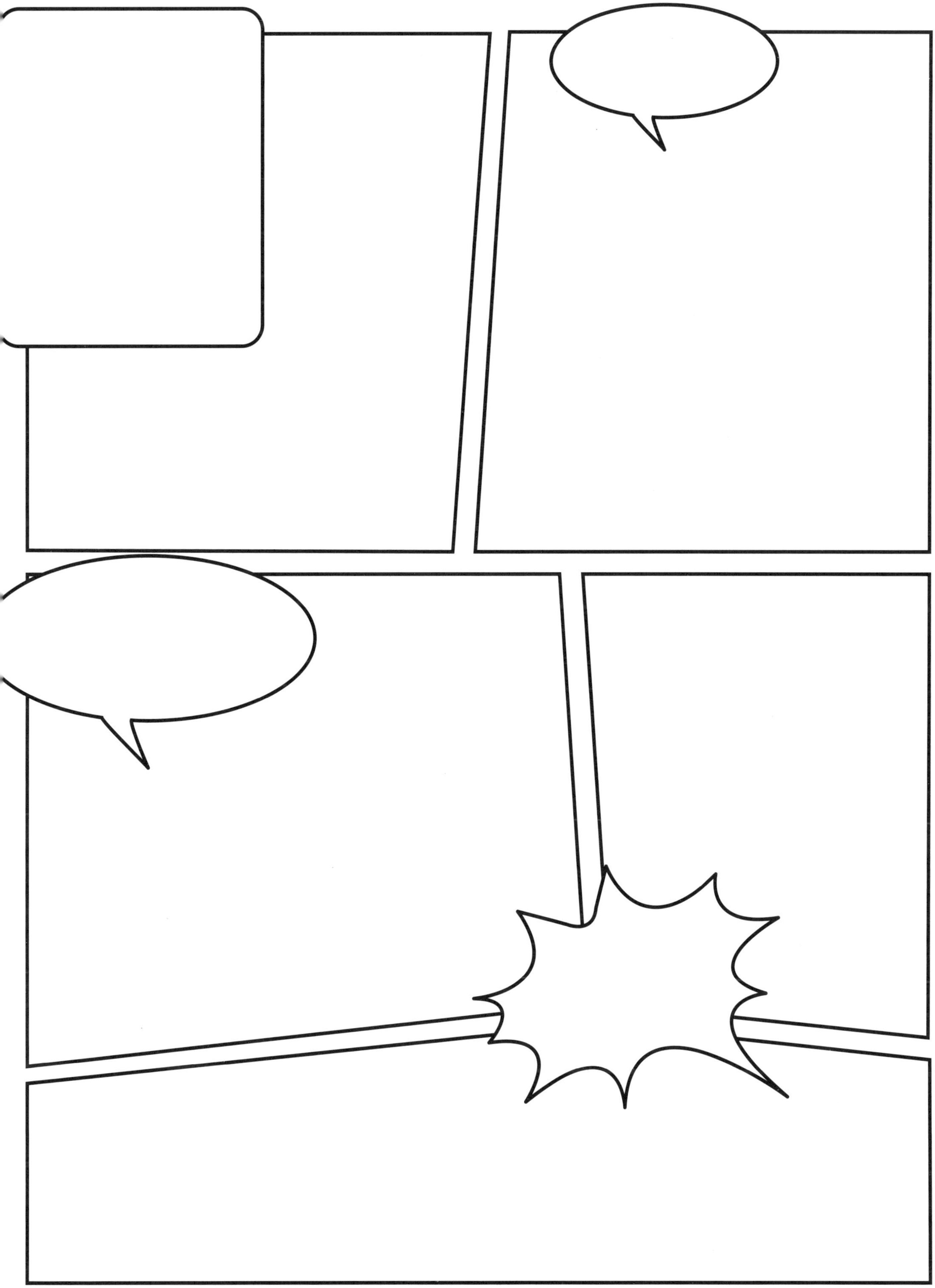

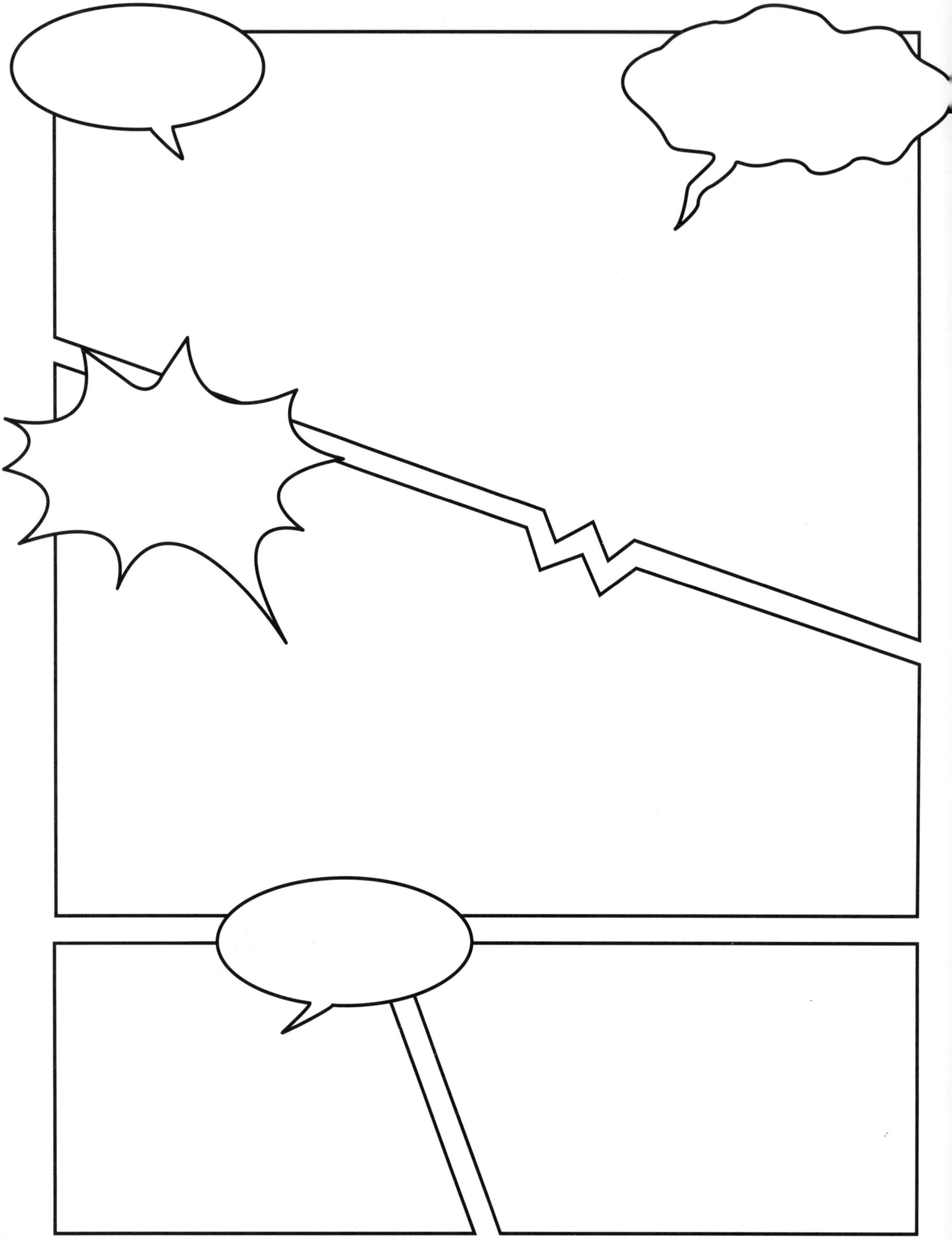

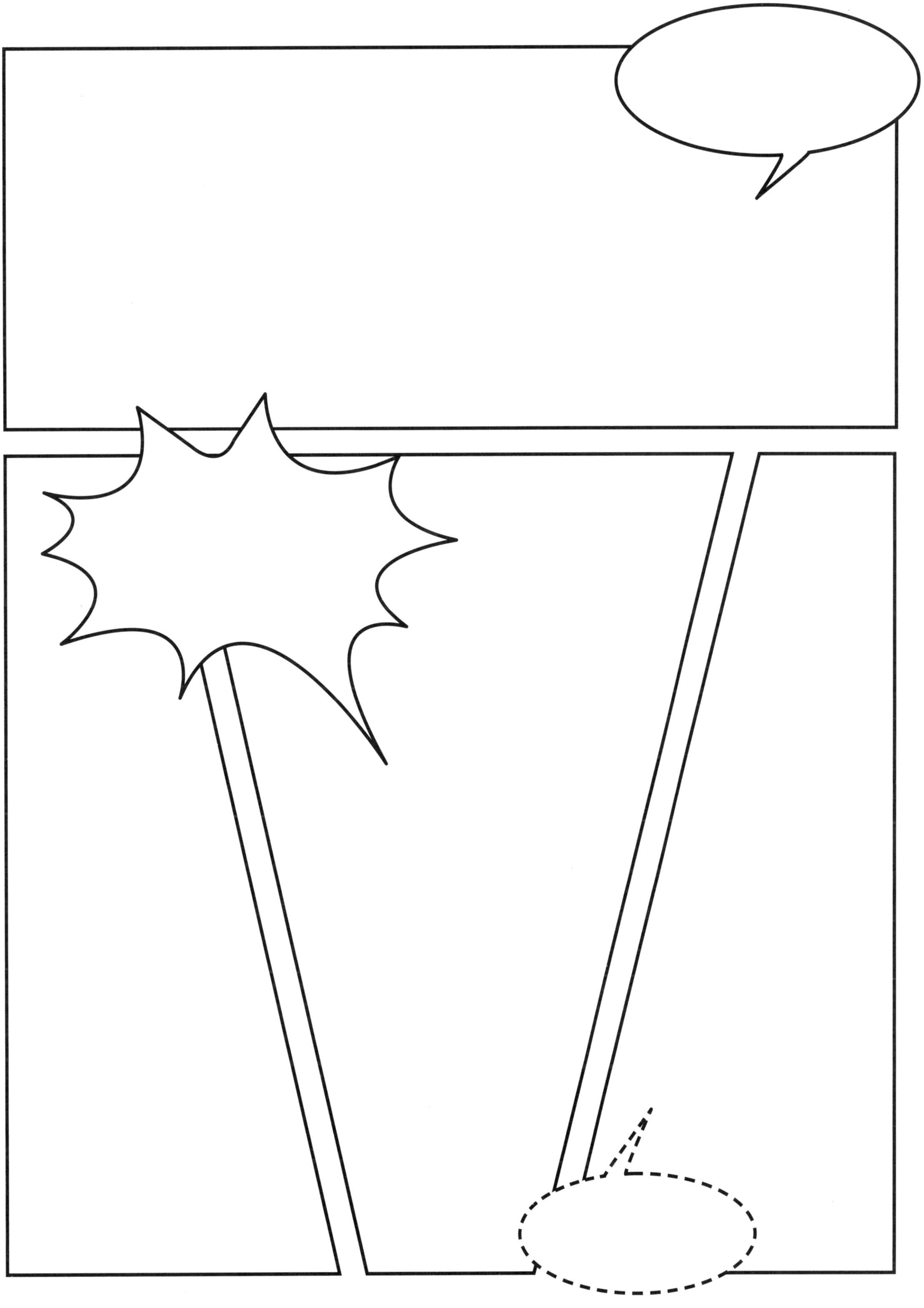

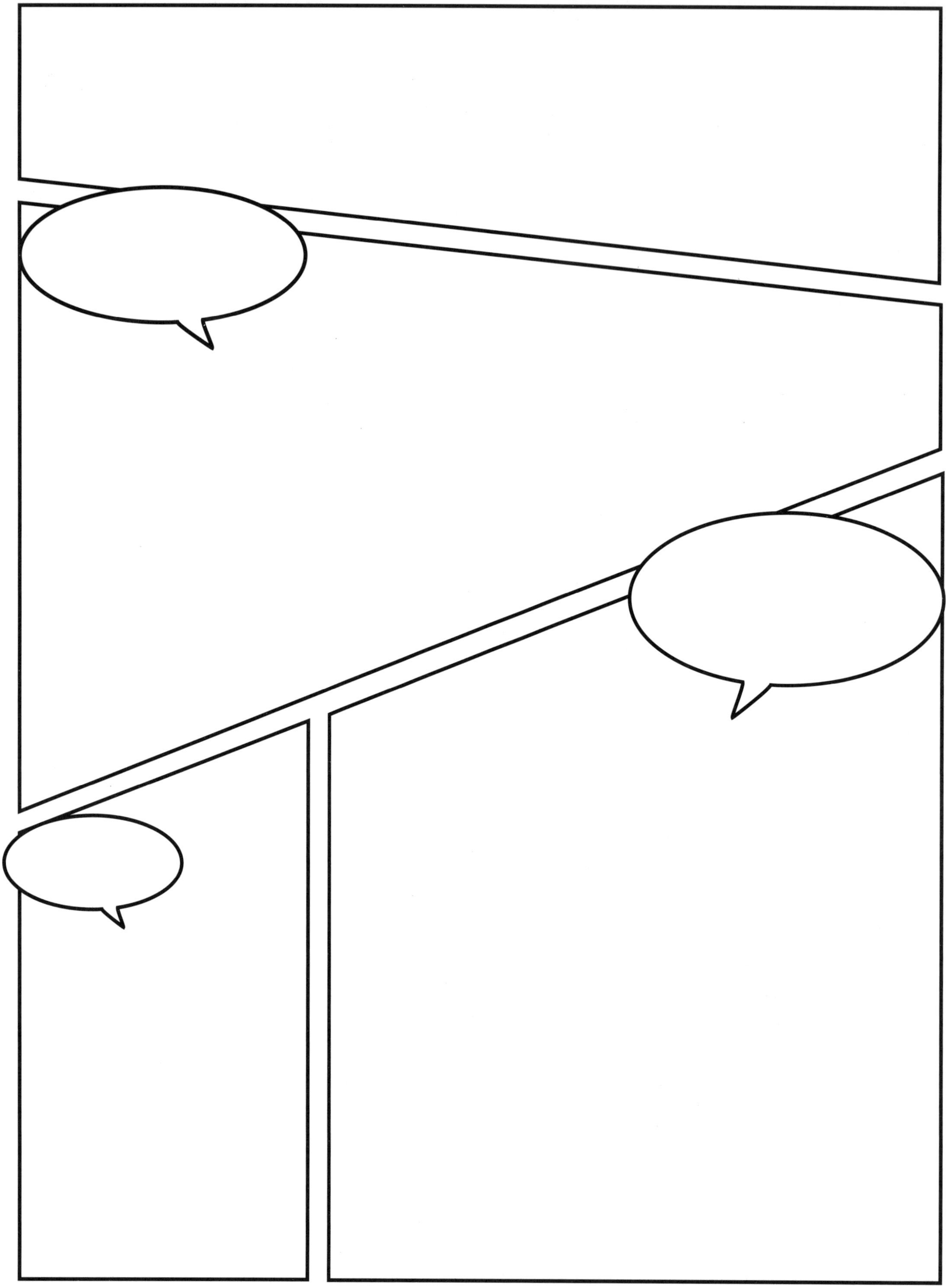

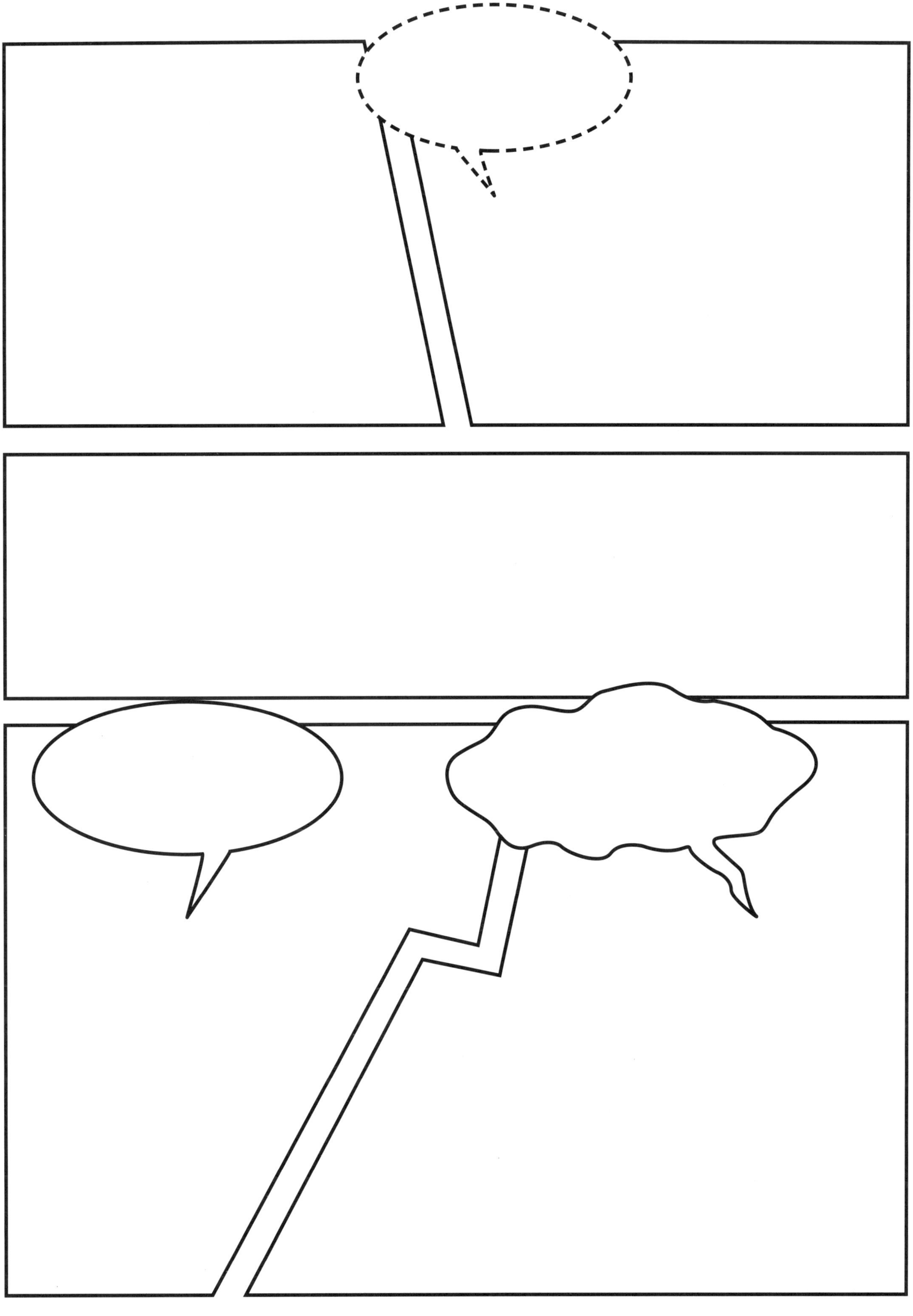

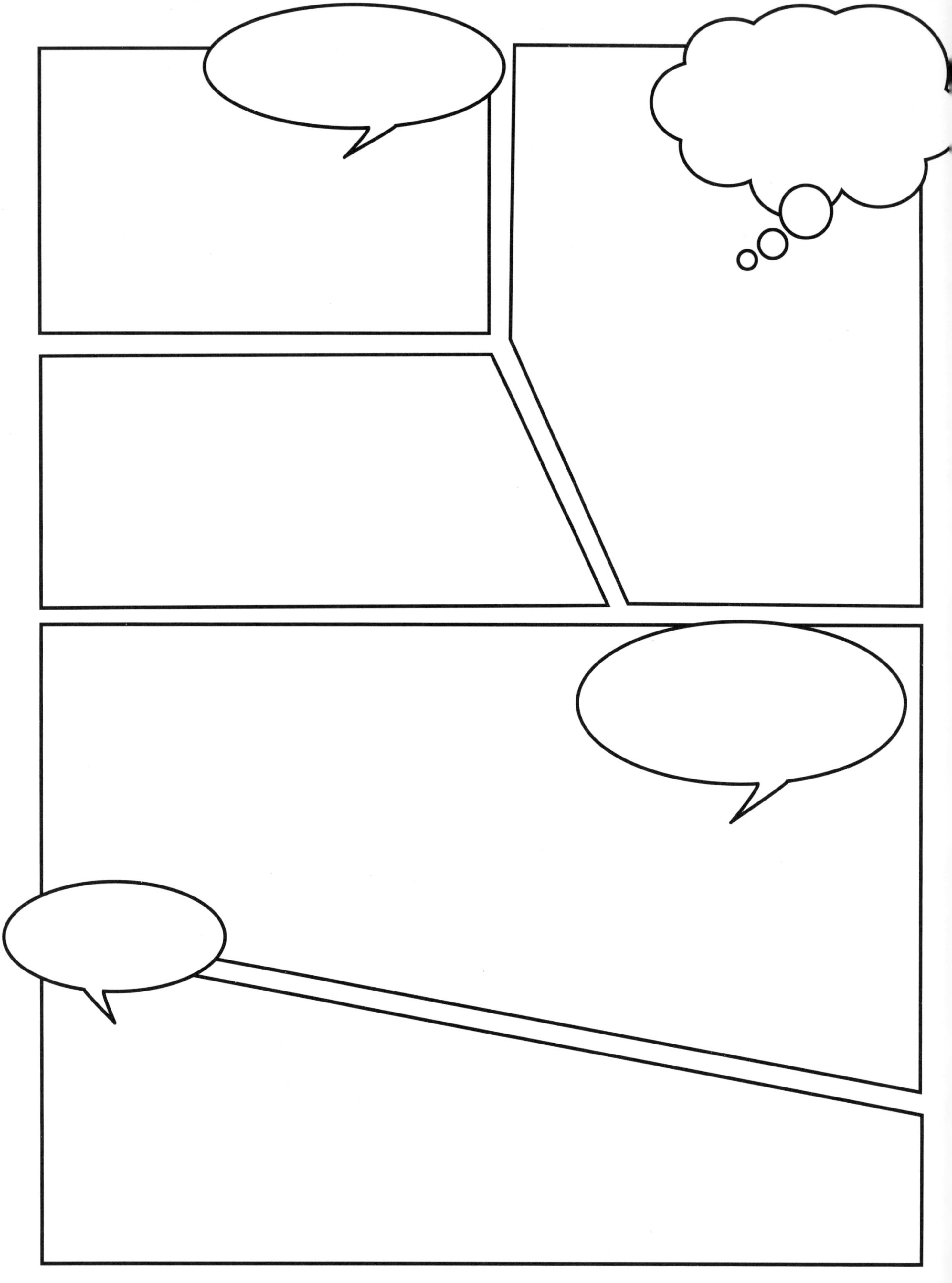

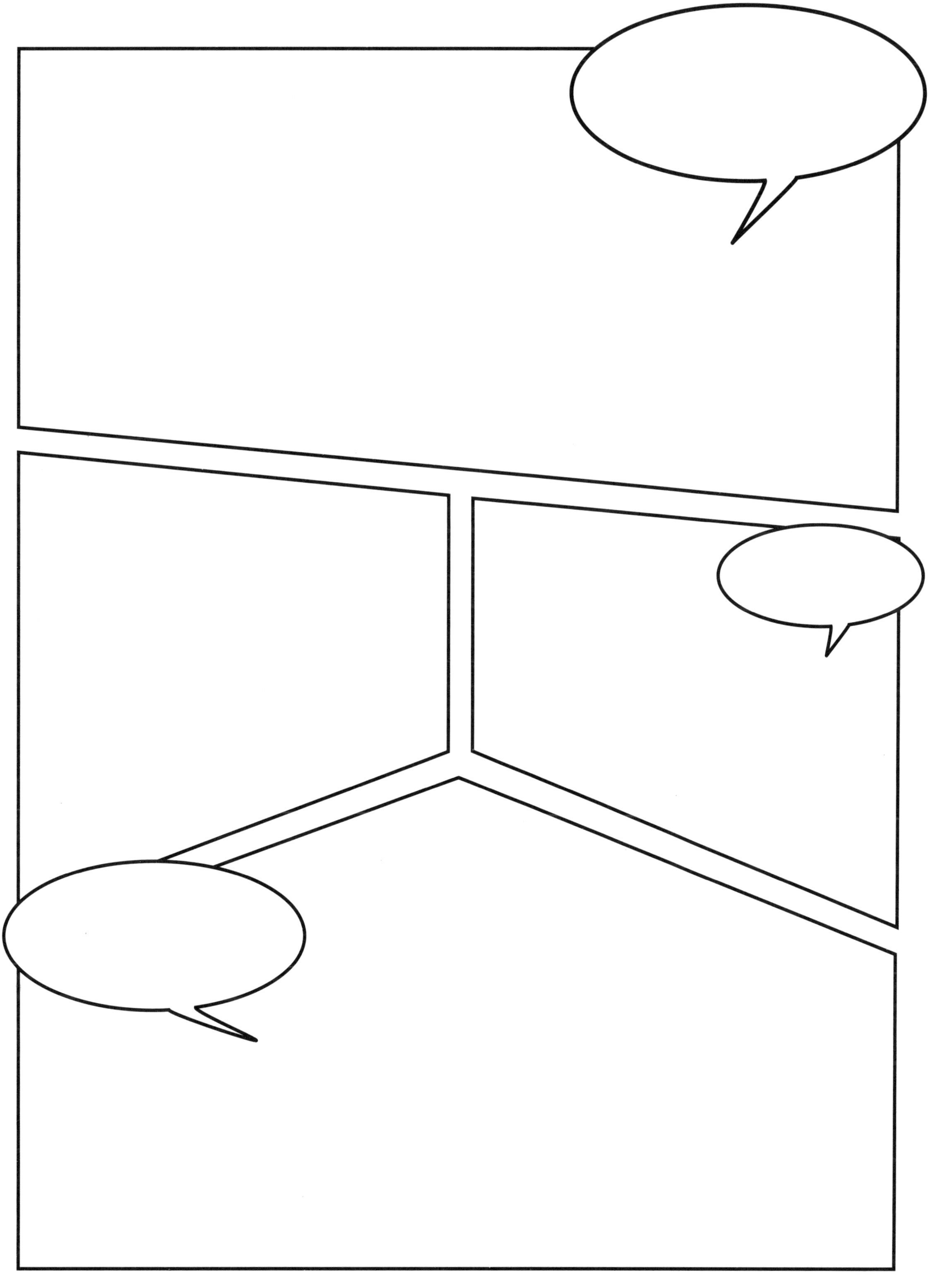

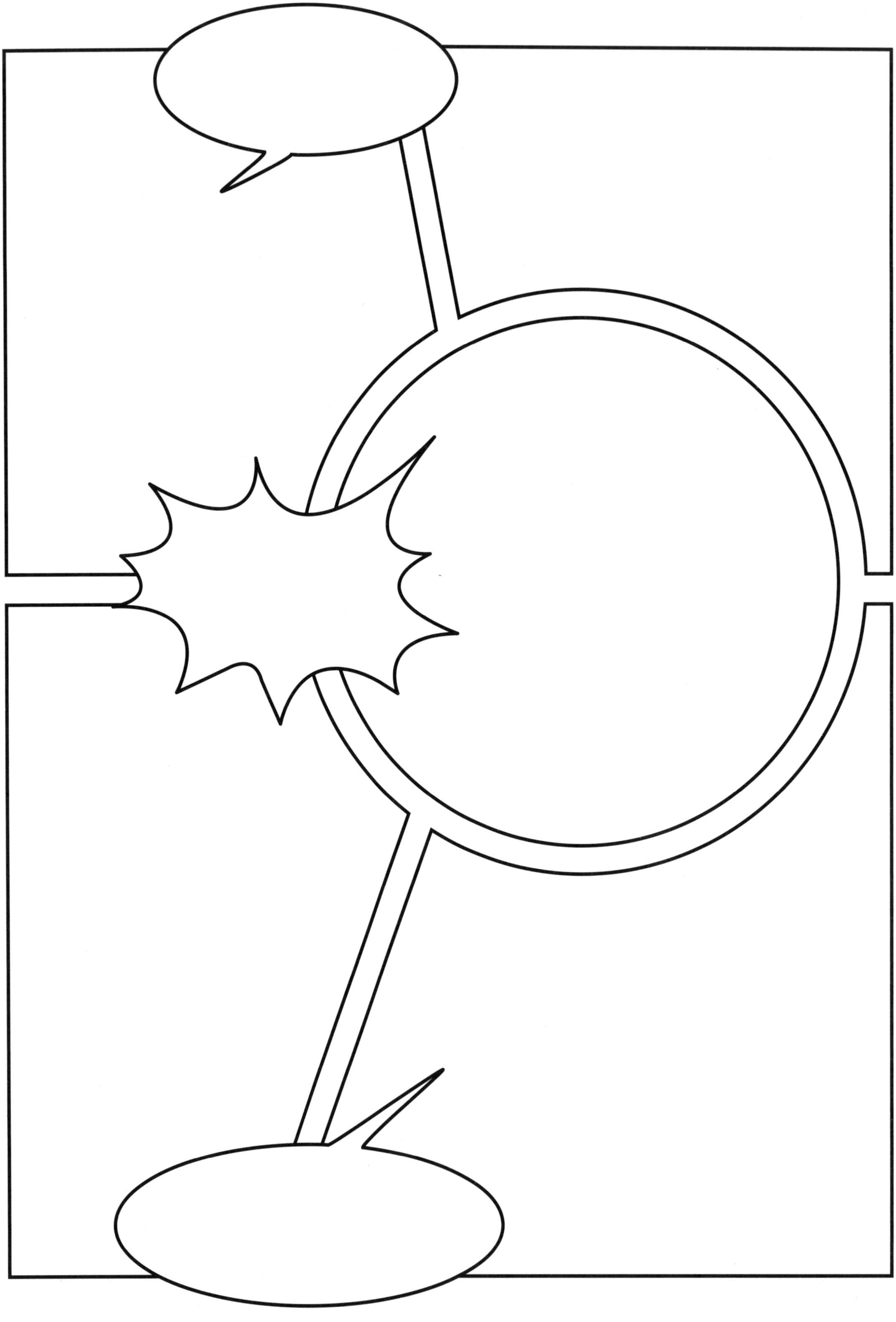

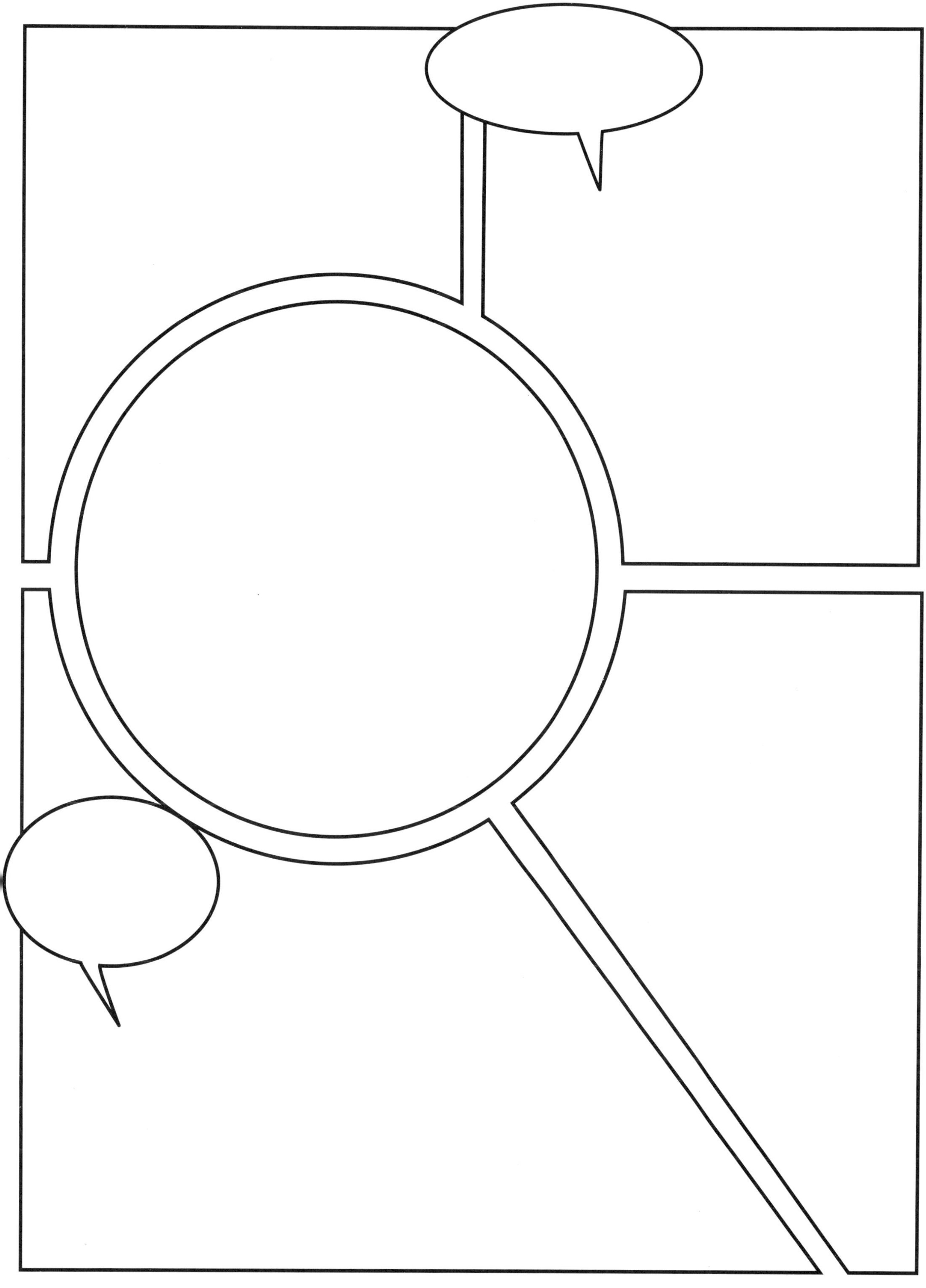

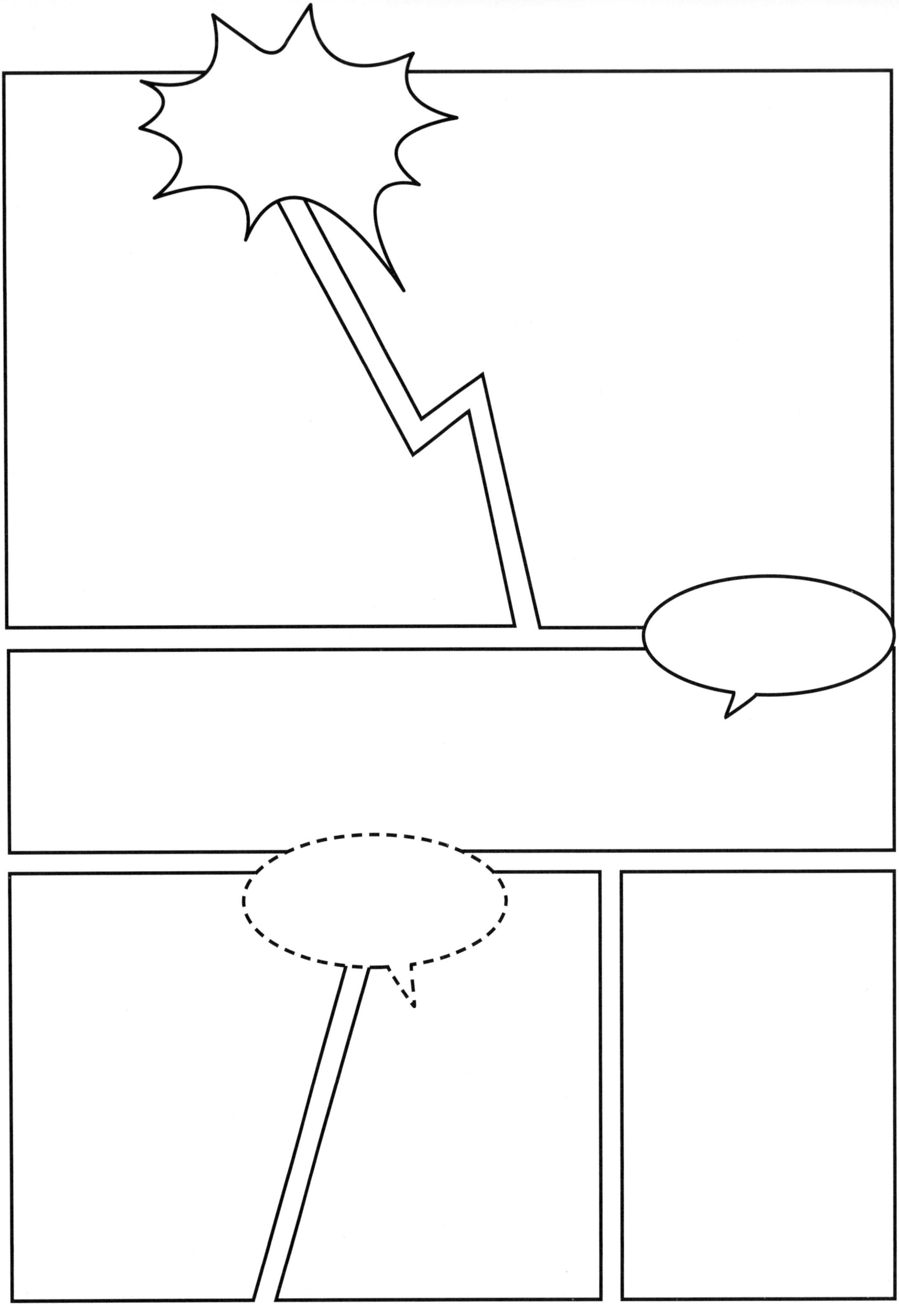

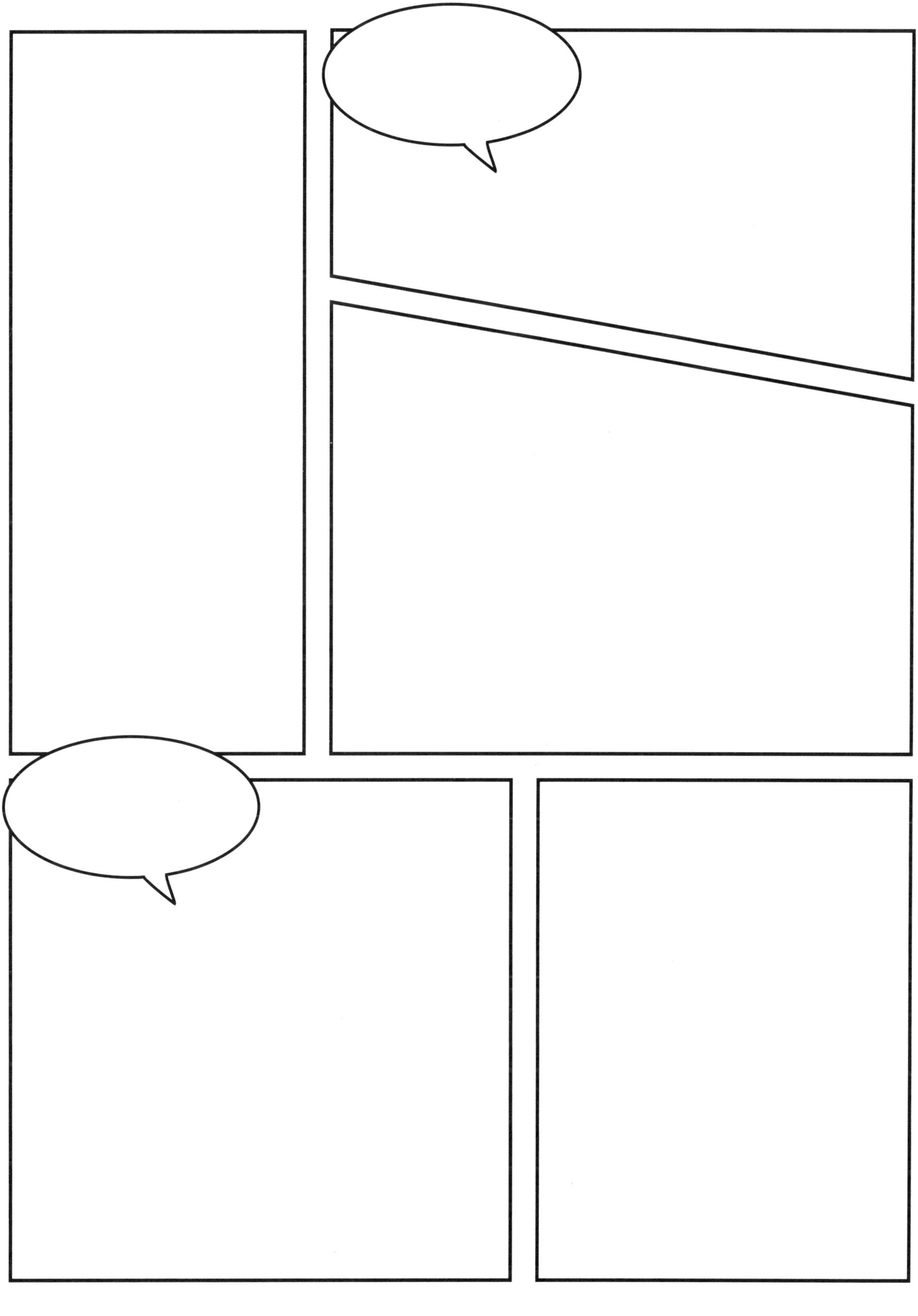

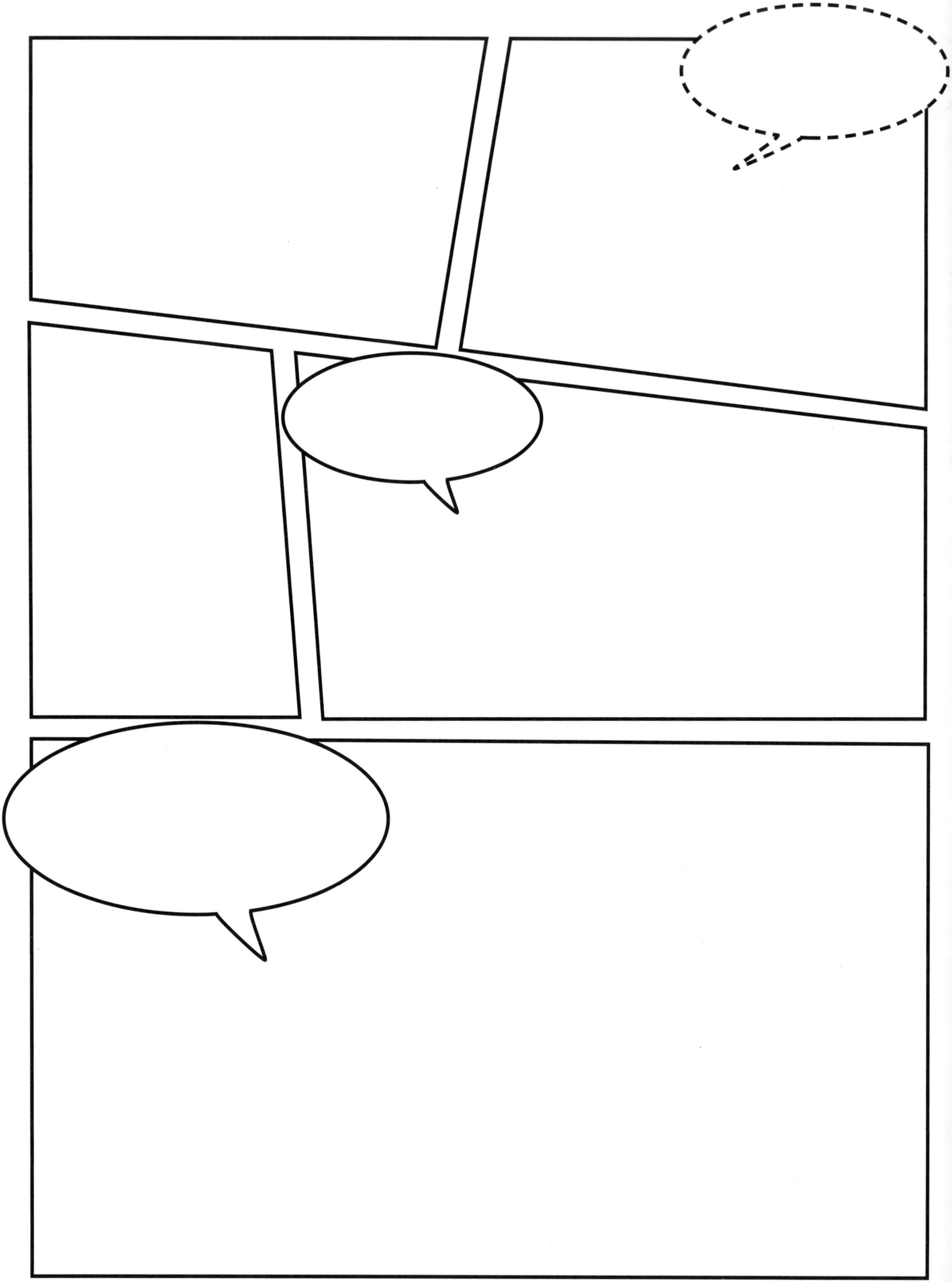

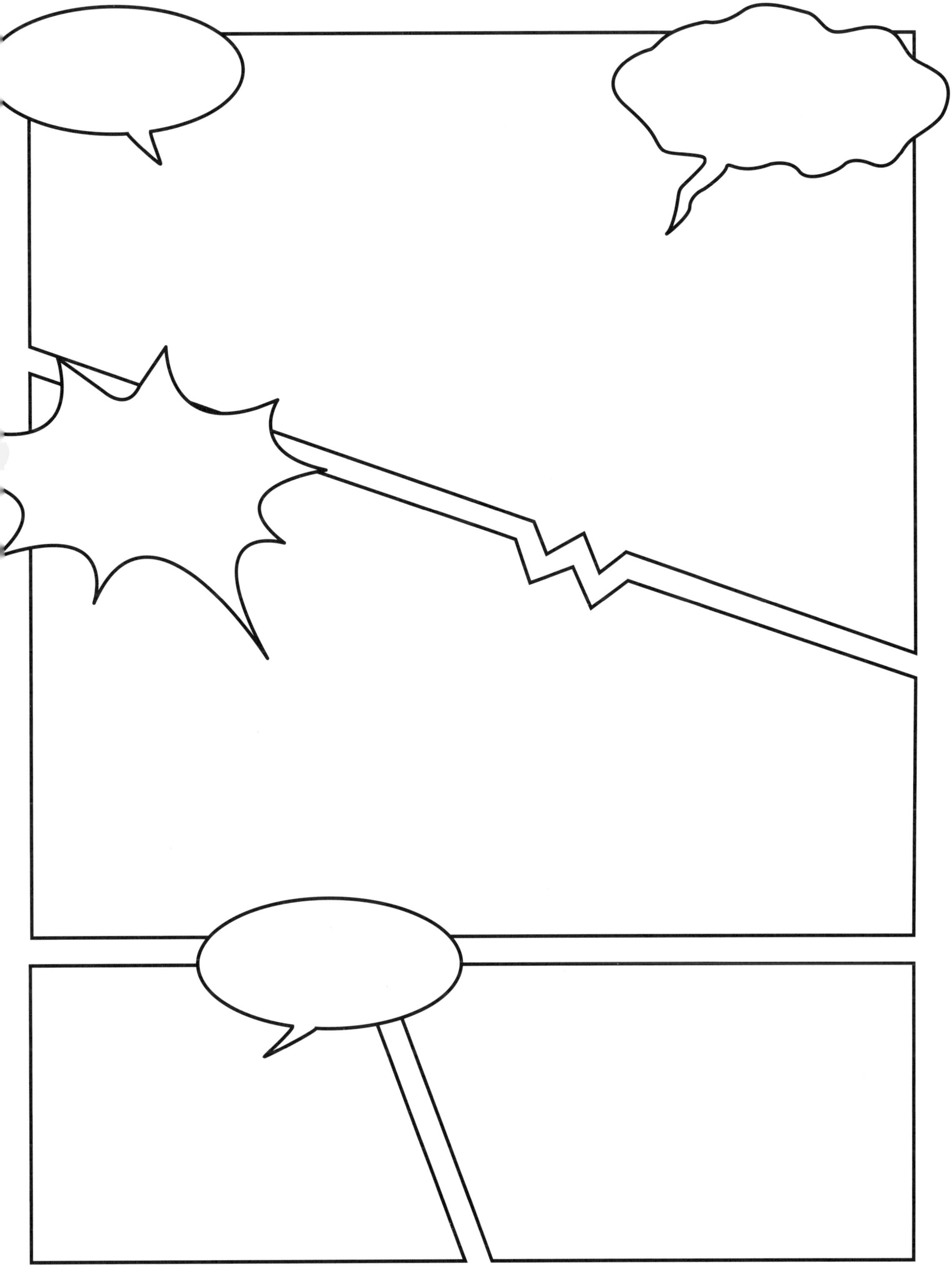

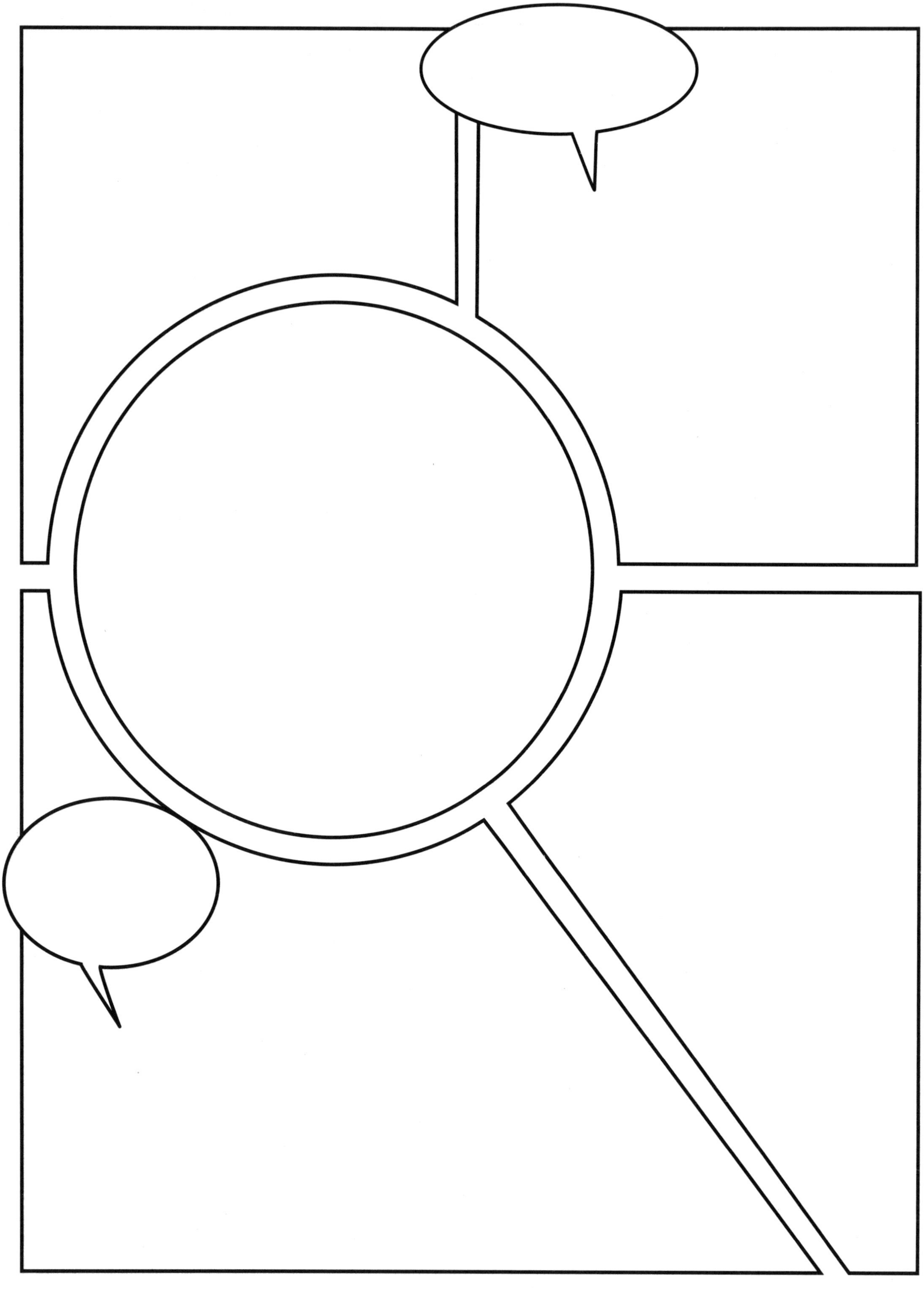

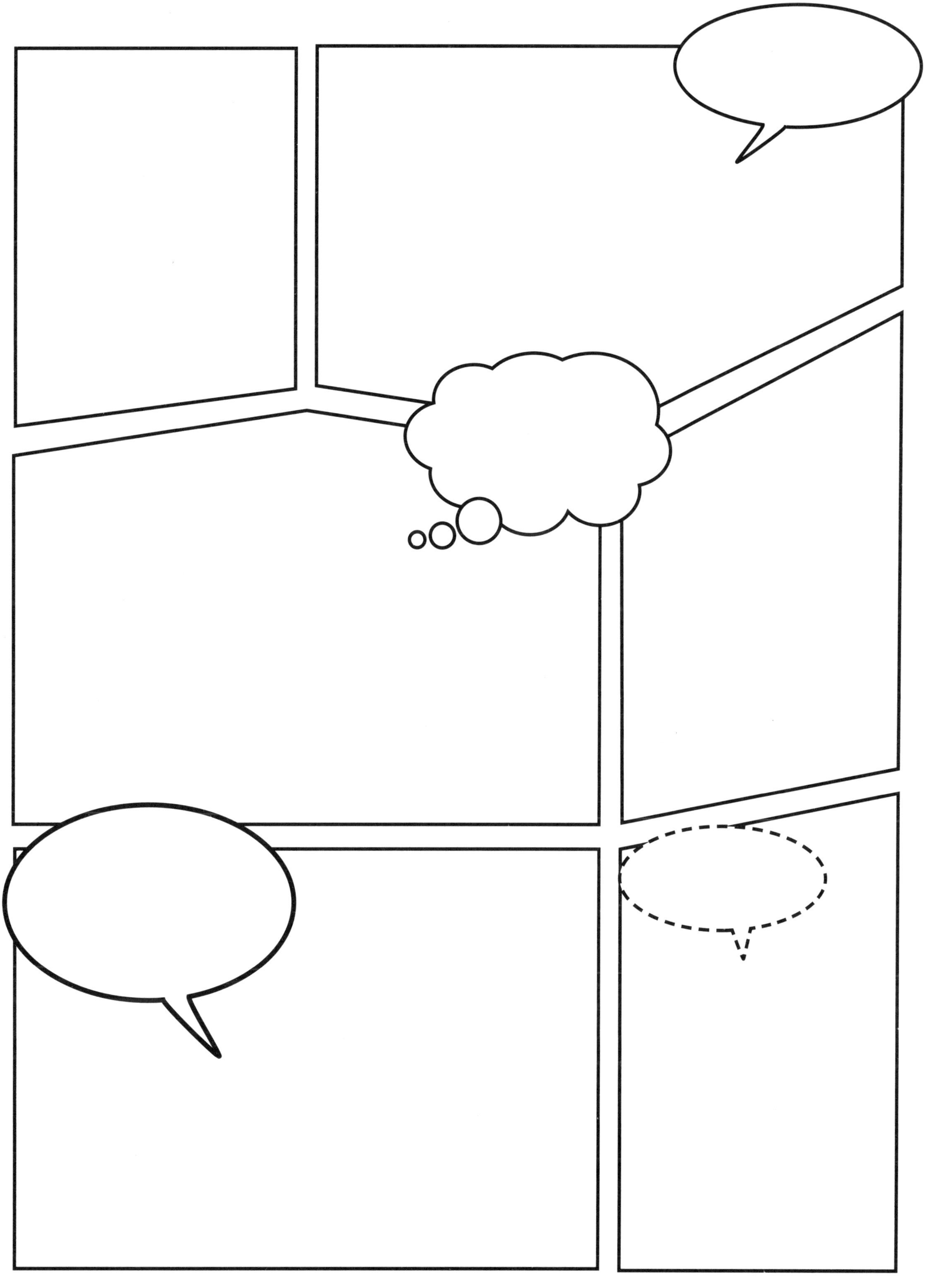

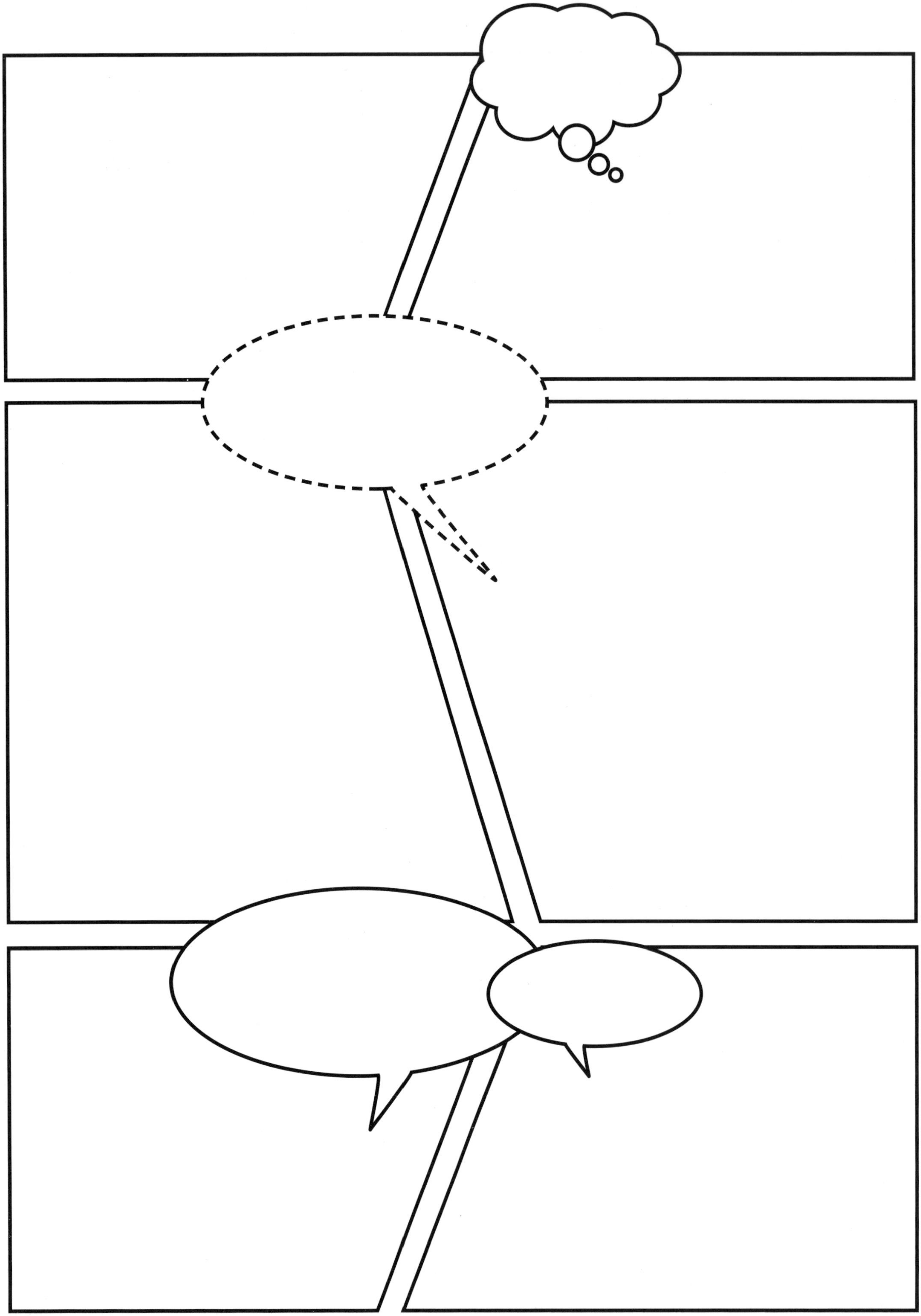

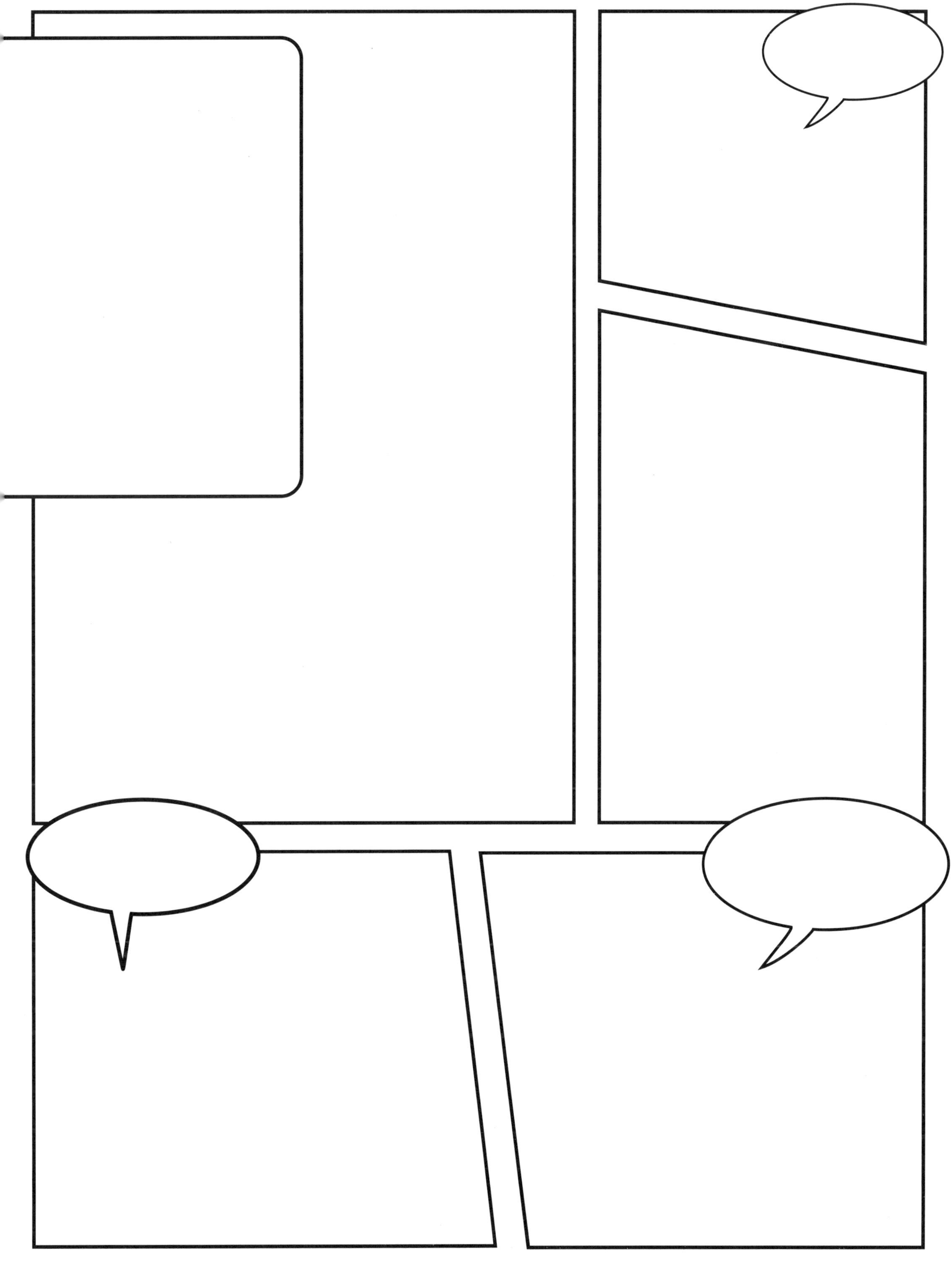

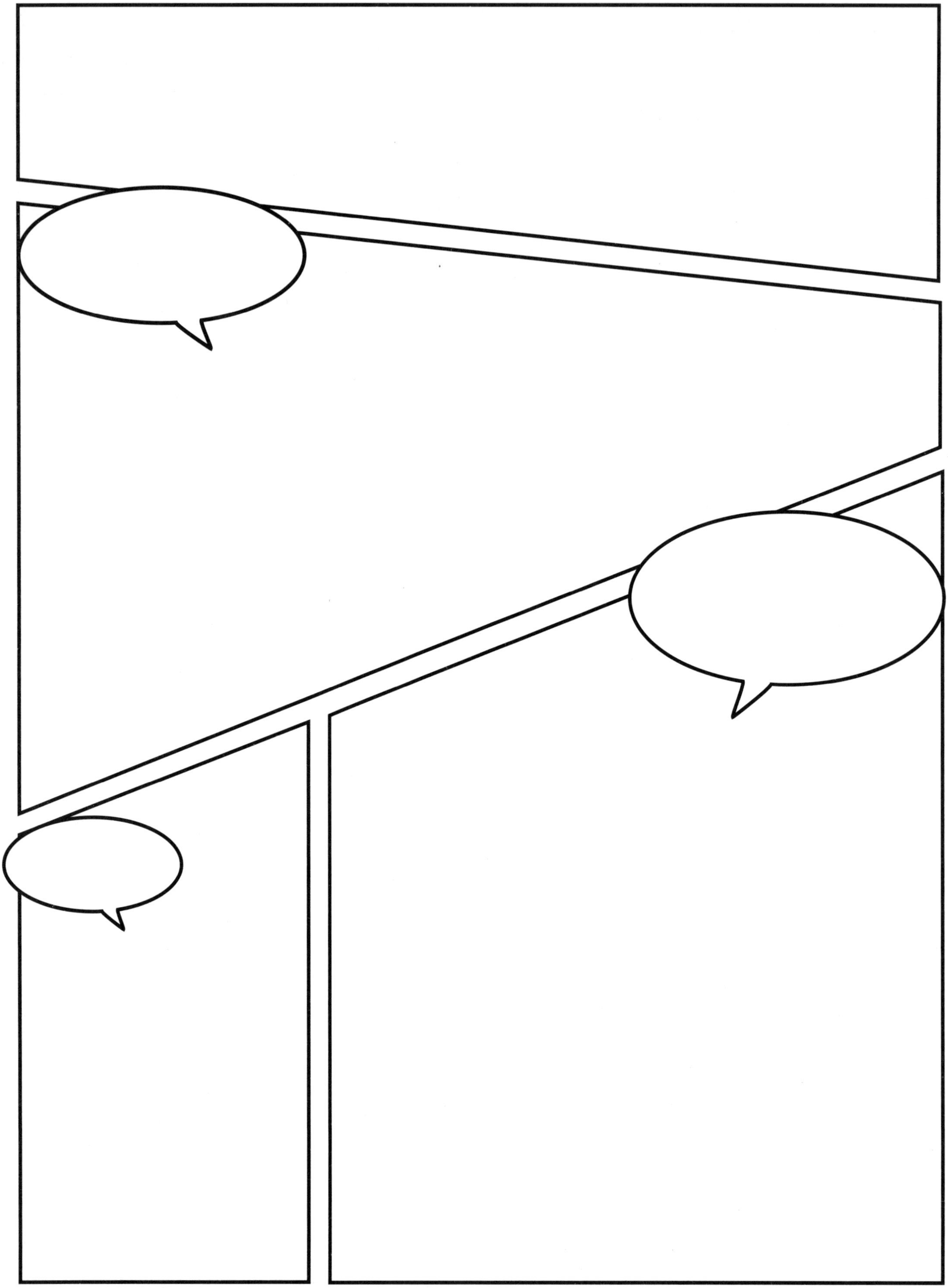

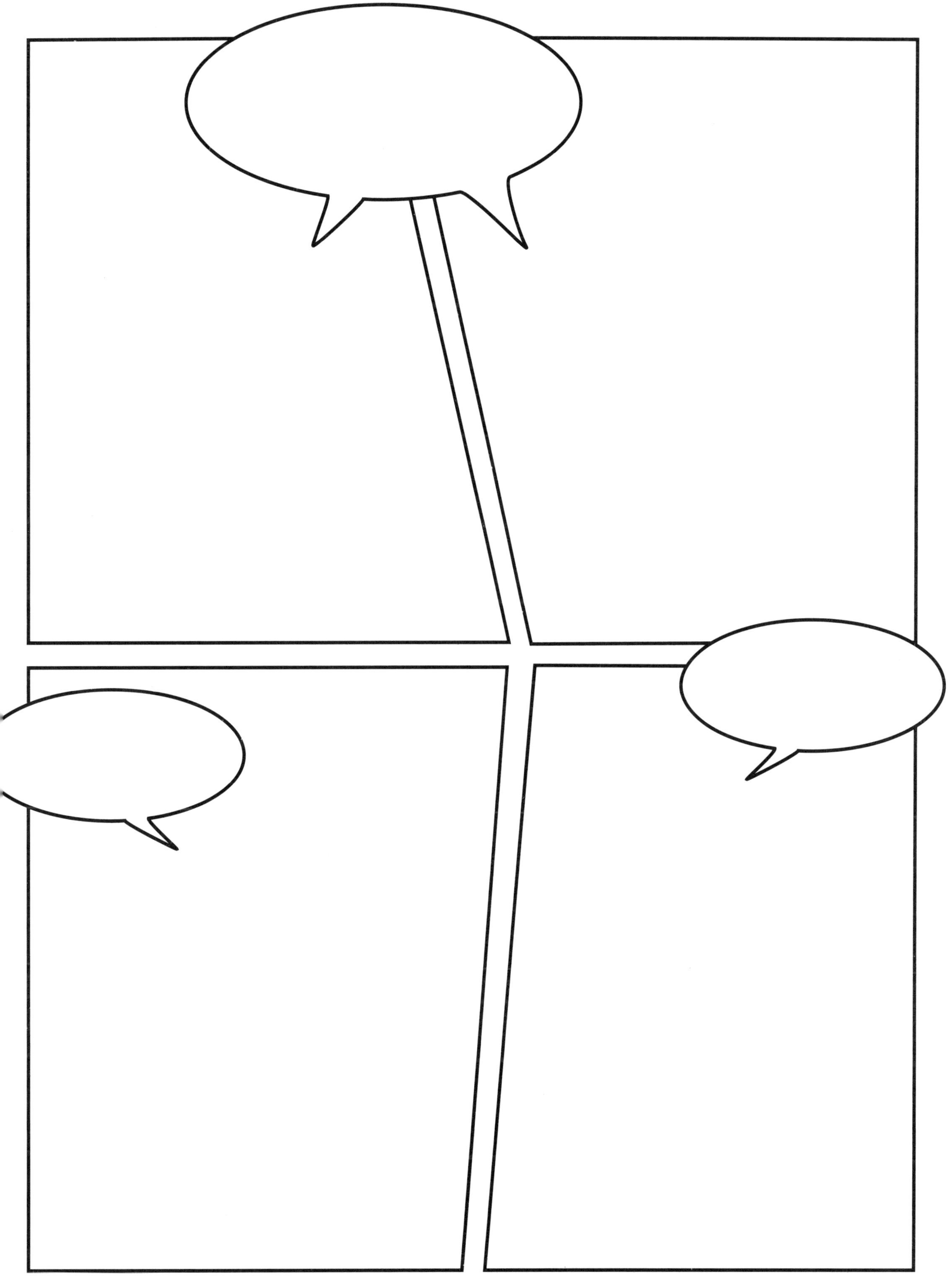

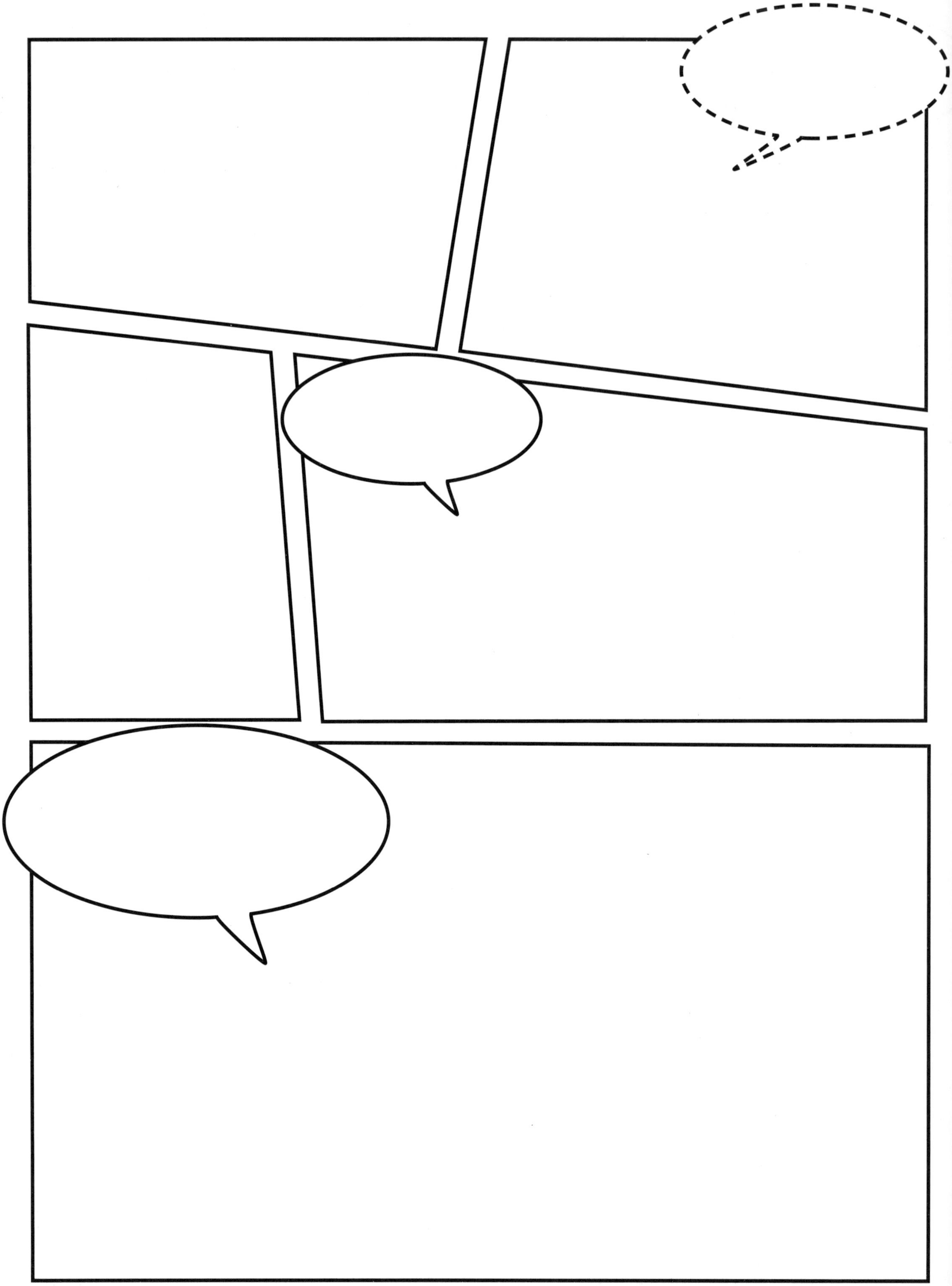

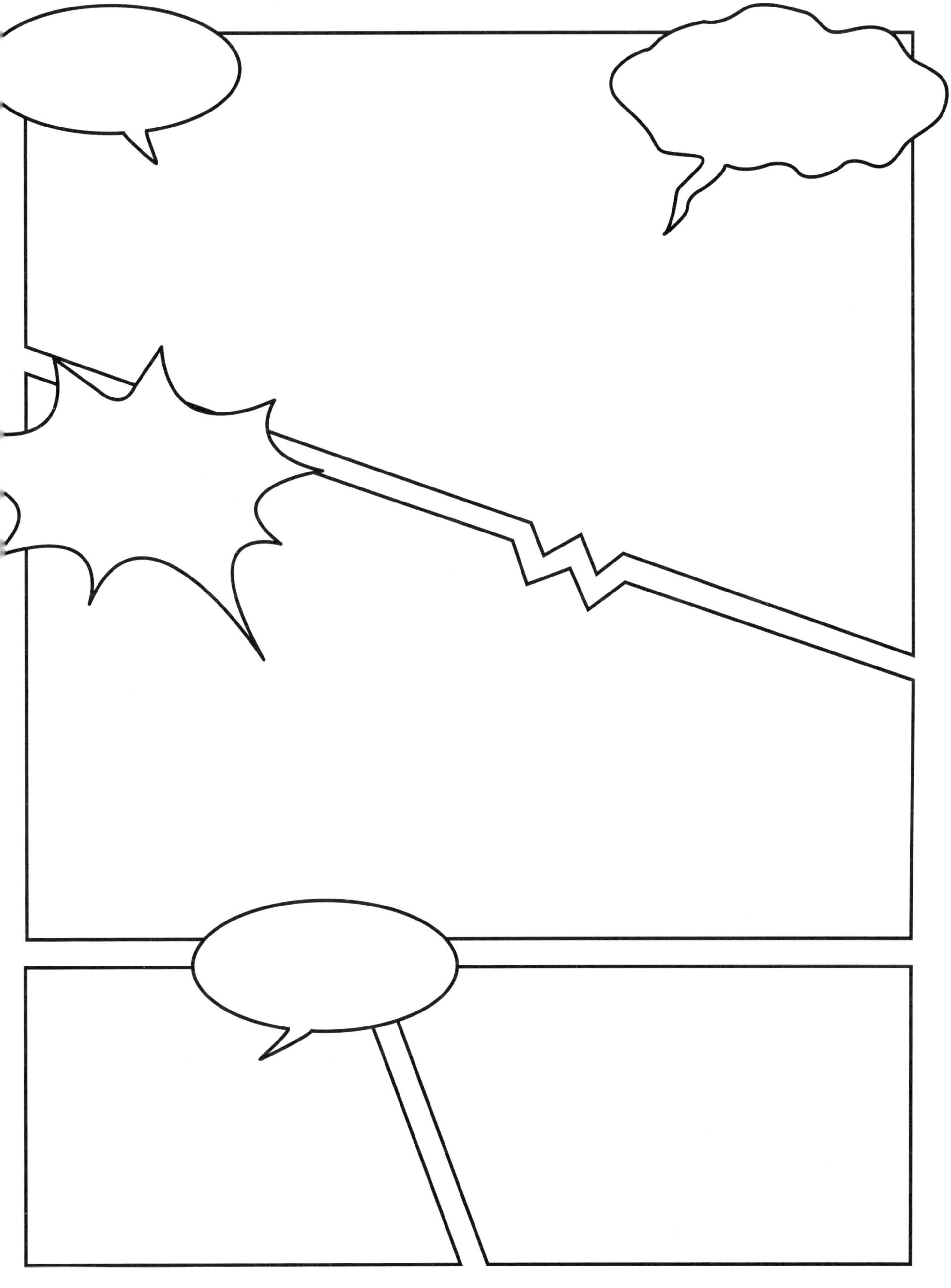

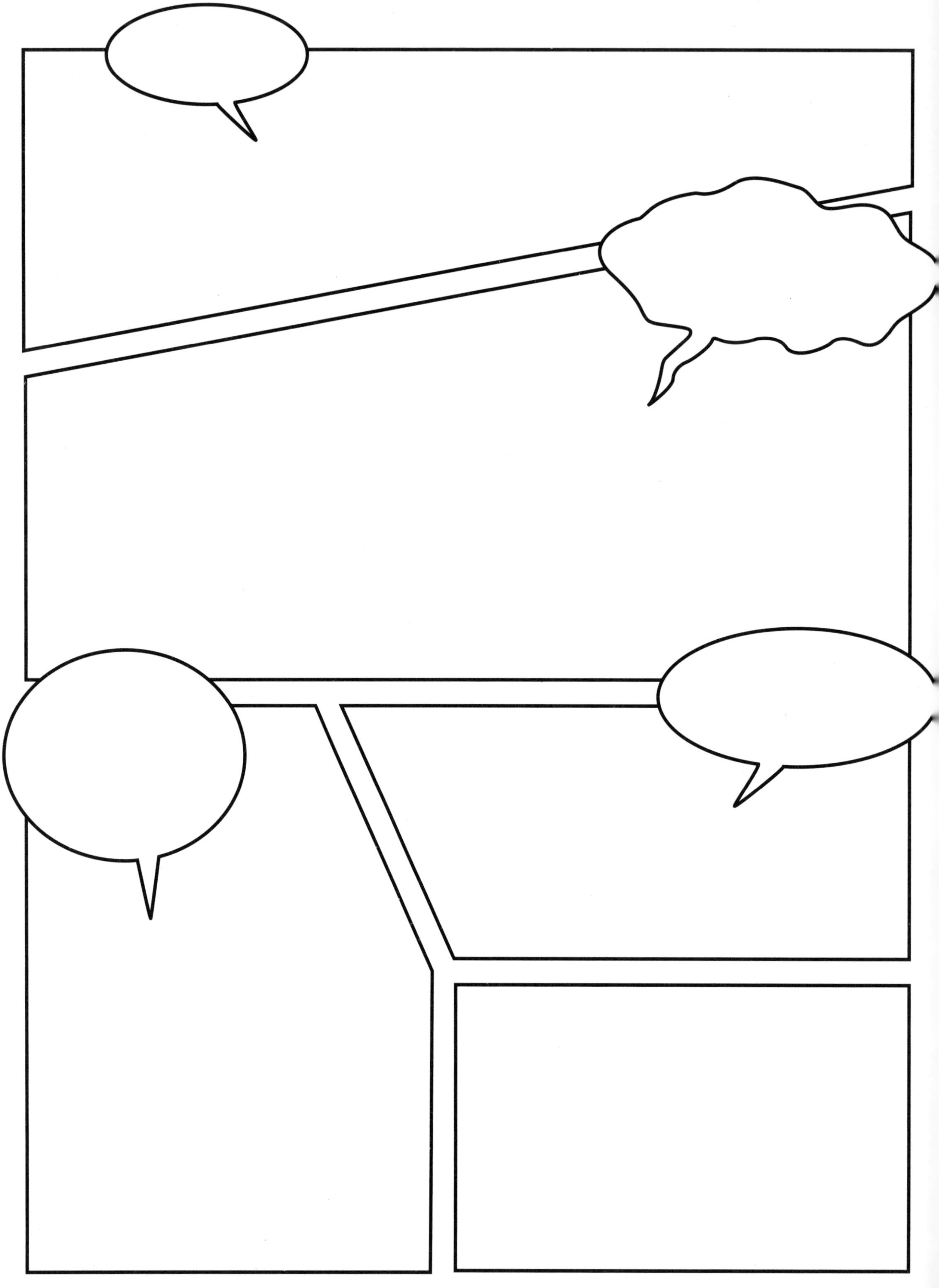

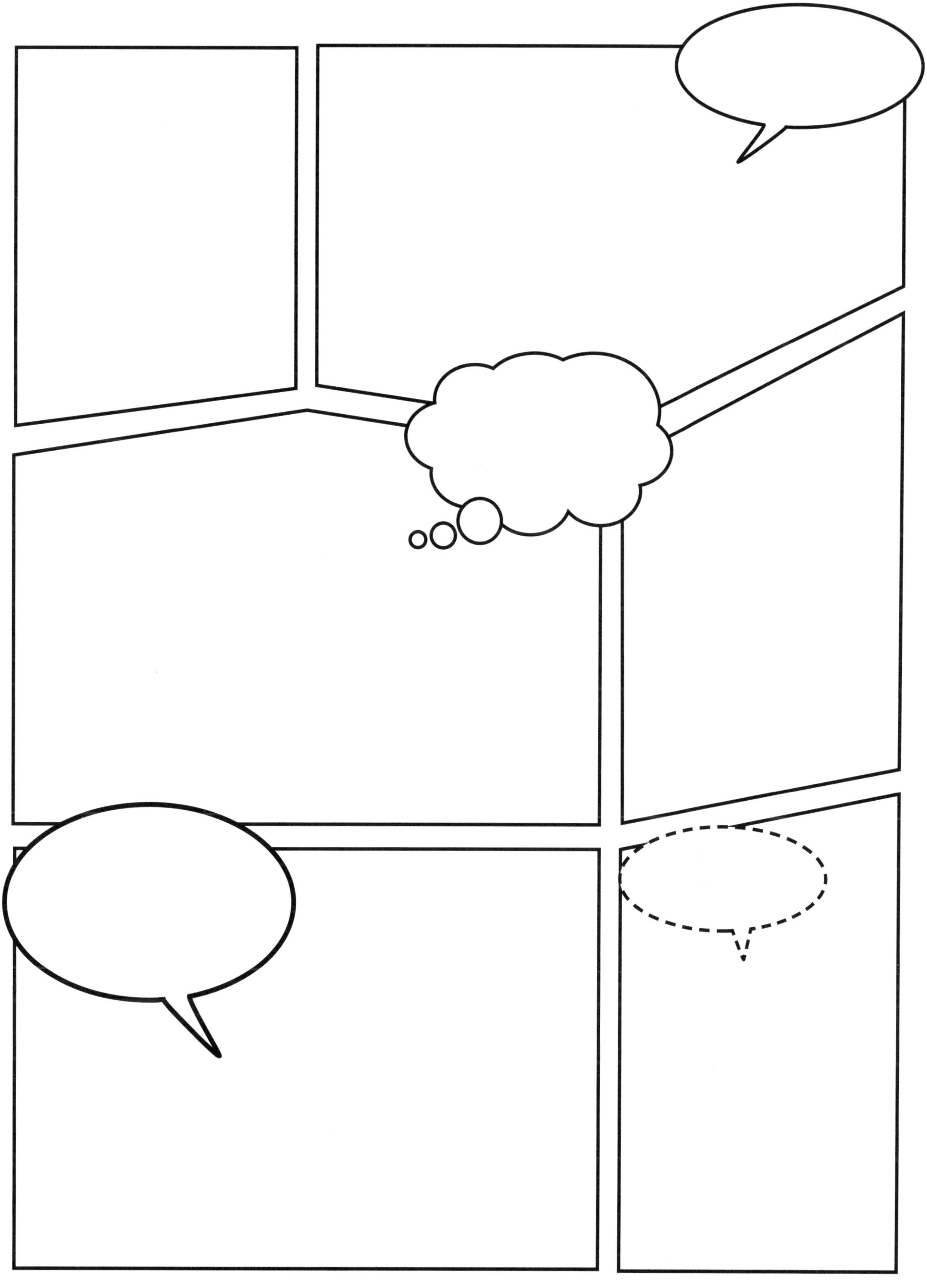

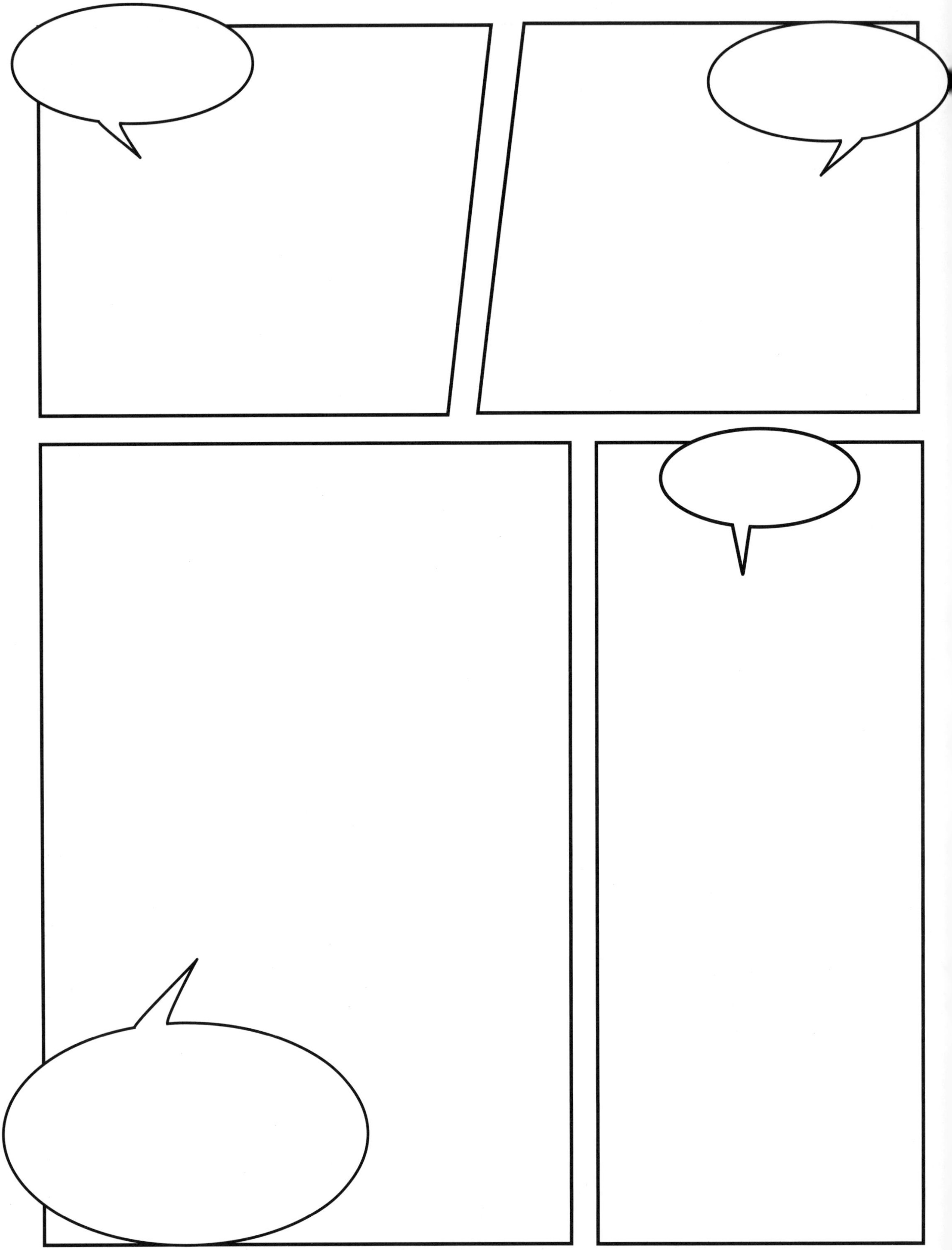

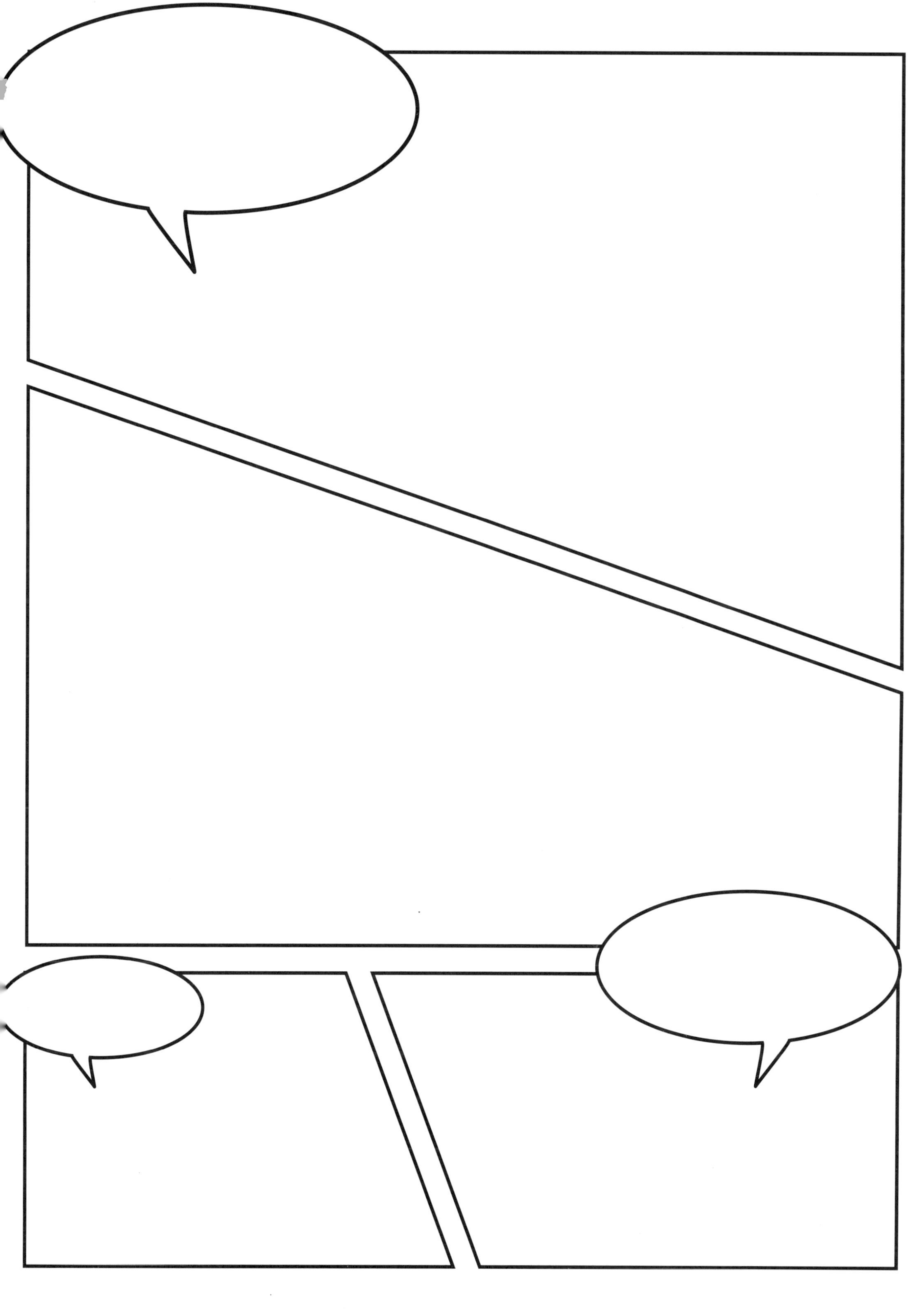

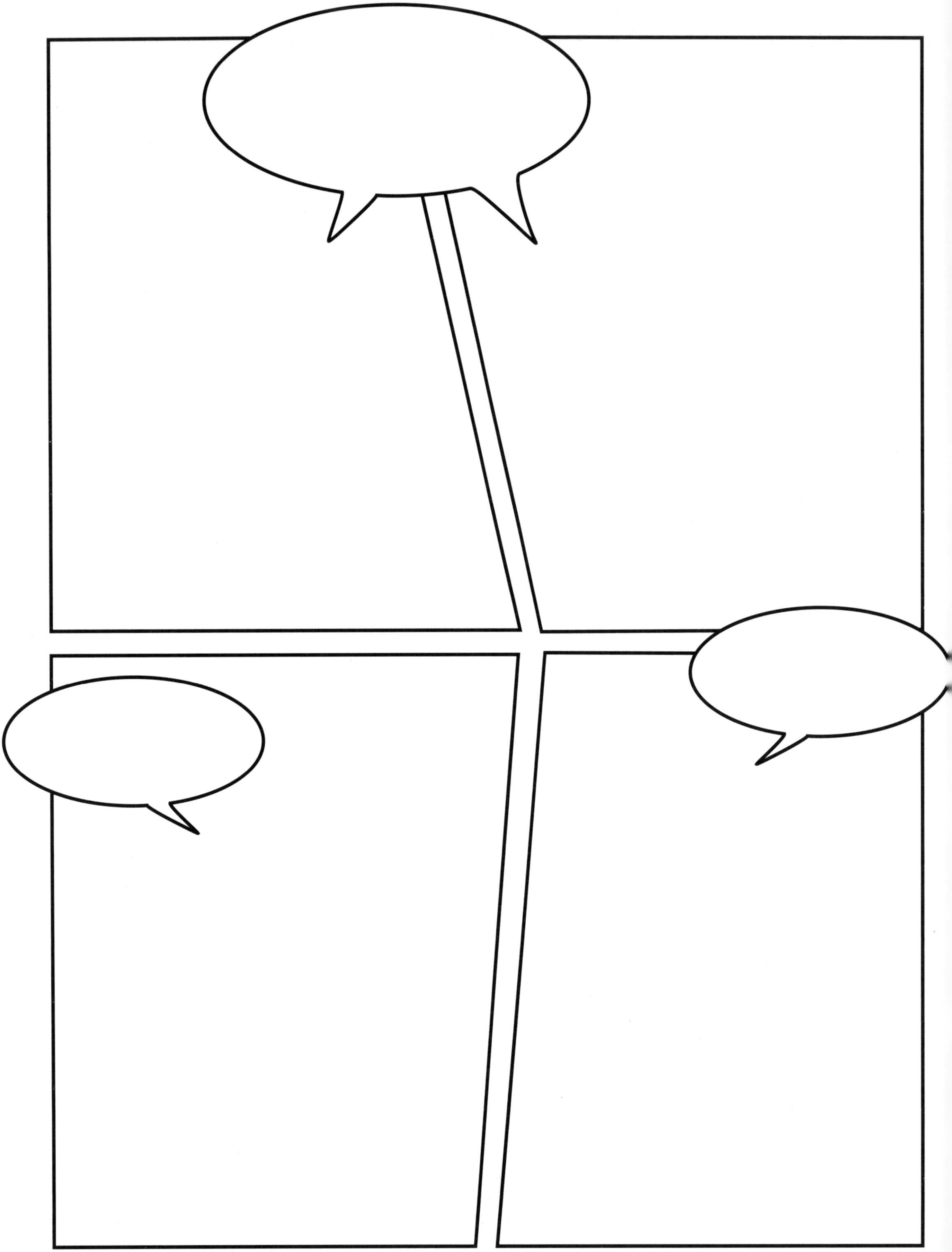

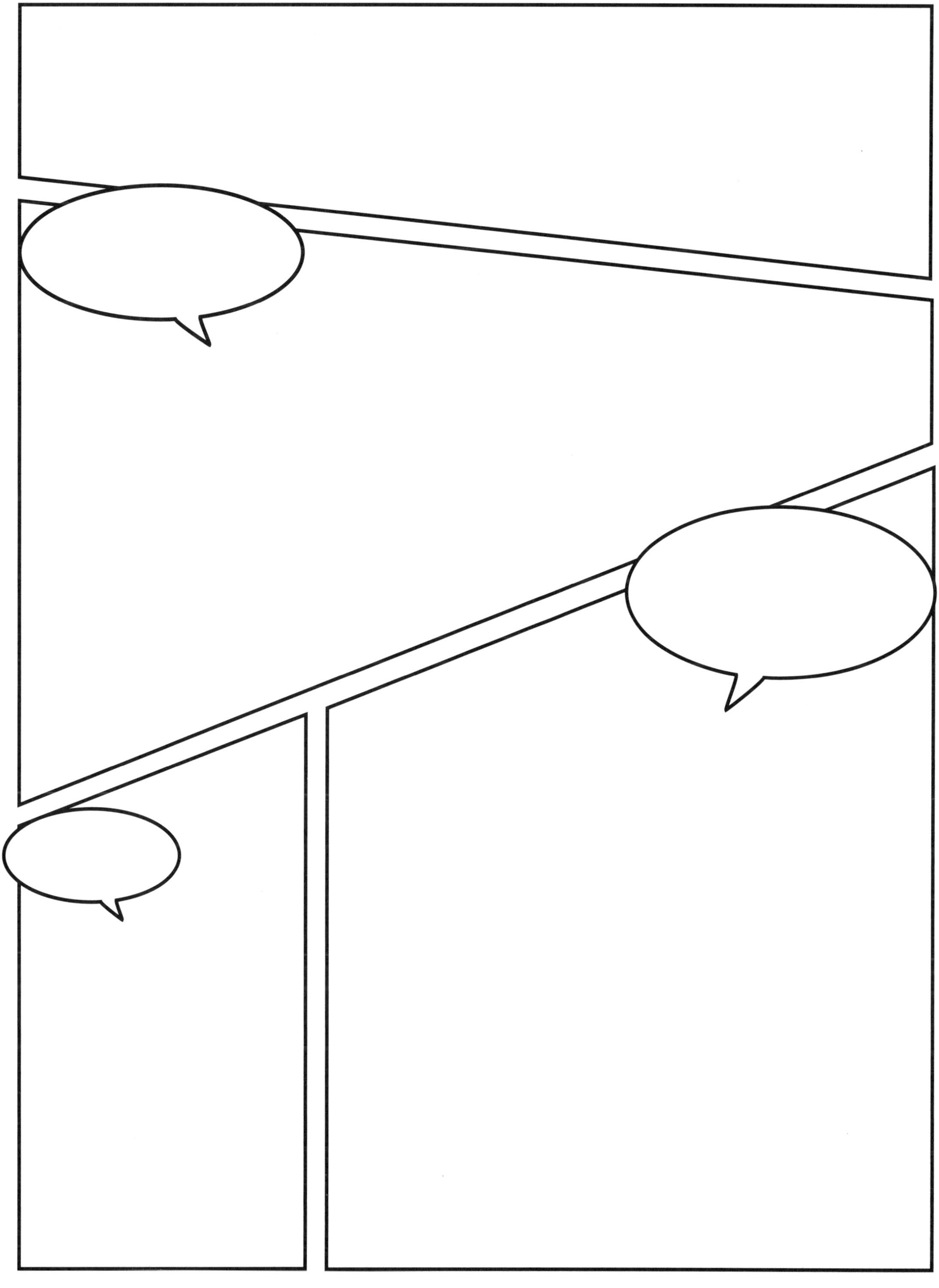

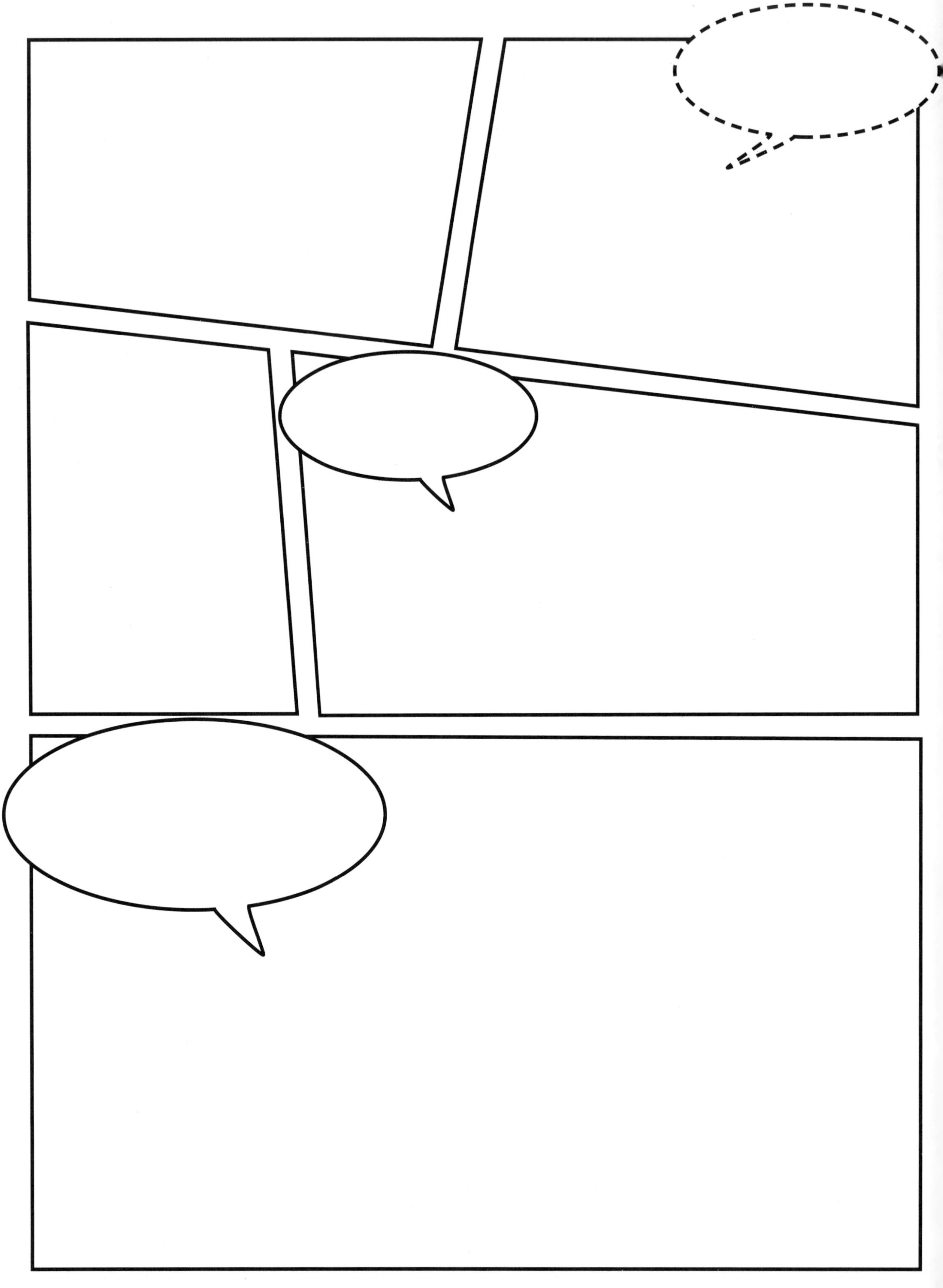

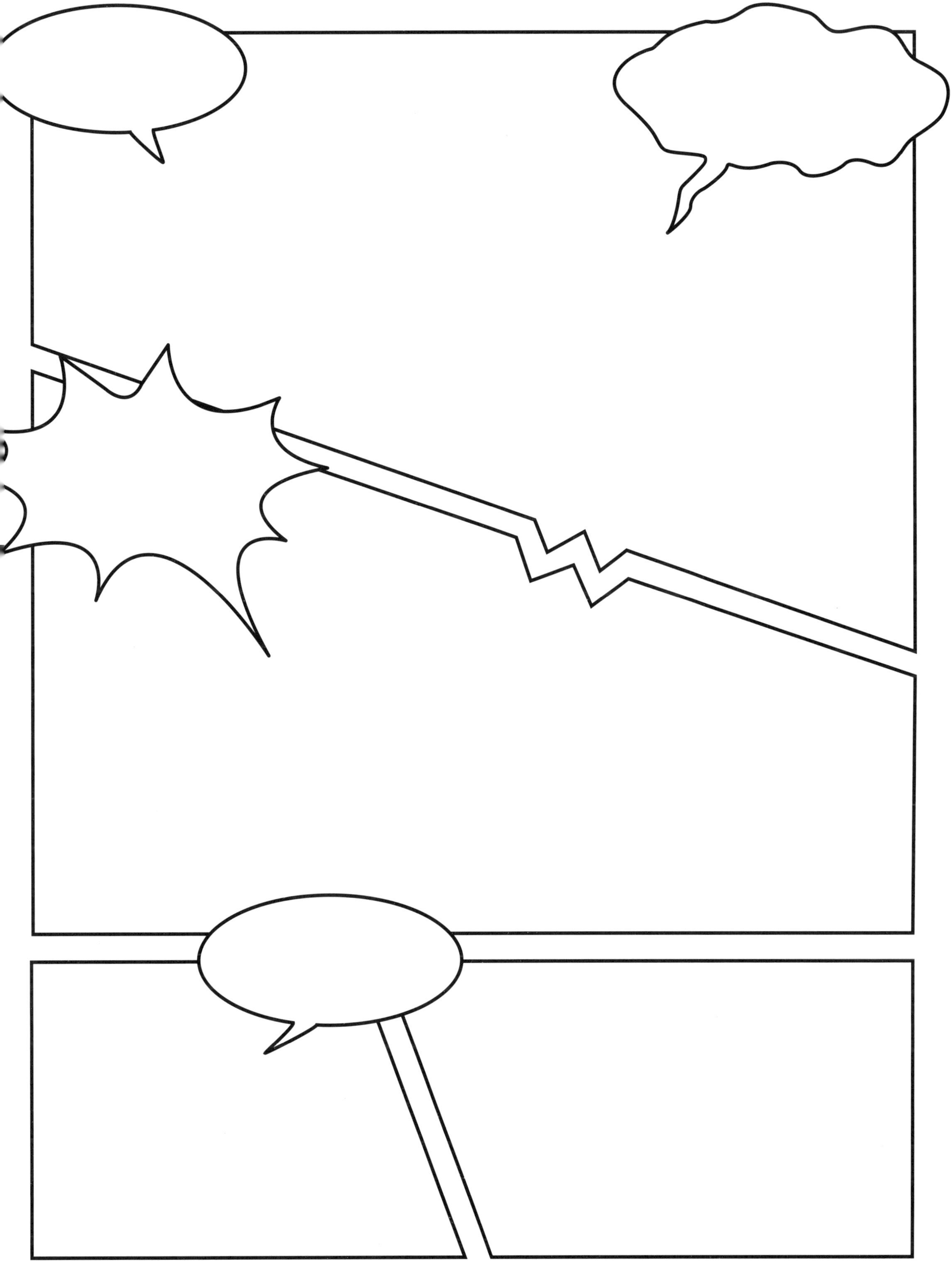

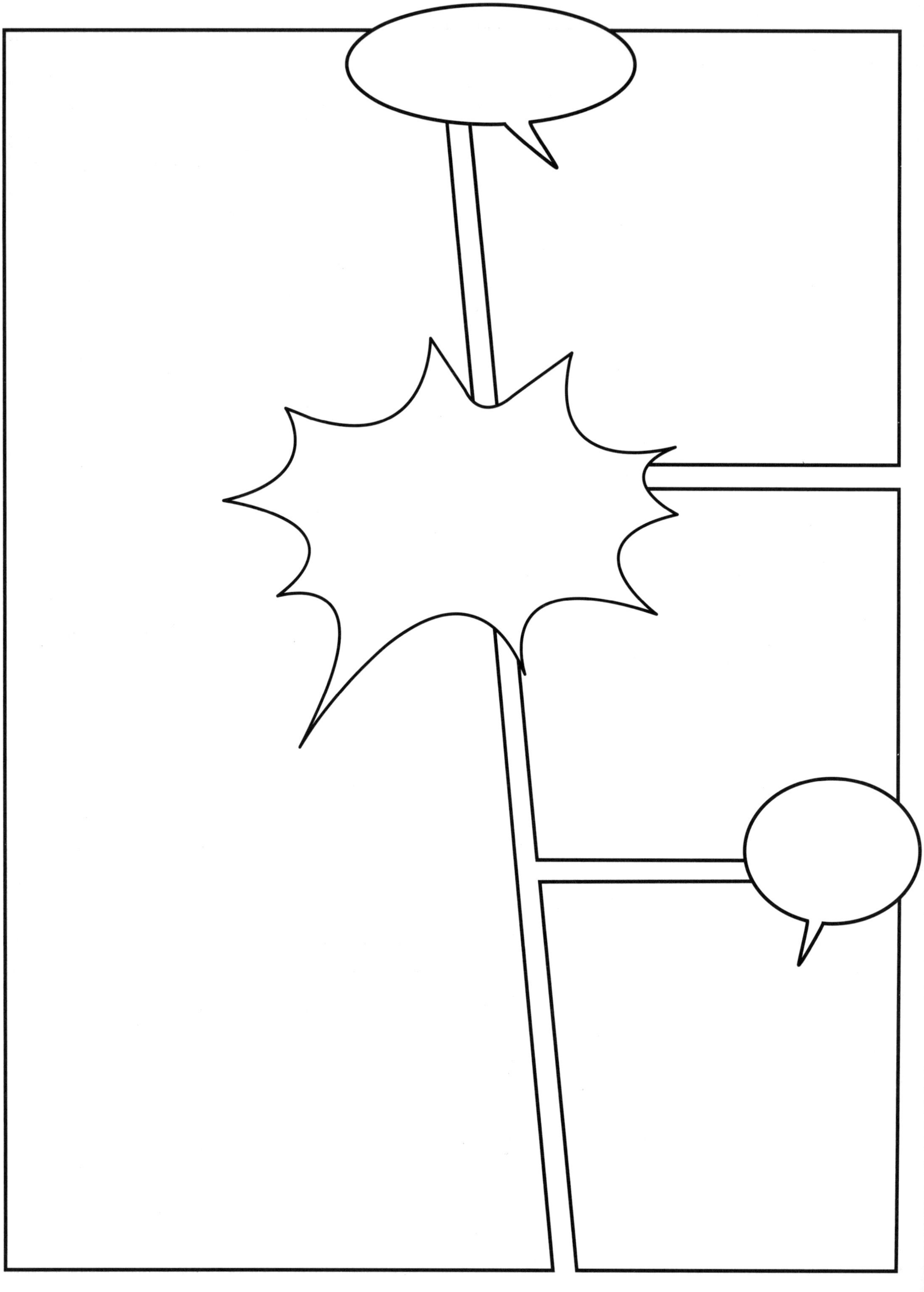

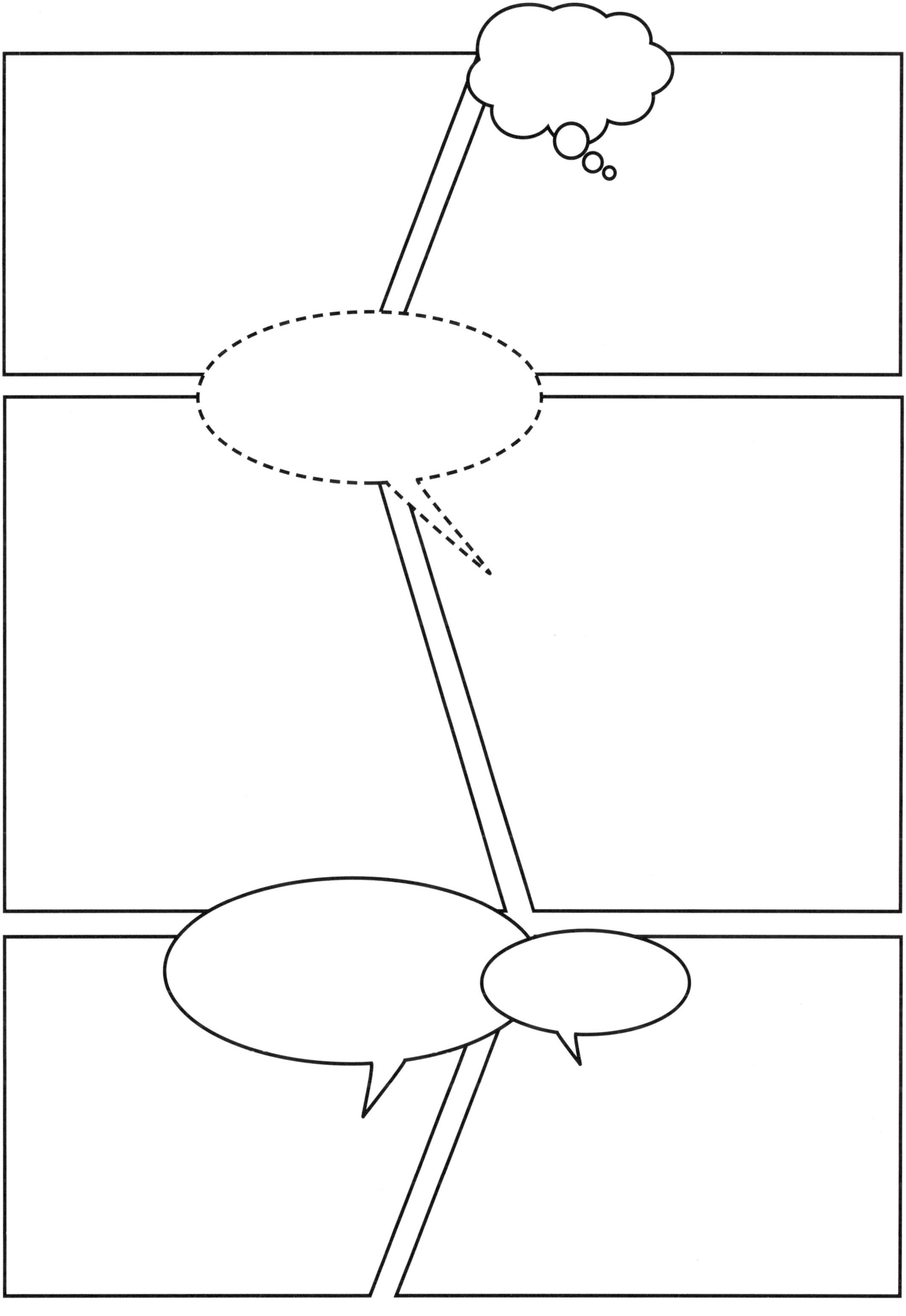

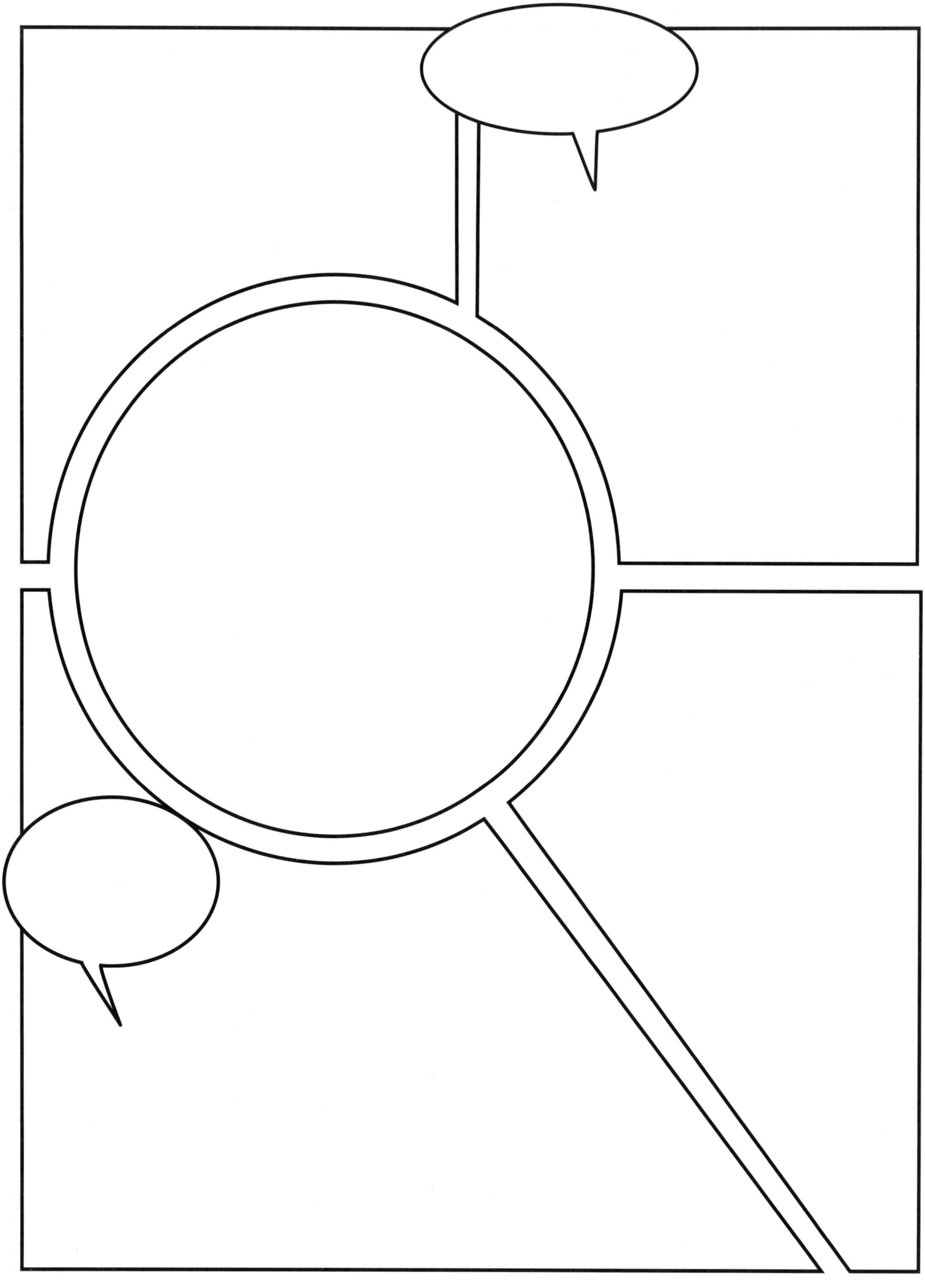

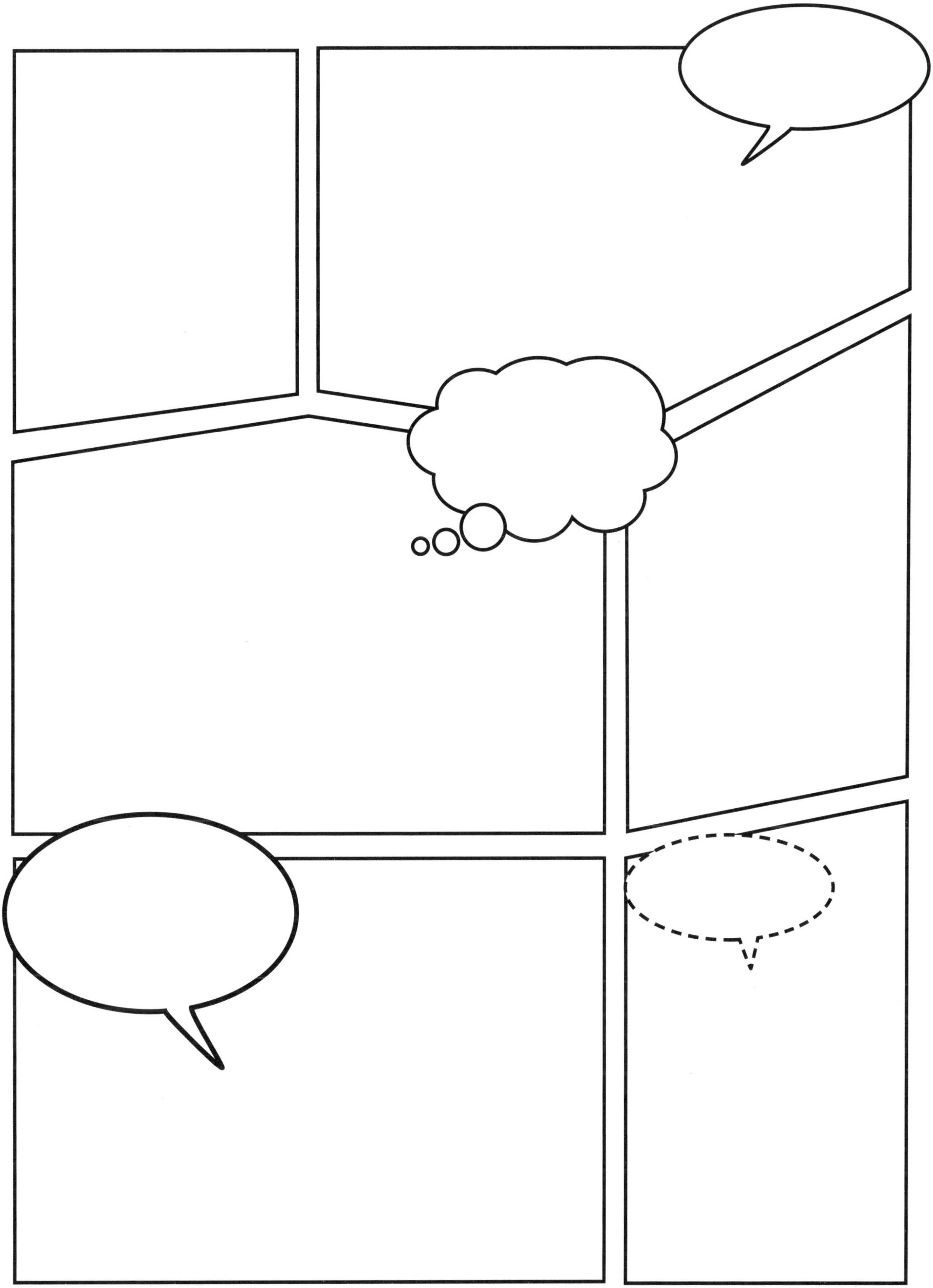

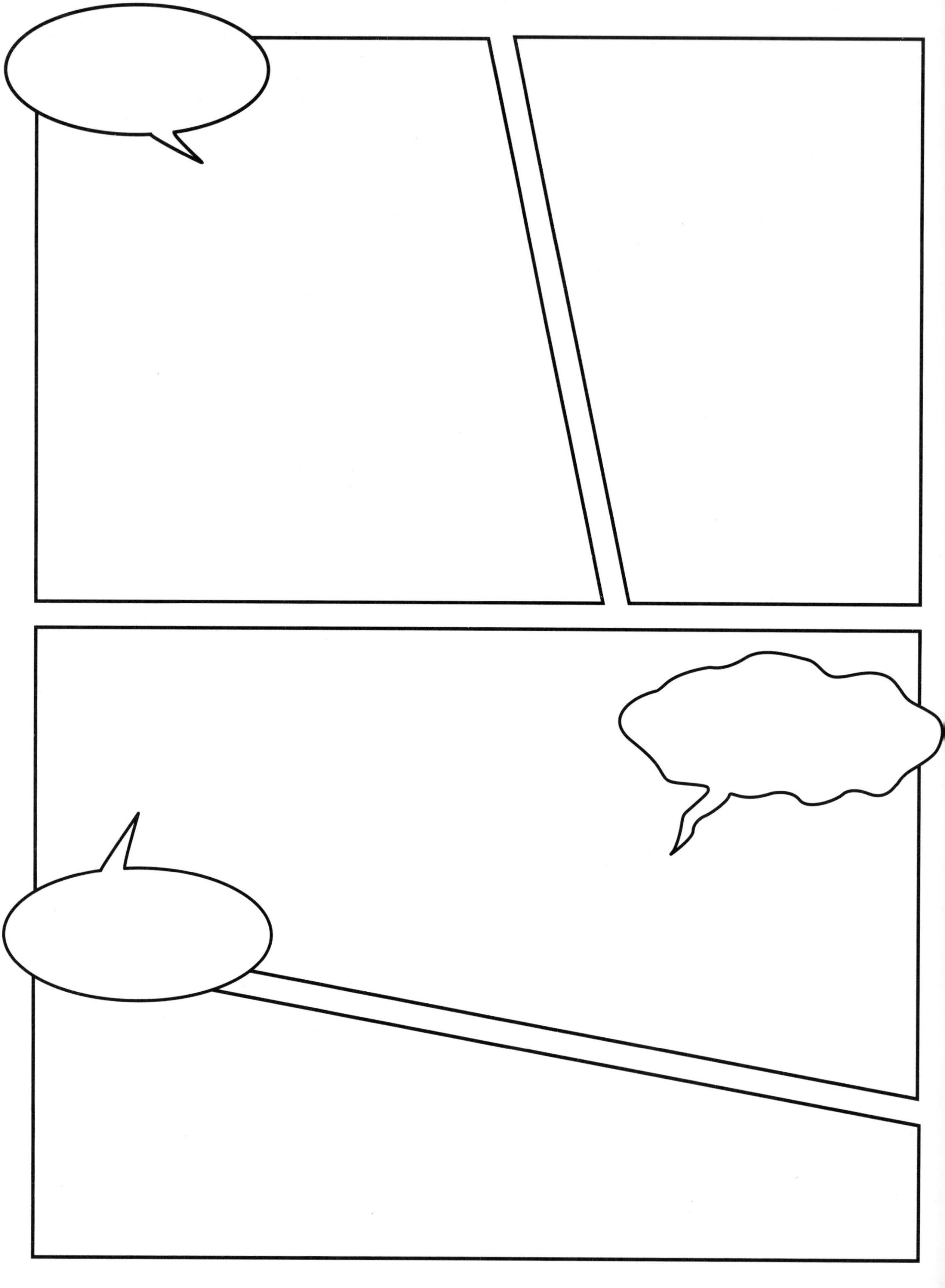

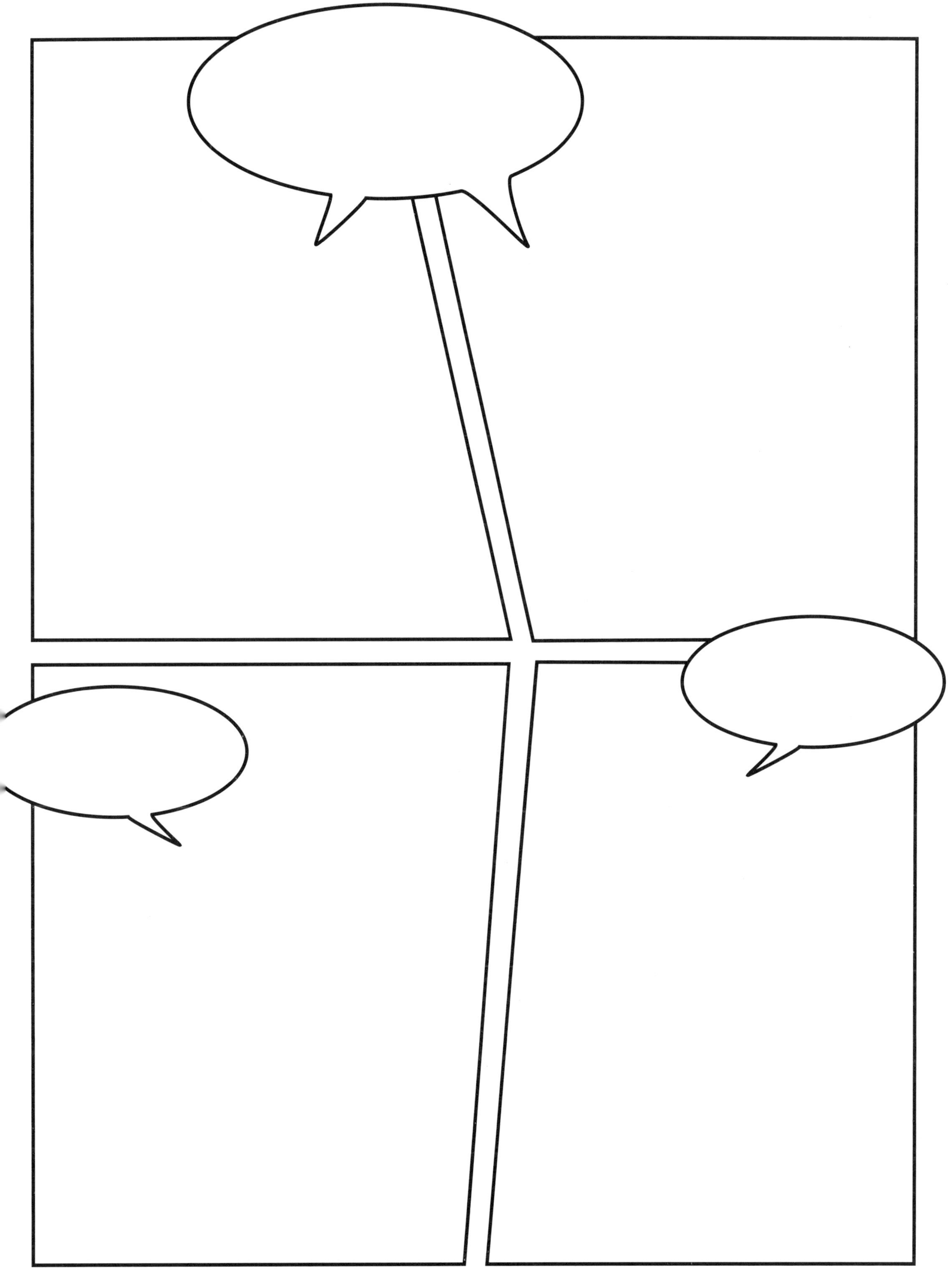

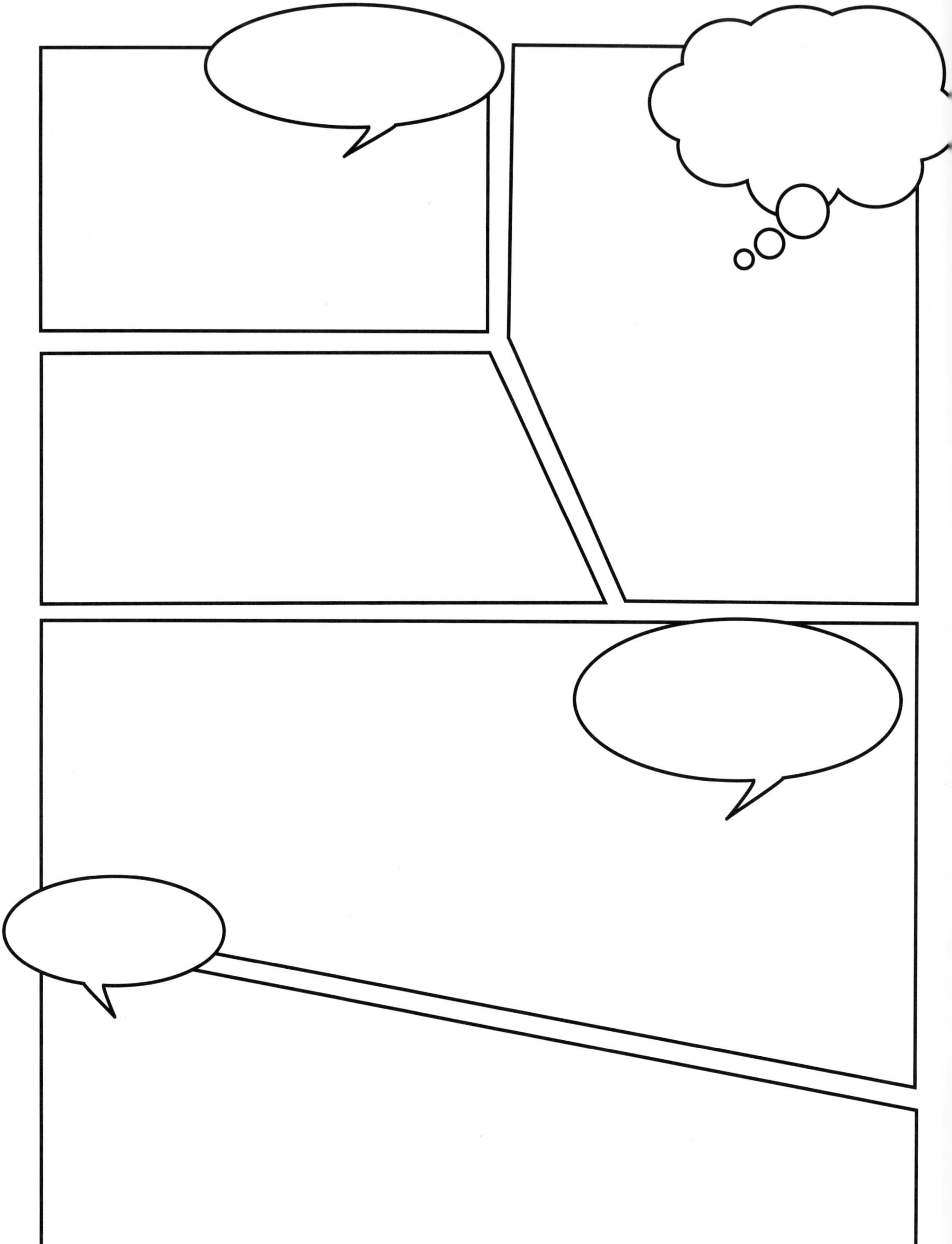

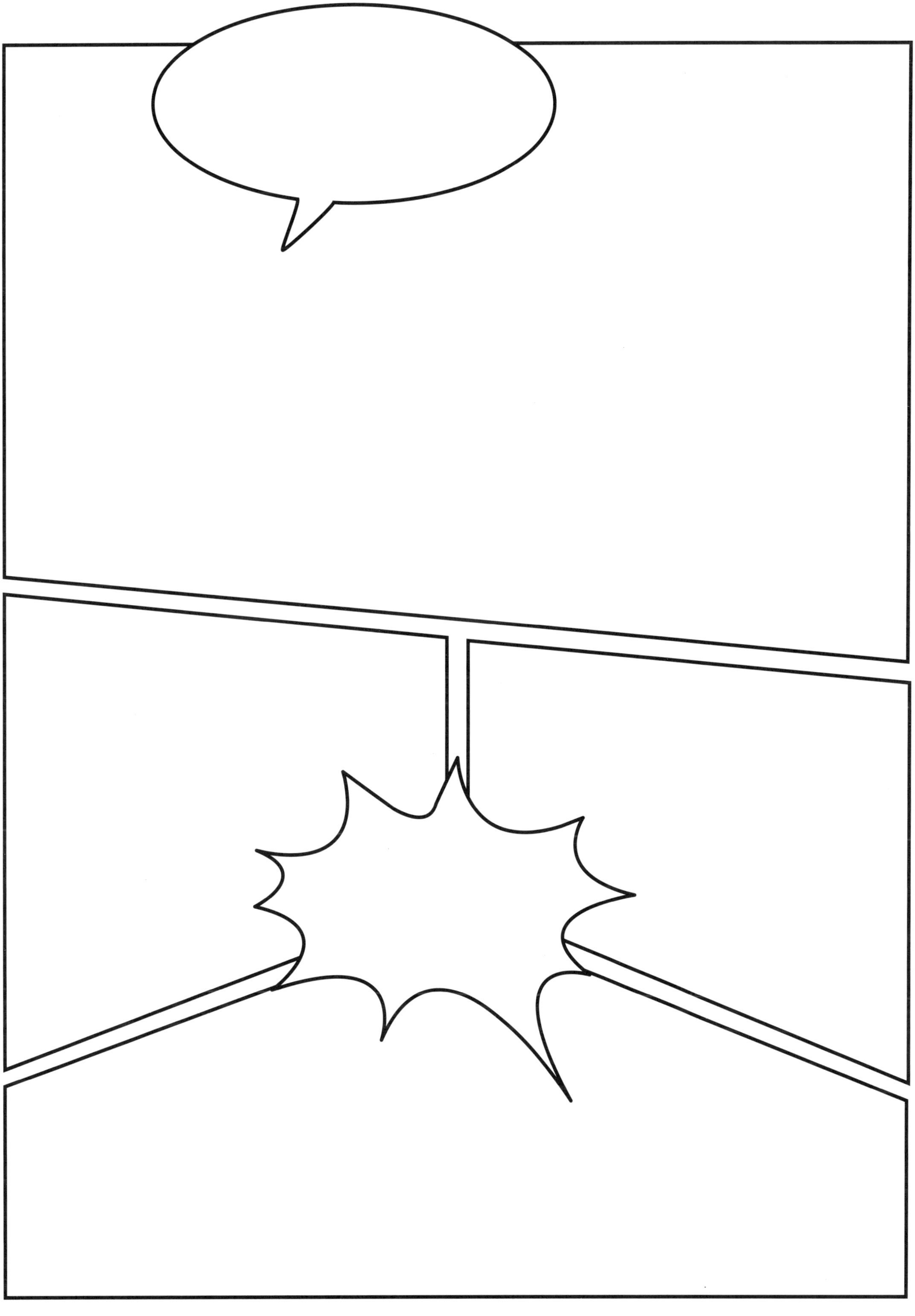

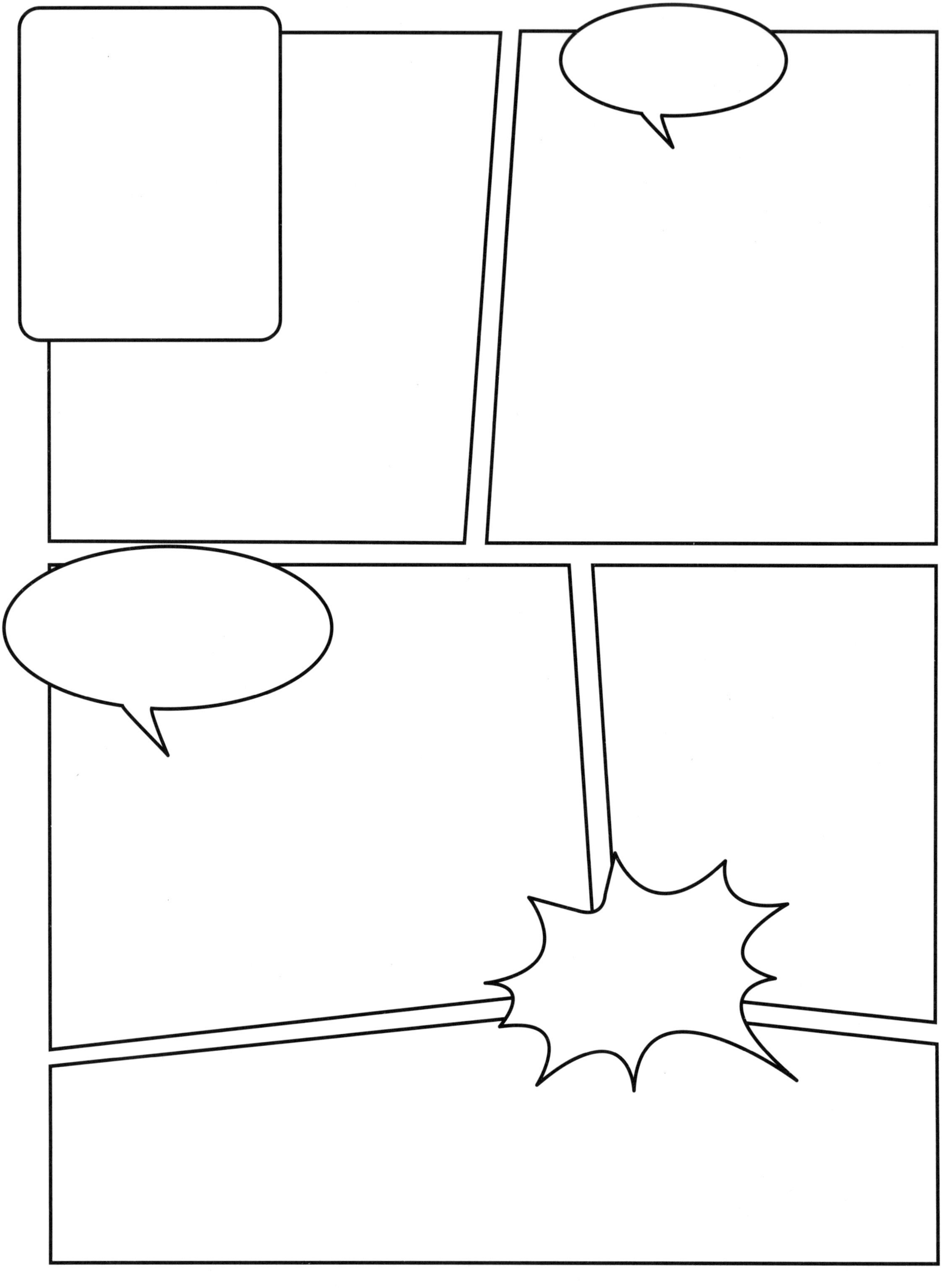

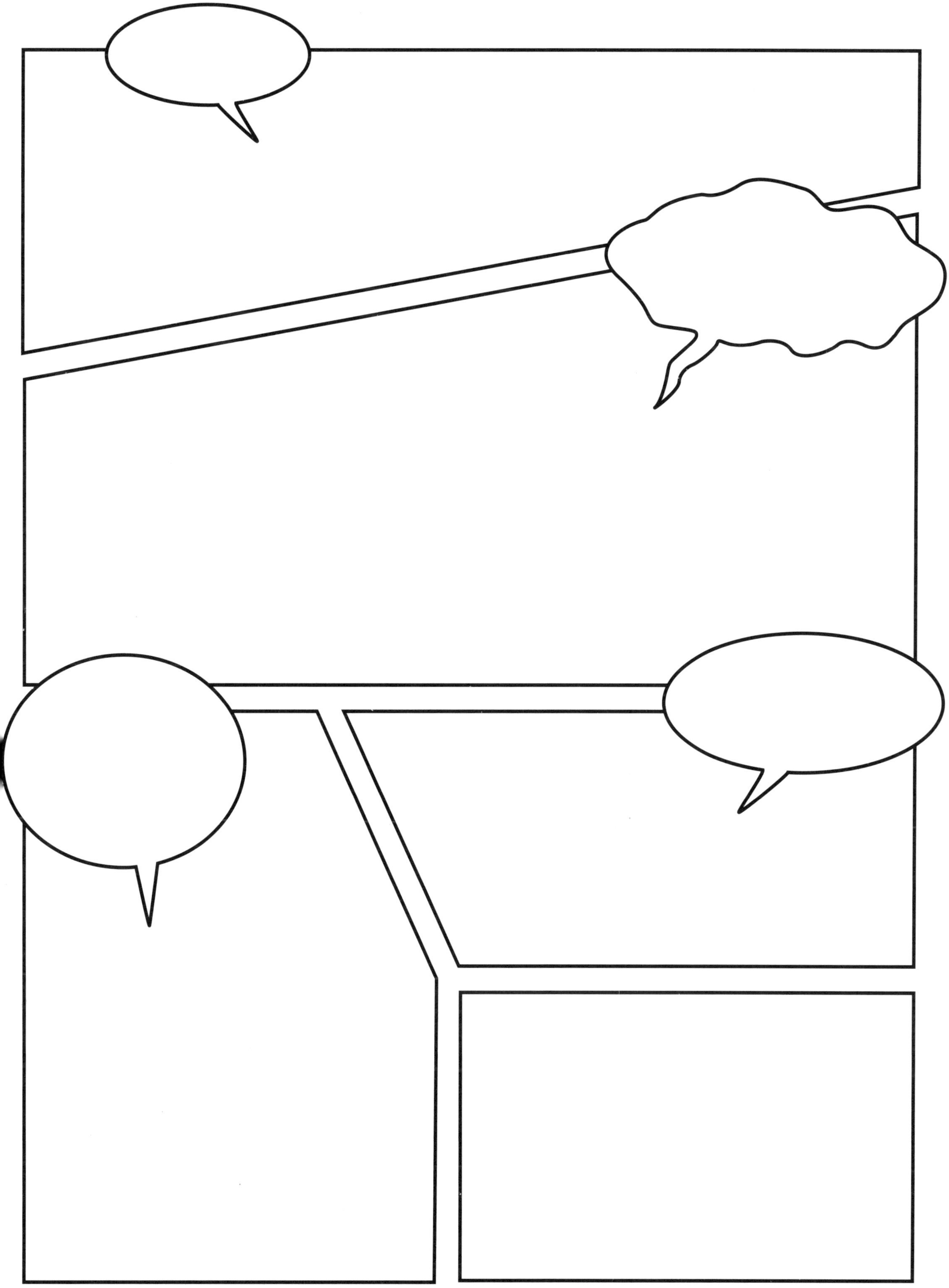

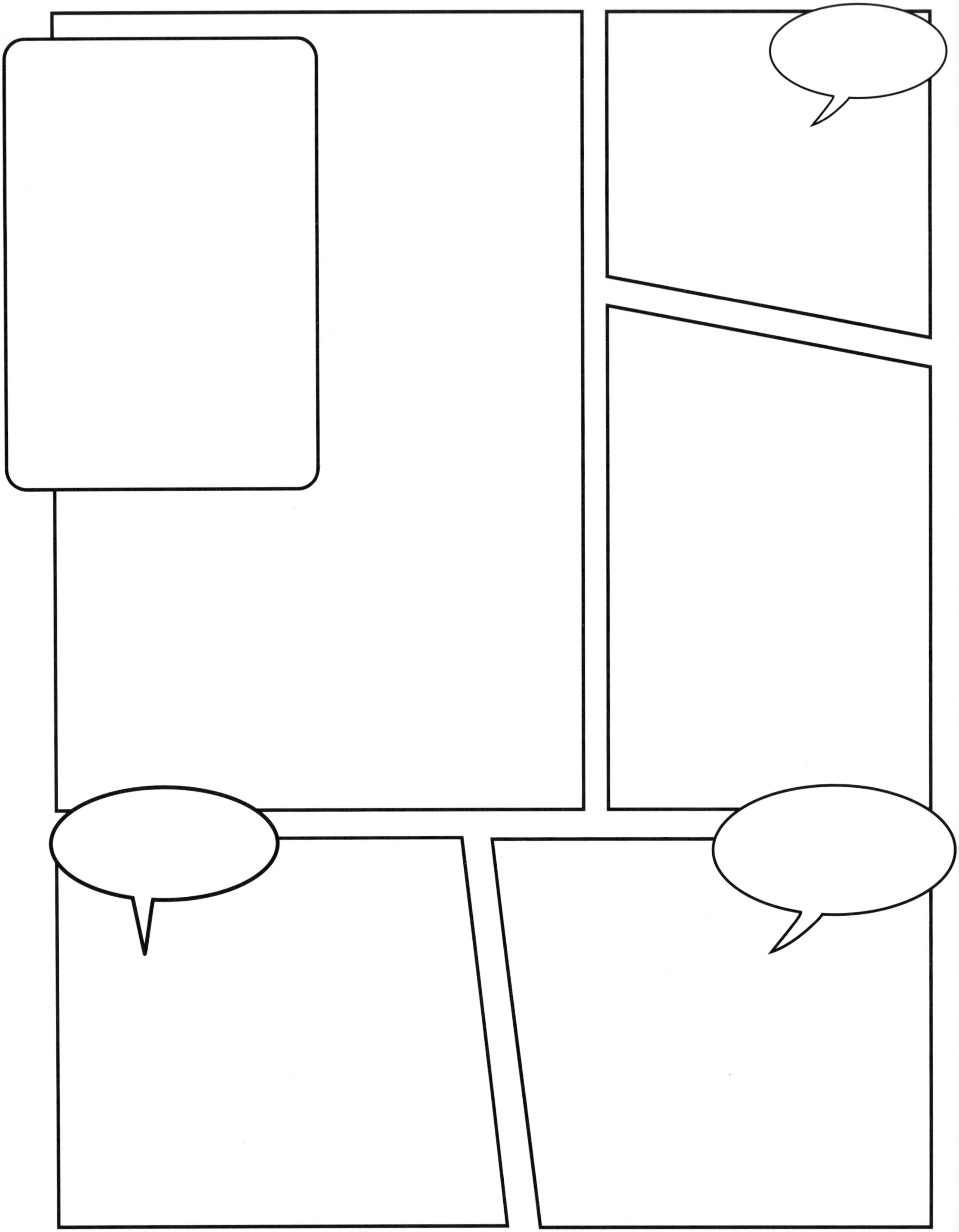

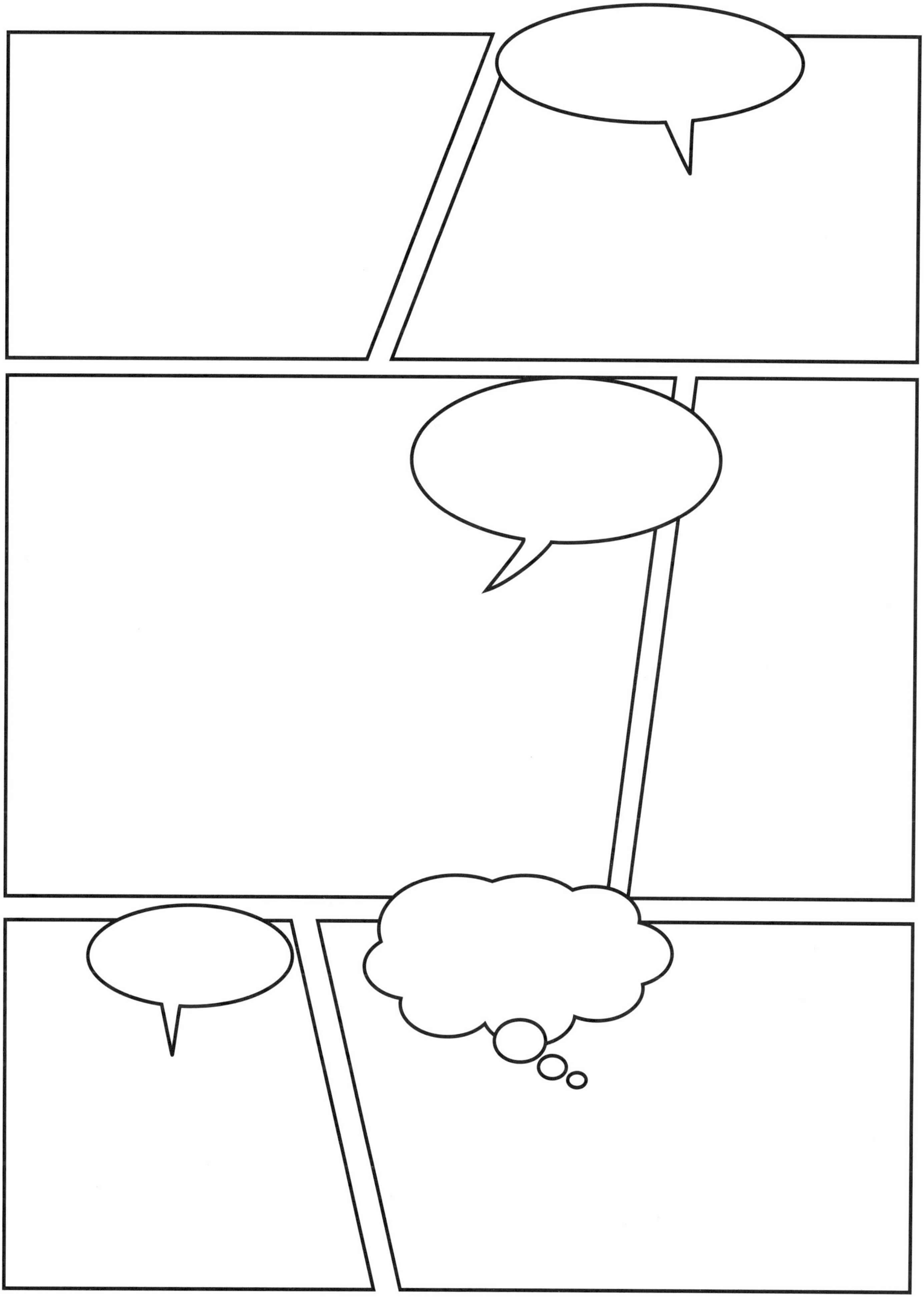

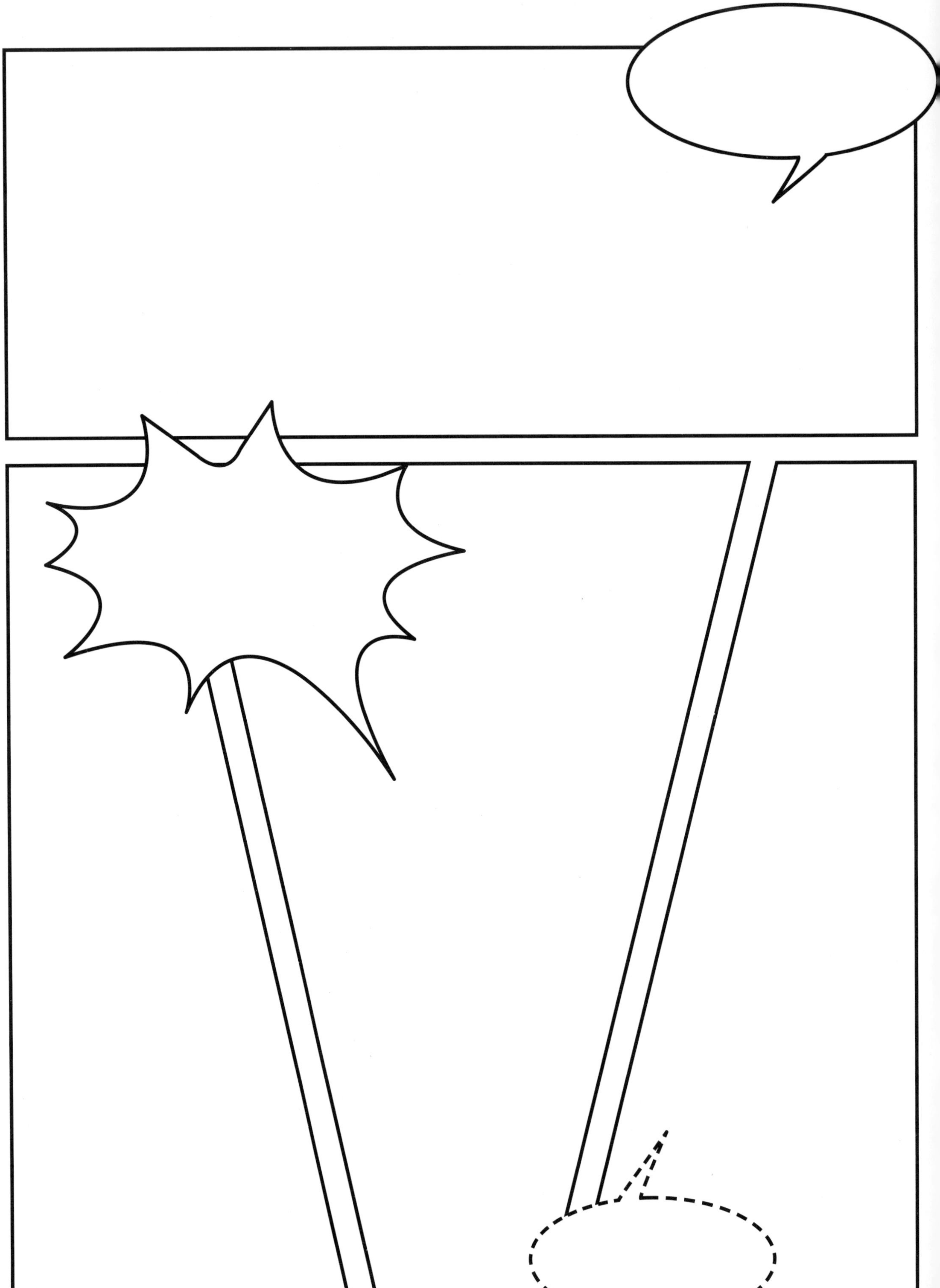

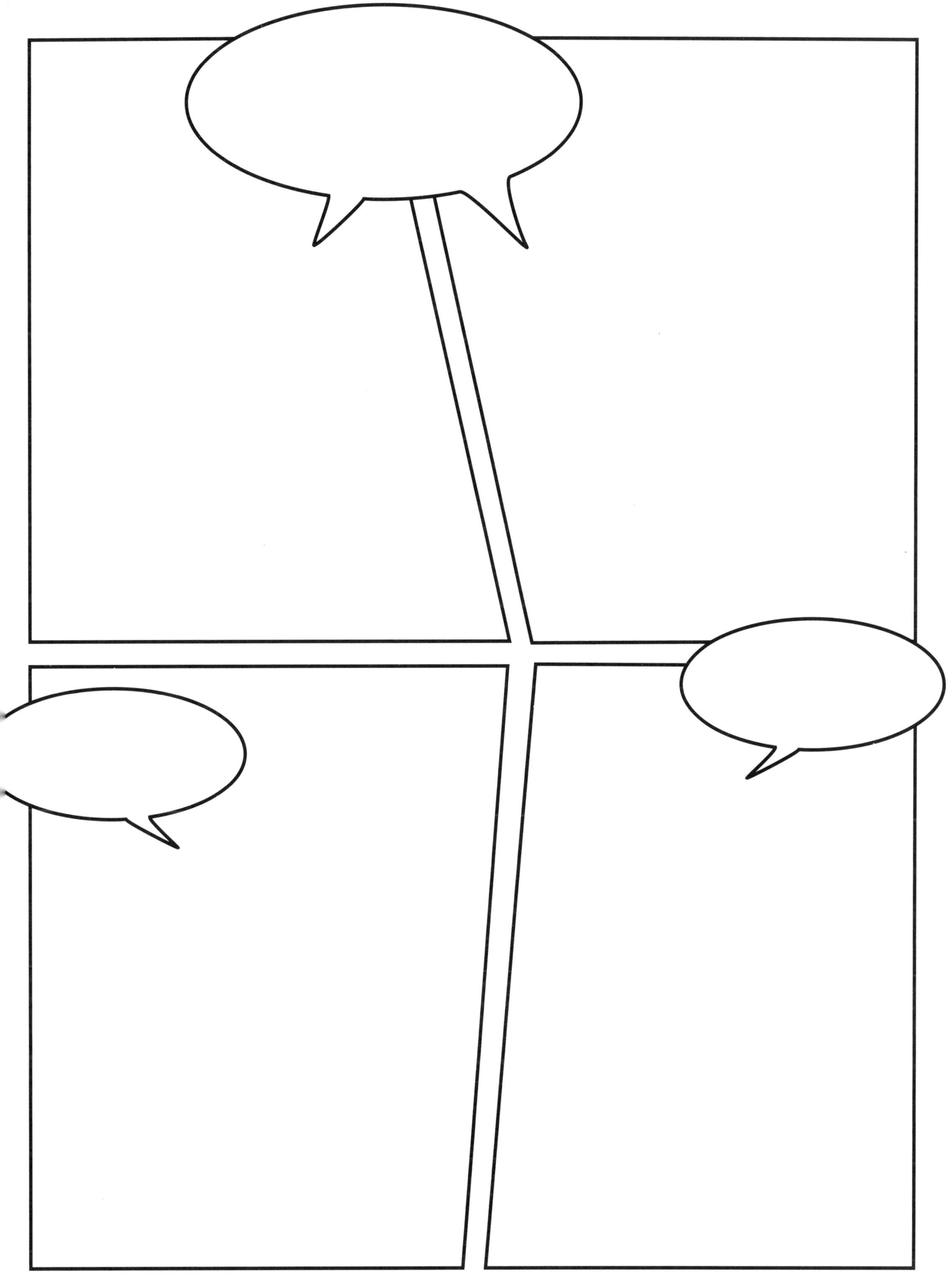

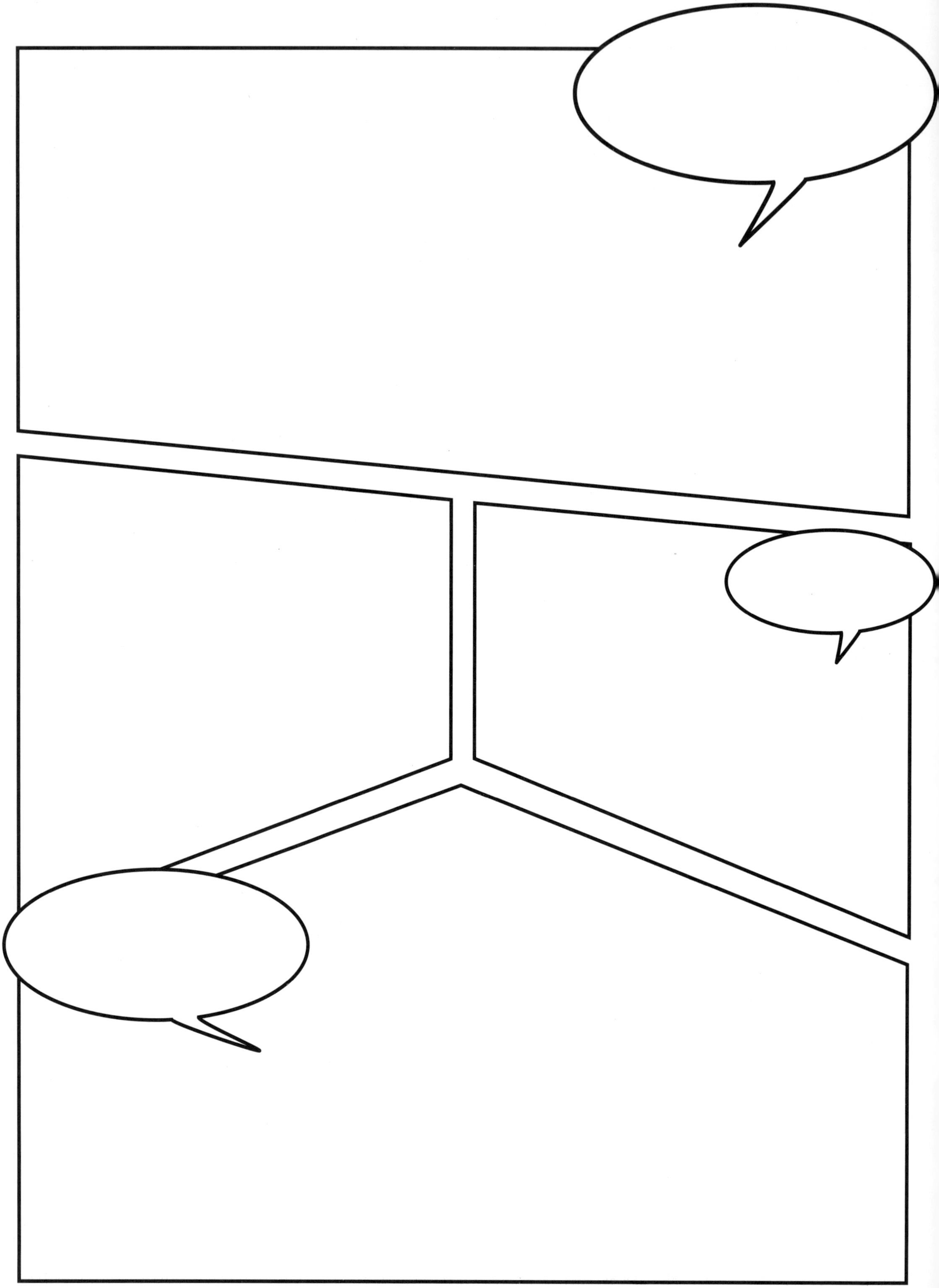

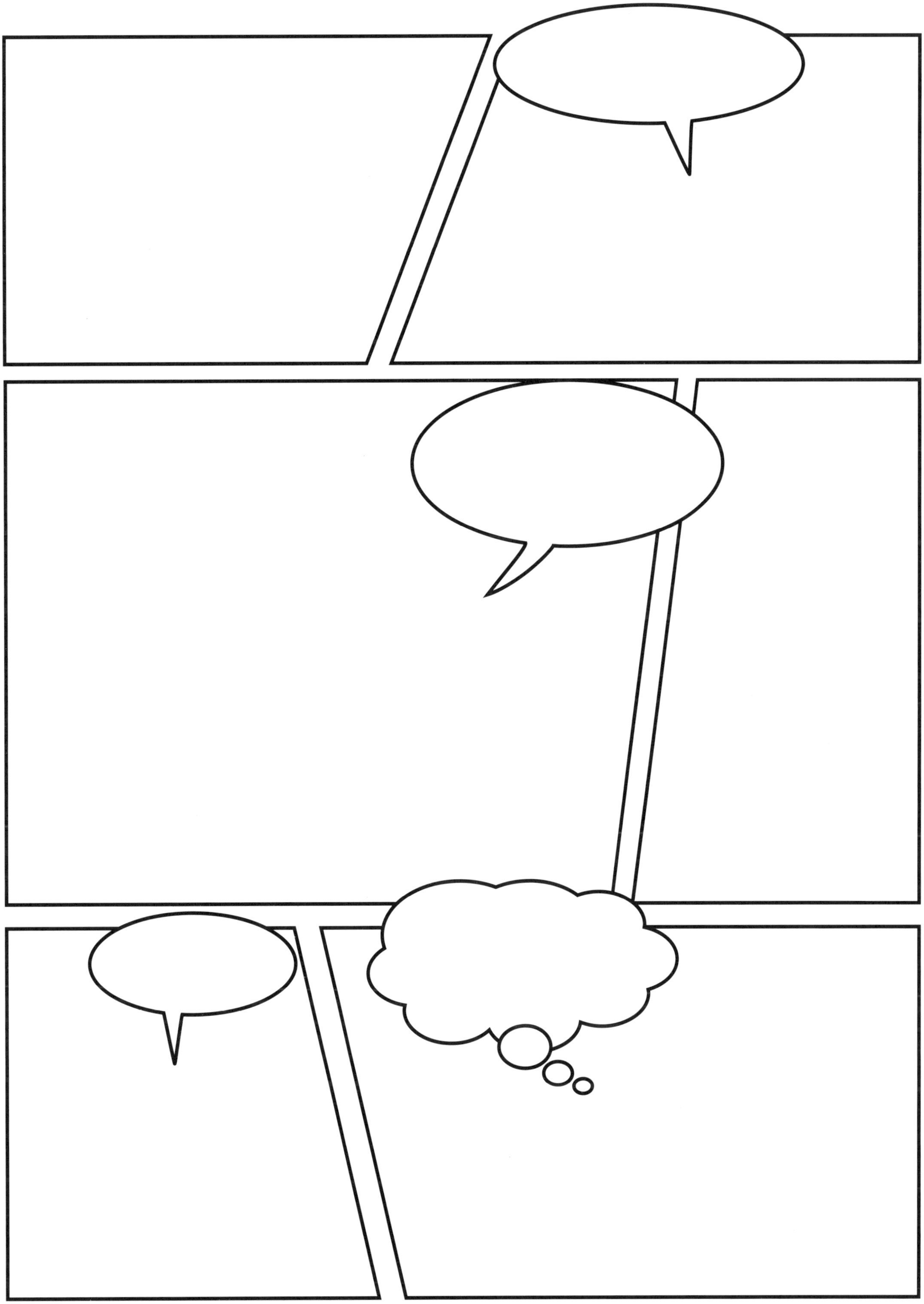

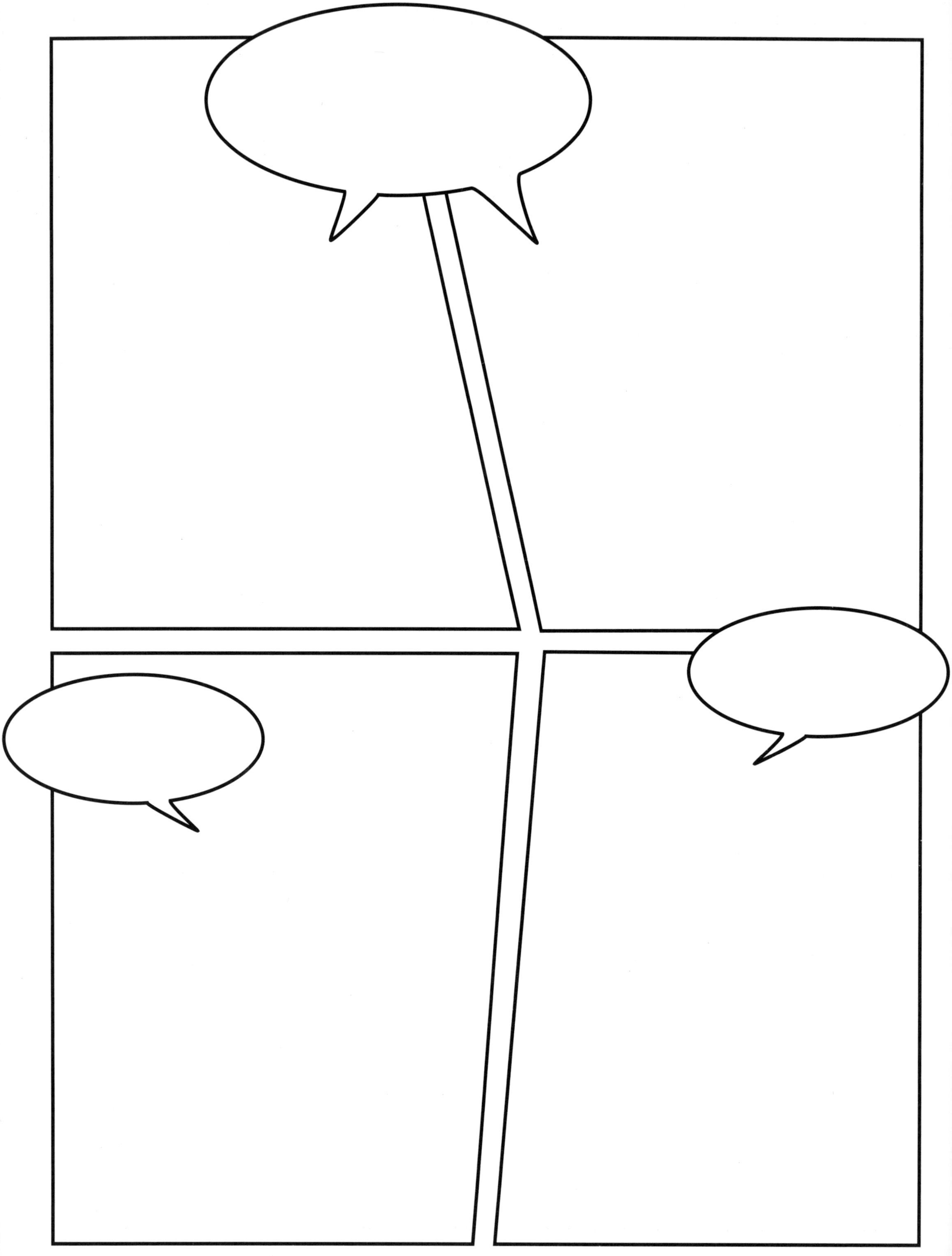

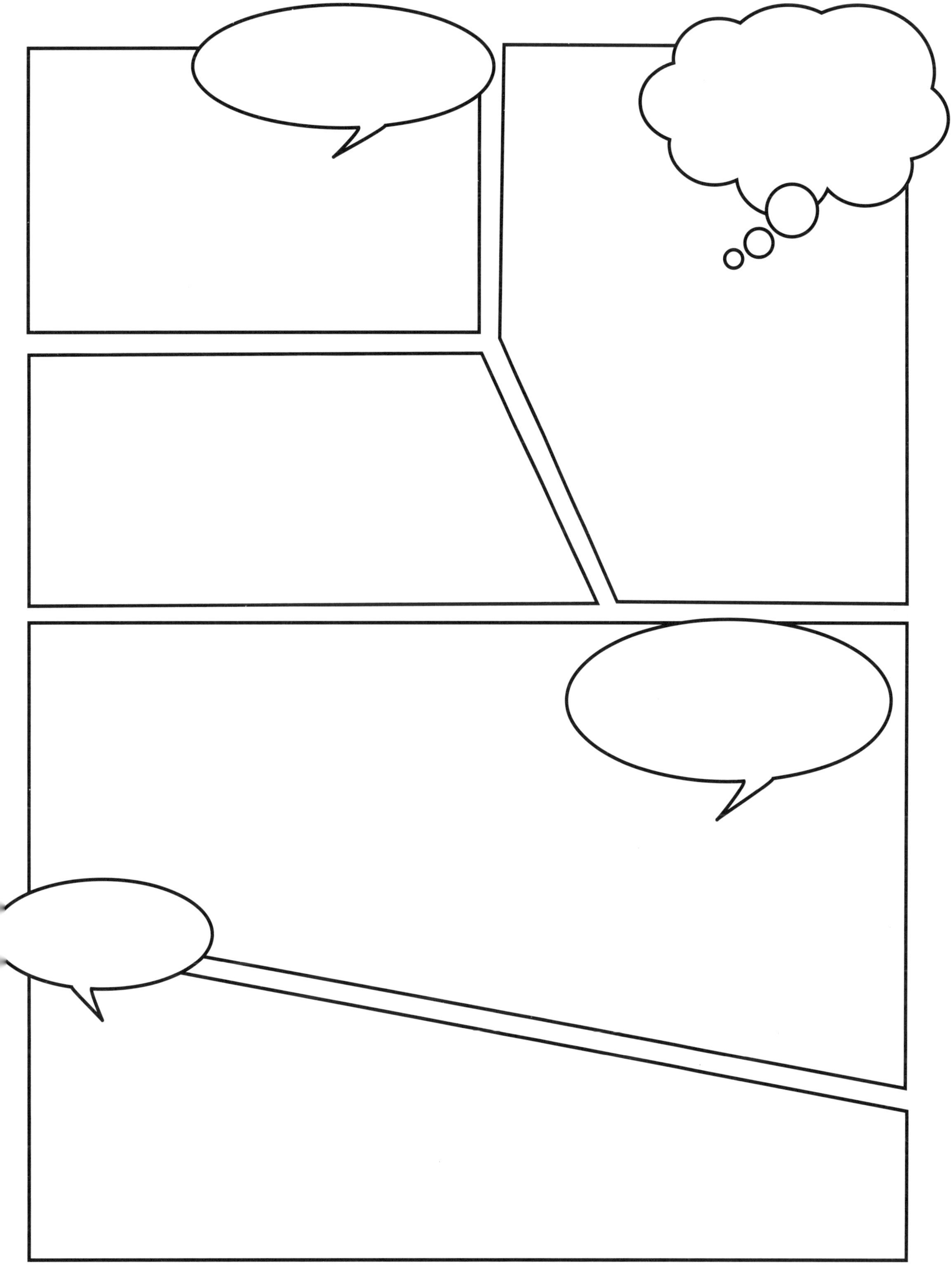

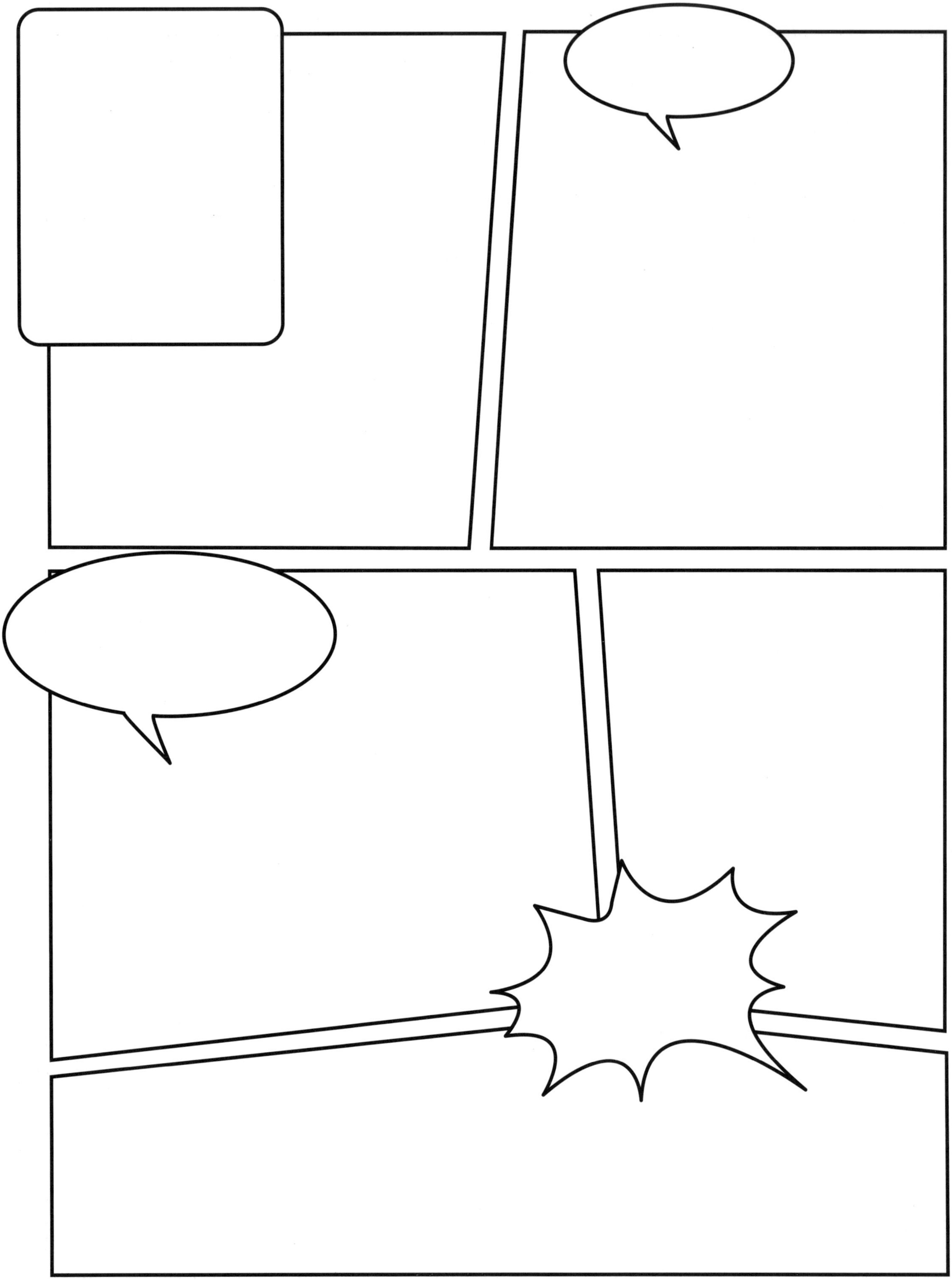

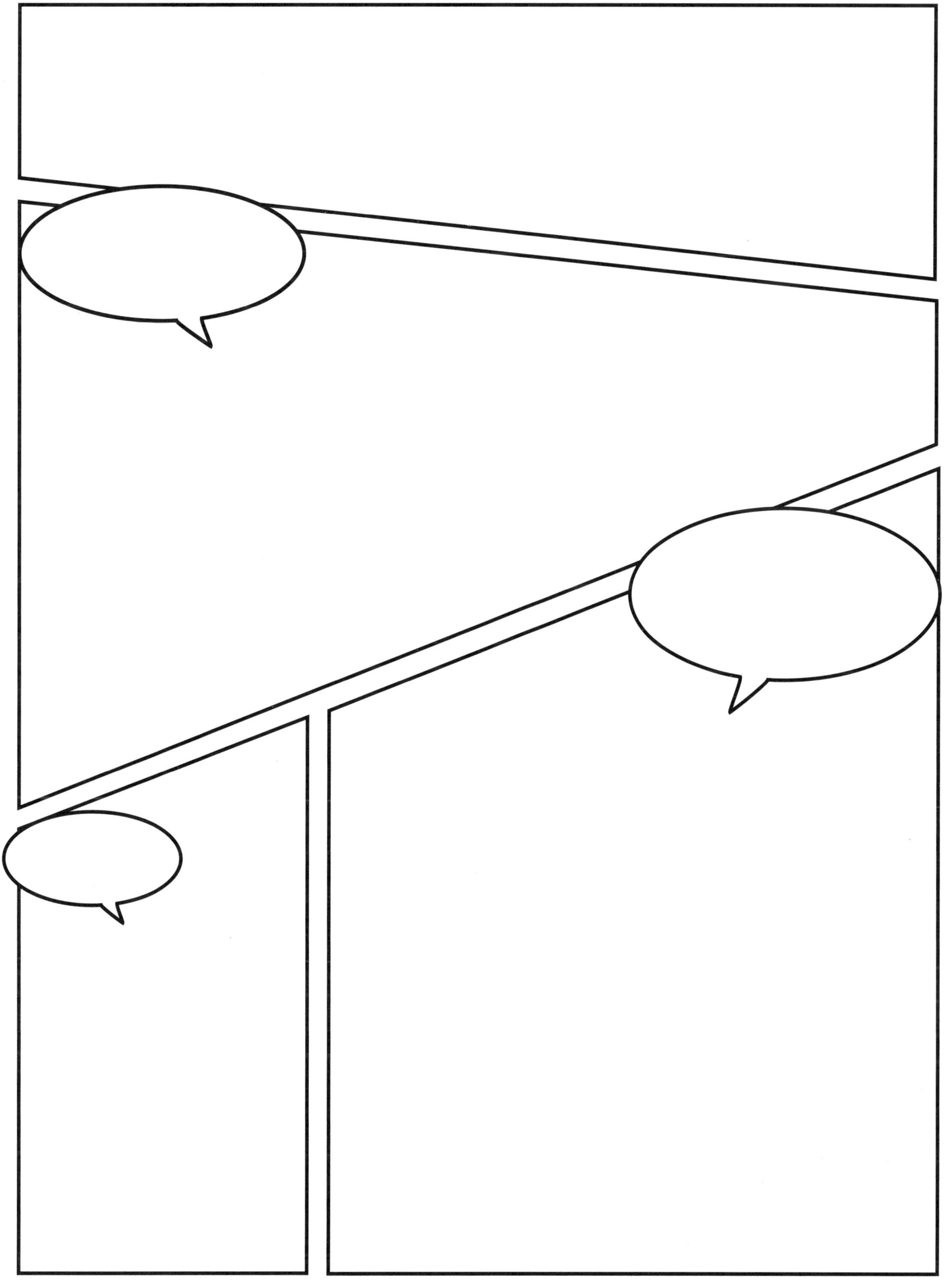

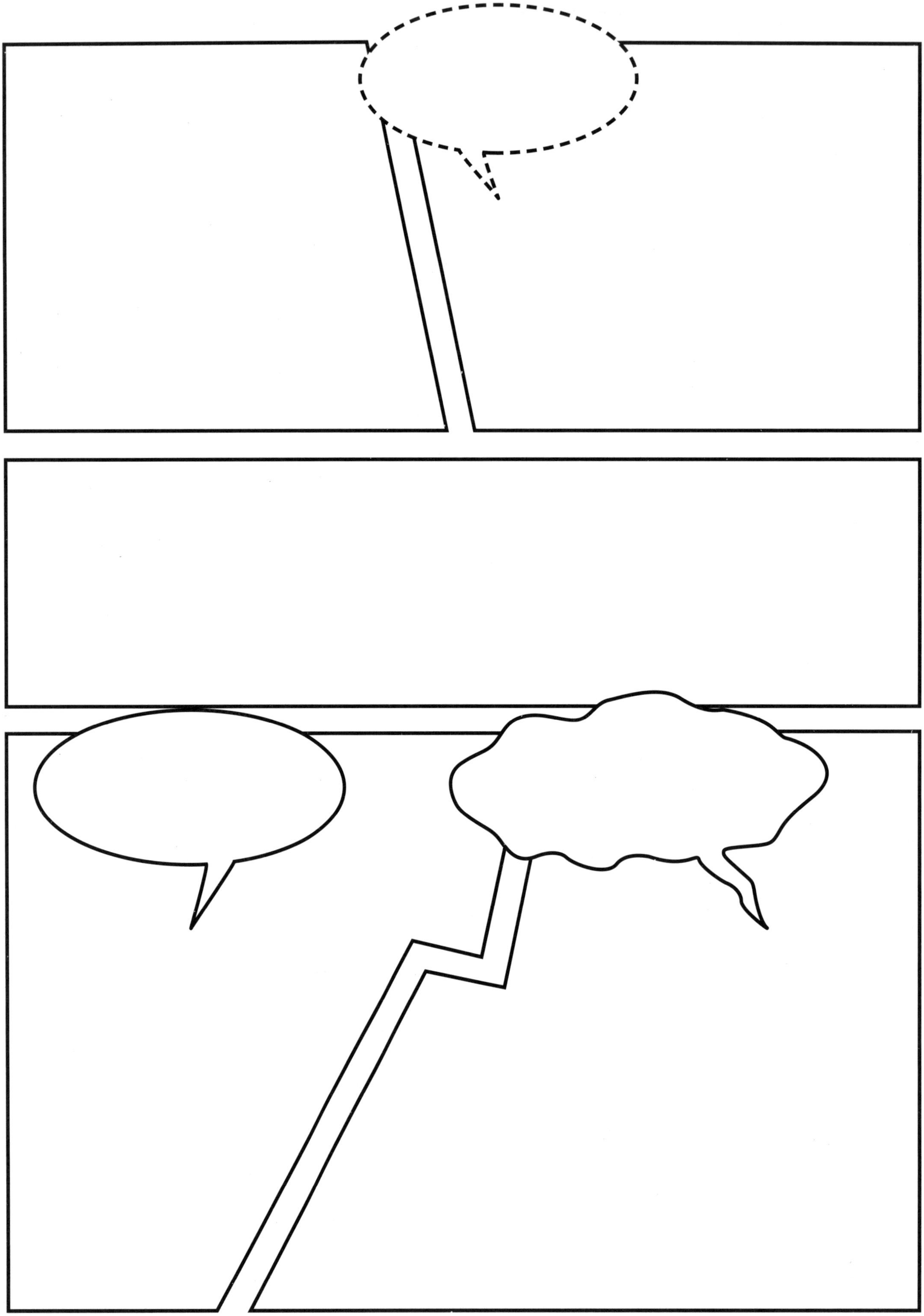

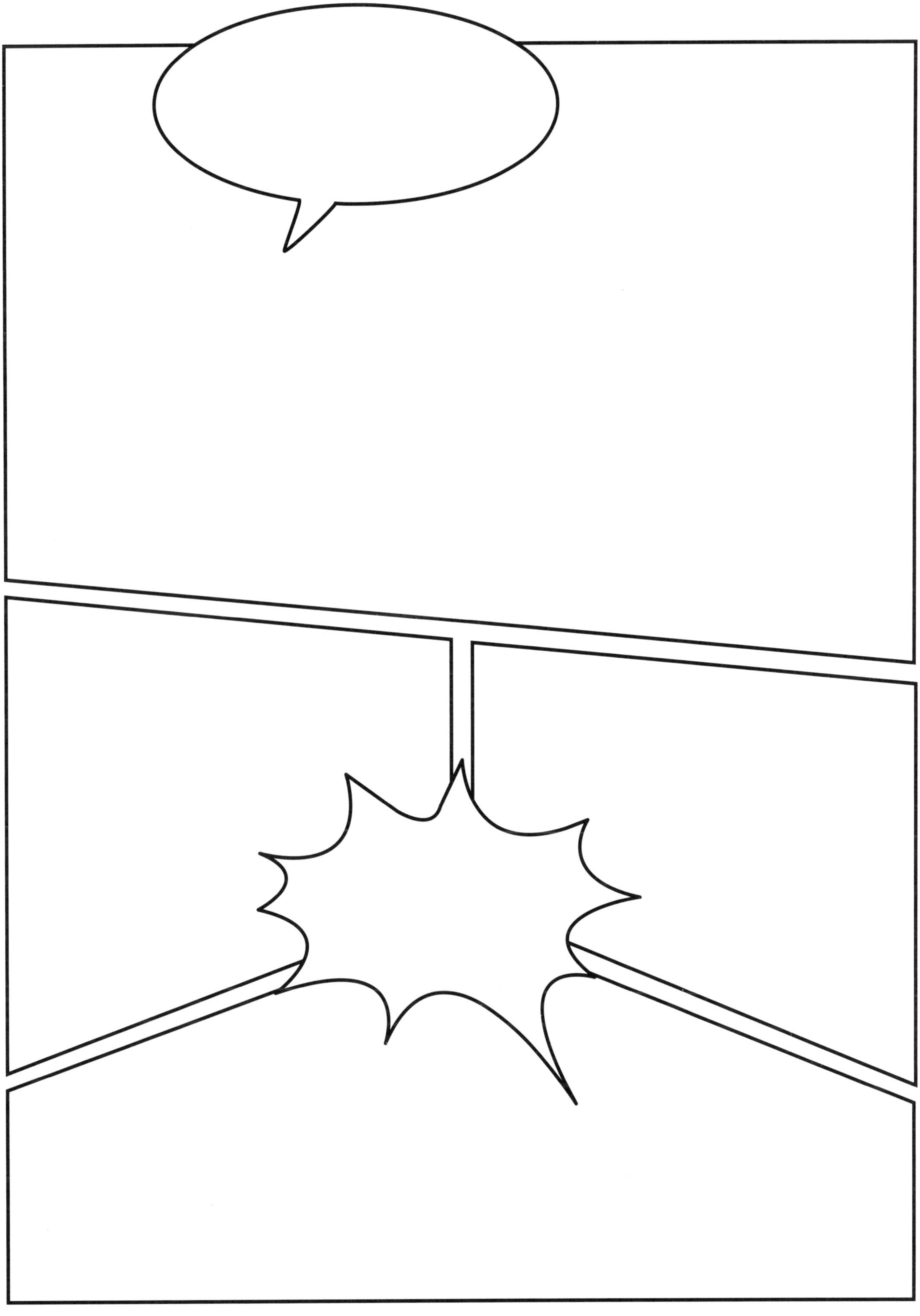

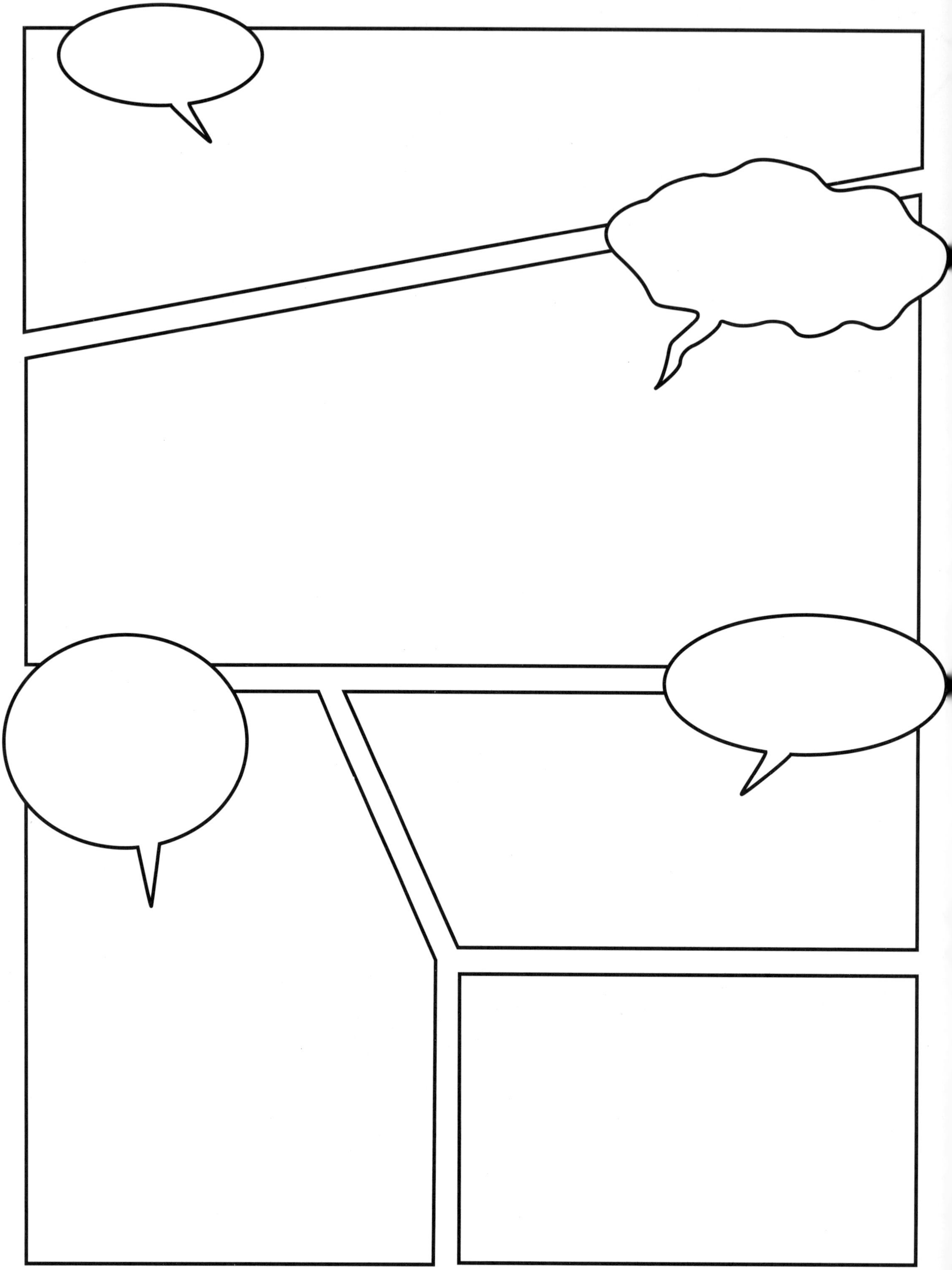

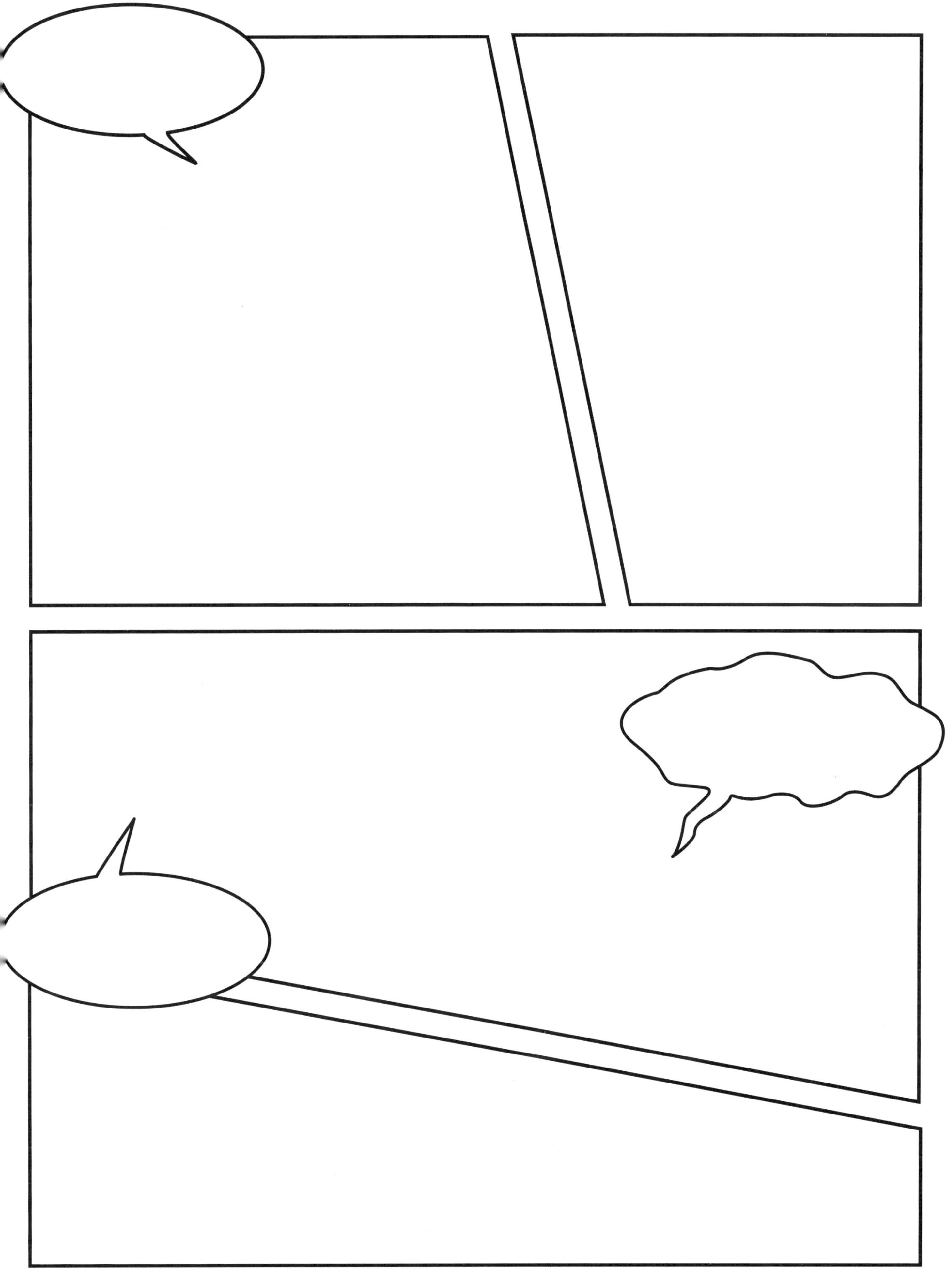